CONTEMPORARY AMERICAN FEDERALISM

Contemporary American Federalism

*The Growth
of National Power*

SECOND EDITION

Joseph F. Zimmerman

STATE UNIVERSITY OF NEW YORK PRESS

Published by

State University of New York Press, Albany

© 2008 State University of New York

All rights reserved

Printed in the United States of America

For information, contact State University of New York Press, Albany, NY
www.sunypress.edu

Production by Ryan Morris
Marketing by Fran Keneston

Library of Congress Cataloging in Publication Data

Zimmerman, Joseph Francis, 1928-
  Contemporary American federalism : the growth of national power /
Joseph F. Zimmerman.
      p.   cm.
  Includes bibliographical references and index.
  ISBN 978-0-7914-7595-9 (hardcover : alk. paper)
  ISBN 978-0-7914-7596-6 (pbk. : alk. paper) 1. Federal government—
United States. I. Title.

JK325.Z56 2008
320.473'049—dc22

                                                        2007050478

10 9 8 7 6 5 4 3 2 1

This book is dedicated with love to
Deirdre Ann Taylor

Contents

Preface

A federal system is inherently more complex than a unitary system with the degree of complexity of a given federal system reflecting the extent of the constitutional concentration of political powers in the national government and in the regional governments, ease or difficulty of the amendment of the constitution, and court interpretation of the powers of the two spheres of government. A thorough understanding of the United States federal system—encompassing national-state, interstate, and state-local relations—necessitates an in-depth study over an extended period of time because of the system's Daedalian nature. The author places particular emphasis on the continuing kaleidoscopic changes in the nature of the system and the adequacy of theories in explaining functioning of the system.

A review of the early books on the United States governmental system reveals they described the constitutional distribution of powers between Congress and the states based on the dual theory of federalism and hence were legalistic in nature. The theory of cooperative federalism came to prominence in the post–World War II period and books generally focused heavily on congressional conditional categorical grants-in-aid to state and local governments, and later block grants and general revenue sharing. Although Congress first used a delegated power in 1790 to supersede the regulatory powers of states in two areas, no book until 1991 focused on congressional enactment of preemption statutes removing regulatory powers from the states.[1] Similarly, no general book on state-local relations was published until 1983 and no general book on interstate relations was published until 1996.[2]

This volume's central intergovernmental theme is the accretion of political power in the United States at the national level. With a few exceptions, Congress prior to 1965 intruded indirectly into traditional state and local government by offering conditional categorical grants-in-aid to state and local governments, and they could avoid the conditions by not applying for and accepting the grants. The explosion in enactment of national preemption statutes—including ones establishing minimum national standards removing regulatory powers from subnational governments commenced in 1965—has worked revolutionary changes in the federal governance system that have profound implications for the three planes of government—national, state, and local—in the nation.

These changes affect the governance role played by voters. Democratic theory is premised on citizens playing an active and informed governance role. The continuing concentration of political power on the national plane reduces citizen participation in policy making because of the large geographical scale of the nation, but increases the influence of economic special interest groups.

Two other intergovernmental themes are emphasized. The health of a federal system is dependent on cooperative relations between sister states and a mechanism for settling interstate controversies. The U.S. Constitution authorizes states to enter into interstate compacts with the consent of Congress and grants original jurisdiction to the U.S. Supreme Court with respect to interstate disputes, a grant made exclusive by Congress in 1789.

State-local relations also are of great significance because local governments provide the bulk of governmental services and are engaged in a broad range of regulatory activities. These governmental units originally were creatures of their respective state government, but today general-purpose local governments in most states possess significant discretionary powers flowing from state constitutional and legislative devolution of powers.

The concluding chapter examines the adequacy of current theories—dual and cooperative—in explaining national-state relations and provides postulates of a more general theory encompassing national-state, interstate, and state-local relations.

Acknowledgments

A scholarly book on a complex subject is never the work of a single individual as the author draws heavily on available literature.

A Herculean effort is required to collect all pertinent literature on a subject as Daedalian as the United States federal system. I am most pleased to acknowledge a sincere debt of gratitude to my research associates—Winston R. Brownlow, Karl Schlegel, and Katherine M. Zuber—who were most proficient in searching the political science and public law literature and locating books, government documents, articles, and unpublished works pertaining to the United States federal system.

I also acknowledge a special debt of gratitude to Addie Napolitano for her expert preparation of the manuscript for publication. Any errors of fact of misinterpretation are my sole responsibility. I also thank my copyeditor, Laura Glenn.

CHAPTER 1

National-State Relations

The United States, with 3,628,150 square miles of territory, is one of the largest and most diverse nations in the world. An understanding of the nation's federal system cannot be gained without knowledge of the nation's diversity. Individual states vary in size from Alaska with 586,400 square miles of territory to Rhode Island with only 1,214 square miles of territory. Equally great population differences are found in the population of the states, ranging in 2004 from 509,294 in Wyoming to 19,254,630 in New York to 36,132,147 in California. Population density ranges from 1.1 per square mile in Alaska to 1,134.4 per square mile in New Jersey. A sharp shift has occurred since 1945 with the fastest-growing states in the south and the west, and several states losing population. New York lost more than 126,000 residents in the year ending on July 1, 2006. Similar differences exist between the populations of local governments ranging from 75 residents in Dixville Notch, New Hampshire, governed by an open town meeting, to more than 8,000,000 in New York City.

Racially, the nation is diverse with whites of various ethnicities constituting 67.9 percent of the population, blacks (African Americans) 15.9 percent, Asian 5.5 percent, American Indian and Alaska natives 0.4 percent, native Hawaiian and other Pacific islanders less than 1.0 percent.

Several states have sizable economies and California has the seventh largest economy in the world with its 2006 gross state product totaling $1,621,843 million compared to $24,178 million in North Dakota. Per capita personal income varied from $24,820 in Louisiana to $47,819 in Connecticut. Tax collections in the United States are large: $2,398,000,000,000 in fiscal year 2007 by the U.S. government and $2,435,084,000,000 by the fifty States and their local governments. Congress annually appropriates approximately $450,000,000,000 in financial assistance to subnational governments.

1

There are significant political cultural differences between the States and often within a state such as New York. These differences affect the functioning of the federal system with respect to the extent of cooperation and conflict between the national government and individual states, and between states. Daniel J. Elazar developed a typology of political culture facilitating an understanding of why government systems differ in various states.[1] The marketplace underlies the individualistic political culture, which "places a premium on limiting community intervention—whether governmental or non-governmental—into private activities to the minimum necessary to keep the market place in proper working order."[2]

Elazar defined the moralistic political culture as one committed to promoting the public interest that may necessitate governmental intervention in private matters in order to achieve goals benefiting the general public.[3] Hence, governmental activism is more common where this type of culture prevails.

The traditionalist political culture "accepts government as an actor with a positive role in the community, but it tries to limit that role to securing the continued maintenance of the existing social order."[4] In such a society, politics tends to be conservative and the role of government is custodial and not activist.

The federal system since 1965 has become more complex and has been characterized by the increasing concentration of political powers in the national government flowing from congressional preemption statutes removing completely or partially regulatory powers from subnational governments and generally broad U.S. Supreme Court interpretations of the scope of the delegated powers of Congress.

NATIONAL GOVERNANCE SYSTEMS

Governments may be classified in terms of the geographical distribution of political power as unitary, confederate, and federal. The terms "confederation" and "federation" were synonymous in the eighteenth century. An understanding of a federal system is promoted by comparing it with the unitary and confederate systems.

A Unitary Government

In a unitary form, one central government wields supreme power over all territorial divisions within the nation. Provinces, cities, counties, and other political units owe their creation and continued existence to the central government and they possess only such powers as the central government grants them. The central government can make a broad or a limited devolution of powers to lower planes of government.

Unitary governments are the most common form in the world and subnational governments are viewed primarily as administrative subdivisions to carry out national policies. Commonly, the national government prescribes in minute detail the policies to be implemented and the procedures to be followed. Since the lower-tier units are subject to more or less continuous supervision and control, the unitary organization is able to achieve a degree of national homogeneity, provide uniformity of policy and administration, and concentrate power swiftly and completely in times of national emergencies and wars.

The major disadvantage of this system may be its inflexibility. Identical policies and methods are applied to all local conditions regardless of their applicability in specific areas; sometimes they are suited ideally to solve certain local problems, but at other times they are unsuitable and unadaptable.

The relationship between a state government and its political subdivisions in the United States historically was unitary. Today, the relationship is unitary in some states and federal in other states as explained in chapter 8.

A Confederation

The reverse of a unitary system, a confederate system is one in which two or more independent states band together to establish a central government agency designed to accomplish certain specific common purposes including typically the conduct of foreign affairs and national defense. Each state retains its sovereignty and control over all persons and things within its boundaries with the exceptions of the powers delegated to the central agency. Hence, a confederacy is a system adaptable readily to regional policy preferences.

A confederation is inherently an unstable form of government since individual states may nullify the acts of the central agency and even withdraw from the confederation. In addition, each state may impose high tariffs on goods from other states and discriminate against noncitizens. The friction resulting from such measures tends to destroy the effectiveness of the confederation.

Despite its disadvantages, this system of government has been an instrument for cooperation in revolutionary emergencies and sometimes has been a prelude to the establishment of a closer and more stable political union. The experience of the United States, which had a confederate form of government in the period 1781 to 1788, illustrates this point and is described in greater detail in chapter 2.

A Federal System

In a federal system, all exercisable governmental powers are divided between a national government and several state (canton, province, land, etc.) governments with the exception of concurrent powers exercisable by either plane of government. This system seeks to combine the advantages of the unitary system and the confederate system, but inherently involves exceedingly complex intergovernmental relations if states possess broad powers. In addition, this system may suffer from some of the disadvantages of the other two systems.

The distribution of political powers is made by means of a written constitution, the national government and each state government in theory are supreme within the respective fields assigned to them, and each possesses certain concurrent powers. Kenneth C. Wheare in 1964 defined "the federal principle" as "the method of dividing powers so that the general and regional governments are each, within a sphere, co-ordinate and independent."[5] The national government, if it so desires, can devolve responsibility for a national function—legislative, executive, administrative—on the states and the U.S. Congress has done so as noted in chapter 9.

Elazar provided a similar comprehensive definition of a federal system: "Federalism can be defined as the mode of political organization that unites smaller polities in an overarching political system by distributing power among general and constituent governments in a manner designed to protect the existence and authority of both."[6] Carl J. Friedrick in 1968 viewed federalism as "the process by which a number of separate political communities enter into arrangements for working out solutions, adopting joint policies, and making joint decisions on joint problems, and conversely, also the process by which a unitary political community become differentiated into a federally organized whole."[7]

Richard H. Leach traced the development of the federal system to seventeenth-century England where "a strong feeling of local autonomy prevailed" which was transplanted to the North American colonies and added: "Federalism took root as well in the working relationship that evolved between the English Crown and government and the colonies during the colonial period. Isolated geographically from England, the colonies were tied governmentally to the other country only loosely, and the nature of the ties varied from time to time and from colony to colony. Nor was a successful attempt every made to rationalize and formalize the relationship."[8]

ADVANTAGES OF A FEDERAL SYSTEM

Supporters of a federal system cite eight advantages inherent in the system. First, uniformity of policy and administration can be achieved in national affairs to the extent needed while states retain control over their respective internal affairs. In particular, the high costs that may be associated with nationally uniform policies are avoided.

Second, the retention of a number of powers by the states acts as a safeguard against undue concentration of governmental authority in the nation that might result in the abridgement of the rights of citizens, in general policies harmful to sections of a geographically large nation, or both. James Madison in *The Federalist Number 51* emphasized the prevention of the overconcentration of political power inherent in a federal system.

> In a single republic, all the power surrendered by the people is submitted to the administration of a single government; and the usurpations are guarded against by a division of the government into distinct and separate departments. In the compound republic of America, the power surrendered by the people is first divided between two distinct governments, and then the portion allotted to each subdivided among distinct and separate departments. Hence a double security arises to the rights of the people. The different governments will control each other at the same time that each will be controlled by itself.[9]

Third, individual states may serve as laboratories of political experimentation for innovations in governmental policies. Successful experiments in individual states have led to sister states and Congress adopting the new policies.[10]

Fourth, states do not have to wait for the national government to formulate and implement a program to solve a problem since each state can use its own good judgment and resources in fashioning a remedy.

Fifth, minorities concentrated within one or more states are able to elect their members to state and local government offices, and to influence national policies through the pressure asserted by their state and local government officers on the national legislature.

Sixth, the political decentralization of power provides citizens with additional opportunities to participate in the governance system. There are more appointed and elected offices in a federal system and most of these offices are located in close proximity to the residences of citizens.

Seventh, Friedrick maintained federalism "enhances consensus in political discussion in the sense that solutions are sought that will reduce the size, resentments, and coercion of defeated minorities as well as of permanent minorities which cannot hope to become majorities . . ."[11]

Eighth, Friedrick also is convinced a federal system "enhances confidence in, and loyalty to a constitutional polity."[12]

Disadvantages of a Federal System

Four major disadvantages of a federal system have been identified. First, the system may be rigid if the power distribution can be changed only by means of a formal constitutional amendment, a process that often is prolonged and typically difficult.

Second, existence of concurrent powers, exercisable by the national government and the regional governments, may result in an uneconomical overlapping of functional responsibilities and divisive conflicts between the two planes of government. Such conflicts are especially apparent in times of rapid economic and social changes when jurisdictional conflicts may delay or prevent effective action by either the national government or regional governments or failure of the two planes of government to integrate their policies. Concentration of authority in one government as in a unitary state would result in greater effectiveness and efficiency during a period of rapid change in contrast to a federal system.

Third, serious problems may be caused by lack of uniformity in important functional areas—including banking, highway safety, insurance, and mental illness—as laws and regulations governing these areas may vary widely among regional governments. Furthermore, problems may be created by the failure of one or more regional government(s) to recognize the public acts and records, such as contracts and divorces, of another regional government.

Fourth, an English socialist, Harold J. Laski, wrote in 1939 that federalism in the United States was obsolete and could not cope with the problems generated by the Great Depression, and declared nine years later "the States are provinces of which the sovereignty has never since 1789 been real."[13]

Theories of American Federalism

Two theories—dual federalism and cooperative federalism—are prominent in the literature. Most students of federalism today find relatively little explanatory value in the dual federalism theory, but find greater validity in the cooperative theory. Neither theory, however, explains congressional use of coercive preemption powers to remove completely or partially regulatory powers from state and local governments, or relates to interstate relations and state-local relations. Chapter 9 reviews these theories and offers a dynamic kaleidoscopic theory of national-state relations that can be expanded to include interstate relations and state-local relations in states with a constitution establishing an *Imperium in Imperio* by devolving powers to general-purpose local governments.

Dual Federalism
Edward S. Corwin in 1950 utilized the following postulates to define dual federalism:

1. The national government is one of enumerated powers only;
2. Also the purposes which it may constitutionally promote are few;
3. Within their respective spheres, the two centers of government are "sovereign" and hence equal;
4. The relation of the two centers with each other is one of tension rather than collaboration.[14]

A fifth postulate could be added: One plane of government does not employ coercive powers against the other plane.

The U.S. Constitution suggests this theory. Section 8 of Article I delegates specific powers to Congress and the Tenth Amendment stipulates "the powers not delegated to the United States by the Constitution, nor prohibited by it to the States are reserved to the States respectively, or to the people." In addition, the Fourteenth Amendment provides for dual citizenship by stipulating "all persons born or naturalized in the United States and subject to the jurisdiction thereof, are citizens of the United States and of the State wherein they reside."

Dual federalism sometimes is described as a layer cake, thereby suggesting the national government and a state each possesses sovereign powers and may determine and implement policies within their respective competences unimpeded by the other plane. The dual federation theory incorporates a simplistic and static model of national-state relations by explaining changes in such relations can be accomplished only by formal amendment of the U.S. Constitution. John C. Calhoun of South Carolina early in the nineteenth century promoted this viewpoint that was popular in the southern states.[15]

COOPERATIVE FEDERALISM

James Madison of Virginia, considered by many to be the father of the U.S. Constitution, made clear in 1799 there was no intent to establish a system of dual federalism. In an address prepared on behalf of the Virginia Assembly, he wrote the national government "can not be maintained without the co-operation of the States."[16]

Elazar demonstrated conclusively a rigid dual system of federalism never existed in the United States and cooperation has been a hallmark of national-state relations since the early years of the nineteenth century to 1913.[17] Cooperative federalism implies the existence of two planes of government which is the essential feature of dual federalism, but differs from it in terms of extensive interplane cooperation. Whereas a number of the examples of such cooperation cited by Elazar during the early decades of the federal system were relatively minor, cooperation became extensive in the twentieth century, particularly in the period after World War II. In large measure, the cooperation was recognition of the fact most major multifaceted governmental problems no longer are exclusively national problems, or state problems, or local problems. In addition, cooperation was the product of the Congress's offer of pecuniary inducements to the states to execute national policies, a subject analyzed in detail in chapter 6. The theory of cooperative federalism is based in part on the postulate that one plane of government does not coerce or encroach on the sphere of the other plane.

This theory retains greater explanatory value than the theory of dual federalism as numerous national-state relations, including ones structured by national preemption statutes, are cooperative in nature. The national government provides many services free of charge to state and local governments, including the Federal Bureau of Investigation's fingerprint service and specialized training programs conducted by various national departments and agencies.

President Lyndon B. Johnson in the 1960s employed the term creative federalism to describe an aspect of his "Great Society" programs involving the mobilization of local government and private resources, along with national and state resources, to solve public problems on a cooperative basis.

The theory of cooperative federalism is helpful in promoting an understanding of the system, yet fails to explain congressional structuring of national-state relations by the coercive use of formal preemption powers, cross-cutting sanctions, cross-over sanctions, and tax sanctions explained in chapters 4 and 6.

THE EVOLVING FEDERAL SYSTEM

The 1788 campaign on ratification of the proposed U.S. Constitution centered on the question of whether an all-powerful Congress would be established that would be a threat to the civil liberties of citizens, a subject examined in chapter 2. The price for ratification in several states was the promise by proponents that the first order of business of the new Congress would be the proposal of a bill of rights as amendments to the constitution. Only a small number of opponents of the proposed fundamental document expressed fear that the delegated powers of Congress would be a threat to the states by encroaching on their sphere of powers and regulating them as polities. The proliferation of preemption statutes in the 1970s and 1980s led to a major debate relative to the original intent of the constitution's framers, a topic reviewed in chapter 5.

The ratified Bill of Rights has been effective in preventing congressional abridgement of the civil rights of citizens, but the Tenth Amendment—designed to prevent congressional abridgement of the states' reserved powers—generally proved to be ineffective in the 1970s and 1980s, as documented in chapter 5. Ratification of the Fourteenth Amendment led to judicial incorporation of most of the civil liberties provisions of the Bill of Rights into the amendment in the twentieth century, thereby protecting these liberties from abridgement by states and their political subdivisions.

The unamended constitution implied, without expressly stipulating, the existence of dual sovereignty and the Tenth Amendment was drafted and ratified to incorporate dual sovereignty expressly into the constitution. Under this constitutional conception, Congress and national courts would be powerless to regulate the states and local governments in their capacities as polities.

The Tenth Amendment, however, did not freeze national-state relations. Ratification of the Fourteenth and Fifteenth Amendments and the U.S. Supreme Court's generally broad interpretation of the scope of Congress's delegated powers enable Congress to encroach on many of the traditional reserved powers of the states as explained in chapters 4 and 5.

In 1988, Justice William J. Brennan of the U.S. Supreme Court in *South Carolina v. Baker* opined: "Any federal regulation demands compliance. That a State wishing to engage in [a] certain activity must take administrative and sometimes legislative action to comply with federal standards regulating that activity is a commonplace that presents no constitutional defect."[18]

In terms of its nature, the federal system has evolved from one exhibiting chiefly dual federalism features in 1789 to a system with a number of characteristics of a unitary system with Congress acting as a central government exercising nearly plenary regulatory powers in several traditional areas of state and local government responsibility. To a degree, cooperative federalism appears to have been a transitional phase between an essentially dual federalism phase and today's more coercive phase.

Conflict between the national plane and the subnational plane is inherent in a federal system. Conflict, of course, does not have to involve coercion of one plane by the other plane, but a mechanism other than the court system is essential if a permanent solution to a conflict is to be found. Arthur N. Holcombe in 1955 wrote:

> The coercion of States, which are members of a federal system by the government of the system in order that they may perform the obligations of membership in a satisfactory manner, presents one of the most difficult problems of federal politics. For a principal purpose of a federation is to secure peace and freedom from forcible constraint for the federated States, and the coercion of a State by its own federal government seems to be incompatible with the nature of a well-ordered federal union.[19]

Although Congress enacted 164 complete and partial preemption statutes removing regulatory powers from subnational governments between 1790 and 1964, these statutes did not regulate states as polities. A revolution in national-subnational relations commenced in 1965 when Congress enacted the first minimum standards preemption statute—*Water Quality Act of 1965*—that is described in greater detail in chapter 4.[20] Minimum standards statutes regulate private and subnational governmental activities and provide a state will lose completely authority to regulate the preempted functional area if the state fails to develop a regulatory program with standards at least as stringent as the national standards in each preempted area and an adequate enforcement plan. The number of preemption statutes reached 589 by March 1, 2008.

State government officers have protested strongly against the use of preemption powers by Congress and have filed suits challenging the constitutionality of several major preemption statutes. In general, the U.S. Supreme Court has upheld the constitutionality of such statutes (see chapter 5). Justice Harry A. Blackman in 1985 in *Garcia v. San Antonio Metropolitan Transit Authority* suggested states should utilize the political process, rather than the courts, to seek the amendment or repeal of preemption statutes. State officers accepted his advice and increased their lobbying activities in Congress seeking enactment of preemption relief statutes, a subject examined in greater detail in chapter 4.

There would be no confusion relative to the respective responsibility of Congress and the states if the dual federalism theory served as the basis for the federal system. In general, there was relatively little confusion concerning the responsibilities of the two planes of government until Congress developed seventeen types of complete preemption statutes and eleven types of partial preemption statutes (See chapters 4–5).[21] Enactment of these statutes has blurred the responsibility for a number of regulatory activities since both planes may share responsibility or shift responsibility from one plane to the other plane. The confused responsibility problem is examined in chapter 4 and the referee role of the U.S. Supreme Court in terms of national-state power conflicts is highlighted in chapter 5.

AN OVERVIEW

Chapter 2 focuses on experience with the Articles of Confederation and Perpetual union; the first national governance document; the Philadelphia constitutional convention of 1787, which was called to revise the defects in the articles revealed by experience; and the campaign to convince at least nine of the thirteen states to ratify the proposed U.S. Constitution.

The U.S. Constitution is examined relative to the division off powers between Congress and the states in chapter 3. Powers are classified as enumerated congressional powers, reserved or residual state powers, concurrent powers exercisable by Congress and the states, and prohibited powers. The chapter also describes national guarantees to the states, national dependence on the states, admission of new states by Congress to the Union, expansion of national powers, and national government assistance to states and their political subdivisions.

The subject of chapter 4 is congressional preemption of the regulatory authority of the states, one of the three principal methods by which power has become more centralized in the national government. The chapter examines the major reasons for the sharp increase in the number of preemption statutes since 1965, preemption relief statutes, the confused responsibility problem, national powers delegated to governors of the states, and costs that the states and local governments must finance because of national mandates and restraints incorporated in preemption statutes.

Chapter 5 is devoted to an explanation of the dual judicial system, the exclusive and concurrent jurisdictions of national and state courts, congressional intent to preempt state and local government laws, and major federalism court decisions.

Intergovernmental fiscal relations is the subject of chapter 6 that describes the respective taxing powers of Congress and state legislatures, governmental tax immunity, state taxation of the income of nonresidents and multijurisdictional corporations, national direct and indirect financial assistance to subnational governments, and coercion of these governments by Congress.

Inherent in a federal system are relations between the states. Chapter 7 explains the provisions in the U.S. Constitution relative to suits by one state against another state(s); interstate compacts that can provide for centralization of political power at the regional level; the requirement that each state extend full faith and credit to the statutes, final court decisions, and official records of other states; privileges and immunities of citizens while visiting another state; interstate rendition of fugitives from justice, interstate trade barriers and their removal; and the excise tax rate differential problem involving particularly alcoholic beverages and tobacco products.

Legal and financial relations between a state and its political subdivisions are described in chapter 8 that notes the legal relationship is based on in the unitary principle in some states and on the federal principle in other states. Particular emphasis is placed on state financial assistance to local governments and the state mandate problem.

Chapter 9, the concluding chapter, reviews the accretion of political power at the national level in the United States in the light of the alleged advantages and disadvantages of a federal system outlined in chapter 1, focuses on dynamic metamorphic national-state relations and the current powers of the states, and concludes with an outline of the key postulates of a general theory of American federalism.

CHAPTER 2

Establishment of the Federal System

The governmental system of the United States owes much to English institutions and philosophies of government. The idea of popular sovereignty, separation of powers, rule of law, natural rights, and natural law (a universal law transcending man-made laws) were all well developed—though not always in effect—in England and were transplanted by the early settlers in the thirteen colonies.

Each colony, at the beginning of the revolution, organized a de facto government without a constitution and sent representatives to the Second Continental Congress which first met in May 1775 after the Battle of Lexington in Massachusetts. Although no written document invested this Congress with governmental powers, it borrowed money, raised armies, and entered into treaties with foreign nations. New Hampshire on June 15, 1776, was the first colony to declare its independences from the British Crown. And on July 4, 1776, Congress issued a Declaration of Independences, drafted by Thomas Jefferson, and called on each state to draft and adopt a written constitution.

The revolution was not a cataclysmic one sweeping away the existing governmental institutions. Instead, the revolution transferred the sovereign power from the British Crown to the thirteen states. There was no general dissatisfaction with governmental institutions whose heritage was English. The cause of the revolution was economic and involved taxation and trade.

By 1780, eleven states drafted and adopted constitutions, and Connecticut and Rhode Island converted their royal charters into constitutions. These written fundamental documents recognized that governments emanate from the people and derive their powers from the consent of the governed. Each constitution contained a bill, or declaration, of rights protecting individuals against arbitrary acts of government. These bills are traceable in origin to the constitutional political ideas of England—the

13

Magna Charta, the first *Habeas Corpus Act*, the *Bill of Rights of 1689*, the *Habeas Corpus Act of 1679*, the *Act of Settlement of 1701*, and the *English Common Law*.

As an additional guaranty of popular liberties, the state constitutions provided for separation of powers among the three branches of government—the executive, legislative, and judicial—although the separation was not complete. The primacy of the state legislature was common, but definite powers were allotted to the executive and judicial branches to ensure each branch might guard against unreasonable or capricious actions by the other two branches. Thus, the rule of law rather than of men—the limitations placed on the future actions of the government—was implicit in the written state constitutions.

ARTICLES OF CONFEDERATION AND PERPETUAL UNION

The Plymouth Colony, the Massachusetts Bay Colony, Connecticut, and New Haven organized in 1643 the New England Confederacy, the first confederacy in North America. The confederation was formed as a league for mutual defense against Indian attacks, but went out of existence when the danger of such attacks vanished. In 1696, William Penn proposed a league of colonies composed of a royal commissioner and two deputies from each colony, but the league was not formed.

The first major eighteenth-century proposal for a confederacy was the product of a congress held in Albany, New York, in 1754 at the suggestion of the Lords of Trade to provide for mutual defense of the colonies and prevent the Iroquois Indians from supporting the French in Canada. Benjamin Franklin developed a plan, approved unanimously by the congress, providing for a congress composed of one delegate from each colony which would determine strategies for defense and the amount of funds and troops to be supplied by each colony. The so-called Albany Plan, however, was not approved by the colonial legislatures.

The Continental Congress submitted in 1777 the Articles of Confederation and Perpetual Union, providing for a league of amity, to the states for ratification. Since the document provided for a confederation, the articles could not become effective until all thirteen states ratified the articles. Maryland, the thirteenth state, did not ratify the articles until 1781.

The delay in ratification of the articles was due to a dispute over title to lands lying west of the original colonies. The grants of land from the British Crown extended to the west without limit, but encountered French claims in the Mississippi valley. Virginia, for example, claimed the present day states of Kentucky and West Virginia, and the greater part of Illinois,

Indiana, and Ohio as well as a part of northern Michigan, Minnesota, and Wisconsin. Massachusetts, jumping over eastern New York to Oswego, claimed western New York and the lower half of Michigan and the lower half of Wisconsin. And Connecticut claimed what became the northern part of Ohio, Illinois, and Indiana. Territorial disputes continued subsequent to ratification of the U.S. Constitution and two means of settling such disputes were included in the new fundamental document as explained in chapter 8.

The Second Continental Congress on October 10, 1780, sought to end the dispute over land titles by promising that lands ceded to the Union by a state would be "disposed of for the common benefit of the United States and be settled and formed into distinct republican States which shall become members of the Federal Union, . . ."[1] The stalemate was broken in 1781 when New York, which had few territorial claims, and Virginia, which had many land claims, ceded their lands to the Union and the other states followed by ceding lands. The Congress, created by the articles, in 1787 enacted the famous Northwest Ordinance providing for the admission into the Union of parts of the Northwest Territory as states when the population reached 50,000 and prohibiting slavery.[2]

Interestingly, Article XI of the Articles of Confederation and Perpetual Union provided that "Canada acceding to this Confederation, and joining in the measures of the United States, shall be admitted into and entitled to all the advantages of this Union, but no other colony shall be admitted into the same unless such admission be agreed to by the nine States."

The articles were a unique document providing for more than a common defense alliance and stressing the confederation was "perpetual" in nature. The word "government" does not appear in the articles and Martin Diamond maintained "neither the friends nor the enemies of the Confederation regarded the Articles as having created any kind of government at all, weak or otherwise."[3]

Article II of the articles declared: "Each State retains its sovereignty, freedom and independence, and every power, jurisdiction and right which is not by this confederation expressly delegated to the united States in Congress Assembled." Employment of the lower case "u" in "united" was designed to make clear the articles were establishing a league of states and not a government driving its powers from the people. The latter generally were fearful of a supergovernment.

Article III of the fundamental document defined the nature of the governmental system as "a firm league of friendship" and declared the league's purposes were "common defence, the security of their liberties, and their mutual and general welfare, binding themselves to assist each other, against all force offered to, or attacks made upon them, or by any of them, on account of religion, sovereignty, trade, or any other pretence whatever."

The confederation's governing body was a unicameral Congress composed of from one to seven delegates from each of the thirteen states selected and recallable by their respective state legislature for a term not exceeding three years in any six-year period. Regardless of the number of delegates a state sent to Congress, each state had only one vote in Congress.

Congress was authorized to appoint a committee of the states, consisting of one delegate from each state, to meet during the recess of Congress and to appoint a presiding officer entitled the President for a term not exceeding one year during a three-year period. The committee also was delegated various powers, including borrowing money, building and equipping a navy, raising an army, coining money, declaring war, negotiating treaties with other nations, establishing a postal system, fixing the standards of weights and measures, and regulating relations with the Indian tribes. In addition, the committee was authorized to exercise other powers delegated by Congress provided that nine states agreed to the delegation.

There was no separate judicial branch and no separate executive branch. Congress was delegated limited judicial powers to settle boundary disputes among the states and controversies involving private land claims under grants of two or more states.

Congress was handicapped in carrying out its responsibilities by five major defects in the articles that made Congress largely an advisory body. First, Congress lacked the power to levy taxes and was dependent for revenue on funds supplied to the treasury by the states. Many states frequently failed to send their contribution quotas of funds to Congress, and only New York and Pennsylvania paid their proportionate share of the costs of the revolutionary war. Congress lacked funds to pay interest on loans made in the states, France, and Holland, and officers and soldiers who were not paid during the war were demanding back pay. The "continental" paper notes issued by Congress became worthless, and European bankers refused to loan money except at an exorbitant interest rate.

Second, Congress was not granted authority by the articles to enforce its laws and treaties with foreign nations and states were under no legal obligation to respect the laws and the treaties. As a result, it was not possible for Congress to establish uniform laws throughout the thirteen states relative to matters delegated to it. Furthermore, Congress could not force a state to honor a treaty entered into by Congress with a foreign nation. James Madison in 1787 referred to states violating the treaty of peace, the treaty with France, and the treaty with Holland, and added "as yet foreign powers have not been rigorous in animadverting on us."[4]

Third, Congress lacked the power to regulate interstate commerce and individual states, acting in a mercantilistic fashion, commenced to erect trade barriers against other states, thereby strangling commerce among them.

New York, for example, levied fees on all vessels entering its ports from Connecticut and New Jersey, and Virginia limited foreign vessels to specified ports. This defect was the most serious one and generated the most pressure for amendment of the articles.

Fourth, although Congress was authorized to raise and support an army and a navy, Congress lacked the resources to do so. In consequence, Congress was unable to provide for the common defense during a time period when England was entrenched in Canada and Spain was entrenched in the Southwest, and the friendly French monarchy was in danger of collapse and might be unable to provide assistance in the future. In addition, Congress could not preserve harmony within states by suppressing domestic disorders.

An uprising by farmers in western Massachusetts in 1786–1787 hastened the end of the confederacy. Led by Captain Daniel Shays, the farmers were incensed by an epidemic of mortgage foreclosures resulting from the postrevolutionary war depression, currency deflation, and high taxes. Shays's rebellion prevented a sitting of the Supreme Judicial Court in Springfield in 1786 and allowed Shays to control western Massachusetts for approximately five months. The rebellion was suppressed when Boston financiers sent General Benjamin Lincoln with an army to restore state government control in the area. This rebellion generated fear among property owners who desired a stronger national government that would assist states in putting down rebellions.

Fifth, the confederation was in danger of being dissolved. James Madison wrote in 1787 "that a breach of any of the Articles of Confederation by any of the parties to it absolves the other parties from their respective obligations, and gives them a right if they choose to exert it of dissolving the Union altogether."[5]

In March 1785, representatives from Maryland and Virginia developed an agreement on navigation and trade on the Potomac River and the Chesapeake Bay. In ratifying the compact, the Maryland State Legislature proposed that Pennsylvania and Delaware be included in future commercial regulations. Virginia agreed, but widened the application of the compact by inviting all states to attend a convention to consider a uniform system of commerce and trade in 1786 in Annapolis, Maryland.

Nine of the thirteen states appointed commissioners to attend the Annapolis Convention, but only twelve delegates from five states participated. Maryland, the host state, did not participate because its Senate feared the convention might undermine the Articles of Confederation and Perpetual Union. The delegates adopted a resolution, drafted by Alexander Hamilton of New York, memorializing Congress to convene a convention in Philadelphia in May 1787 for the purpose of revising the Articles of Confederation and Perpetual Union. Congress reluctantly approved the resolution on February 21, 1787. The invitation to participate in the convention did not specify the method by which delegates were to be chosen, but all delegates in each state were appointed either by the state legislature or the governor under legislative authorization. A number of delegates were instructed specifically to consider revision of the articles and to take no other action.

THE CONSTITUTIONAL CONVENTION OF 1787

Rhode Island was the only state that failed to send delegates to the Philadelphia Convention, which met from May 25 to September 17, 1787, and selected George Washington as President. Rhode Island insisted changes in the governance system must be made in conformity with Article XIII of the Articles of Confederation and Perpetual Union.

Seventy-four delegates were selected by the states, but nineteen delegates either did not accept the appointments or failed to attend the convention. Fourteen of the remaining fifty-five delegates departed Philadelphia before the convention concluded its work. Delegates had widely differing backgrounds and abilities; thirty-three were lawyers. Twenty-eight delegates had been members of the Continental Congress or the Congress of the confederation, and other delegates helped to draft the constitution of their respective state. Most notable of the delegates were George Washington, Benjamin Franklin, James Madison, and Alexander Hamilton. Conspicuously absent were Thomas Jefferson who was in France on a diplomatic assignment; John Hancock; Samuel Adams; Thomas Paine; John Marshall, who later became Chief Justice of the U.S. Supreme Court; and Patrick Henry. The latter declined to be a delegate from Virginia.

Not unexpectedly, the convention split into factions reflecting philosophical and sectional differences. The former differences focused on the question of whether a stronger national government would be a threat to the individual liberties won by the revolutionary war. The latter differences were based on the nature of the economy in the various sections of the United States.

On May 29, Edmund Randolph of Virginia introduced fifteen resolutions as the basis for a new national government "in which the idea of States should be nearly annihilated."[6] The Randolph Resolution in effect would have created a national government with powers similar to those of the British Government.

If the Articles of Confederation and Perpetual Union permitted their amendment by two-thirds or three-quarters of the states, instead of requiring unanimous approval of the states, it is probable that the articles would have been amended and not replaced by the Constitution. Following five days of negotiations, delegates decided to forgo the revision of the articles and to draft a new constitution for the United States. The decision was made by a vote of six to one; delegates from five states had not arrived at the time of the vote.

One early dispute in the convention involved a proposal that the national legislature be granted the power to veto laws enacted by state legislatures if the laws contravened powers delegated to Congress. James Madison spoke in favor of the negative:

> The necessity of a general government proceeds from the propensity of the States to pursue their particular interests in opposition to the general interest. This propensity will continue to disturb the system, unless effectually controuled. Nothing short of a negative on their laws will controul it. They can pass laws which will accomplish their injurious objects before they can be repealed by the General Legislature or be set aside by the national tribunals. . . . Its utility is sufficiently displayed in the British system. Nothing could maintain the harmony and subordination of the various parts of the empire, but the prerogative by which the Crown stifles in the birth every act of every part tending to discord or encroachment.[7]

It was no surprise when the convention rejected the proposal that the national Congress should be granted the explicit authority to review laws enacted by the state legislatures and to disallow statutes found to encroach on the powers delegated to Congress by the proposed constitution. Establishment of a federal system by the proposed fundamental law automatically reduced the powers of the states and the proposal held the potential for the nearly complete centralization of powers in the national legislature, which could use its judgment to determine whether a state law was *ultra vires*; that is, exceeded the powers of the state legislature. Furthermore, review of state laws by the national legislature in an era of slow communications could prevent the implement of state laws within their competences by a year or more.

Ratification by the states of the Fifteenth Amendment to the U.S. Constitution in 1870 authorized use of veto power by Congress relative to the election laws of the states. The amendment is the constitutional basis for the *Voting Rights Act of 1965*, which requires federal approval of changes in election laws in state and local governments covered by the act, a subject explained in detail in chapter 4.[8]

The issue of the method of representation for states in Congress proved to be very divisive. Early in the convention, Edmund Randolph introduced a plan that was principally the work of Madison. The Randolph plan provided for representation in direct proportion to the number of "free inhabitants" in each state with the result that Virginia would have fifteen or sixteen members and small states, such as Delaware and Rhode Island, each would have only two or three seats.

The fear of small states that the large states would dominate the Union led to a stalemate over the question of the method of apportioning seats in Congress. The small states favored a continuation of the system established by the articles of Confederation and Perpetual Union with each state possessing an equal vote. The large states, on the other hand, argued for representation based on population.

The rival plans were debated in the committee of the whole for several weeks with delegates from the larger states arguing it was unfair to give states that paid the most in taxes the same representation as the states that paid the least in taxes. Delegates from the smaller states countered that deviation from the role of equal representation ultimately would lead to the servitude of the smaller states.

The famous Connecticut Compromise, incorporating key elements of the other two plans, was approved by the convention and provided that each state would have two senators and the number of members of the House of Representatives would be based on population with one exception; each state would have at least one representative regardless of the state's population.

Delegates from the large states did not accept the compromise until an agreement was reach by the convention that the proposed national government would have an executive branch and a judicial branch, and its laws would apply directly to individual citizens.

The Connecticut Compromise, also known as the great compromise, did not end the dispute over representation. Relative to the apportionment of seats in the House of Representatives, there was a major disagreement among the free states and the slave states. The latter wanted slaves to be included in the apportionment population and the free states wanted the apportionment population limited to free inhabitants. A compromise was reached with the agreement the number of free citizens, excluding Indians not taxed, would be increased by "three-fifths of all other persons."

With respect to the election of members of the House of Representation, Madison was concerned state legislatures might abuse their powers if they had sole control over the times, places, and manner of holding elections and stressed "it was impossible to foresee all the abuses that might be made of the discretionary power."[9] As a result of objections by Madison and other delegates, the convention agreed to add Section 4 to

Article I of the proposed constitution providing that "the Congress may at any time by law make or alter such regulations, except as to the places of chusing Senators."

A division existed among delegates relative to the length of the term of office for members of the House of Representatives with a number of delegates favoring a three-year term and other delegates favoring a one-year term. The convention chose the midpoint and the term was set at two years. Another issue involved the question of universal suffrage for white males or a property qualification for voting. The issue was settled by allowing each state to determine voting qualifications.

The northern states favored the immediate ending of the importation of slaves whereas several southern states wanted to be able to continue to import slaves. John Rutledge of South Carolina emphasized: "If the northern States consult their interest, they will not oppose the increase of slaves which will increase the commodities which they will become the carriers" and Charles Pinkney of South Carolina declared his State would not accept a constitution prohibiting the slave trade.[10] The convention settled this controversy after considerable desultory debate by providing that slaves could be imported for an additional twenty years, but Congress could levy a tax of up to ten dollars on each slave imported.

Whether Congress should be delegated the power to levy import and export duties produced a sectional split with many northern delegates favoring the granting of such power to Congress and the southern states opposing such a grant. The industrializing northern states wished to protect their respective economies against foreign competition and viewed the export tax and the import tax as good sources of national government revenues. Eldridge Gerry of Massachusetts, however, expressed strong opposition to delegating the power to tax exports to Congress: "It might be made use of to compel the States to comply with the will of the general government, and to grant it any new powers which might be demanded. We have given it more power already than we know how it will be exercised. It will enable the general government to oppress the States, as much as Ireland is oppressed by Great Britain."[11]

Southern states objected on the grounds such duties would discourage industrialization and they would be paying more than their fair share of the duties since they imported most of their manufactured products and exported most of their products that were agricultural. The compromise ending the disputed provided that Congress could levy only import duties.

The so-called nationalist delegates desired to have a central government with full power to intervene in any state. The agreed-on compromise provided that the national government would guarantee each state a republican form of government and protection against domestic violence and foreign invasion.

In deciding to create a new system of government incorporating elements of the unitary system and the confederate system, the delegates revealed their fear of a centralized government by incorporating in the proposed constitution a number of "checks and balances" to help ensure the sovereignty of the states and prevent the abuse of power. One house of the Congress could check the other house relative to bills, the President could veto bills enacted by Congress subject to an override of vetoes by a two-thirds vote of each house of Congress, and the national courts could check the actions of the other two branches. Relative to the courts, it must be pointed out it was not clear from the Constitution that the courts could invalidate a statue enacted by Congress or a presidential action.

Although many authors refer to the U.S. Constitution as a document incorporating numerous compromises, the reader should be aware that there was no serious opposition to delegating to the Congress fifteen of the eighteen powers contained in Article I. Similarly, there was near unanimous agreement with the specific prohibitions placed on Congress and the states, and the requirement states must obtain the permission of Congress to initiate specified actions.

THE RATIFICATION CAMPAIGN

As noted, the Articles of Confederation and Perpetual Union stipulated they could be amended only by the unanimous consent of the thirteen states. The proposed constitution was not an amendment of the articles, but a replacement fundamental law containing several provisions that were in the articles. In contrast to the latter, the new document reverted to the Declaration of Independence's trust in the people by stipulating in its preamble: "We the People of the United States, in order to form a more perfect union, establish justice, insure domestic tranquility, provide for the common defence, promote the general welfare, and secure the blessings of liberty to ourselves and our posterity, do ordain and establish this Constitution for the United States of America."

Reflecting the preamble and the belief that the people would be disposed more favorably than state legislatures, the framers of the Constitution specified that each state legislature was to provide for the election of delegates to a special convention that would consider ratification of the proposed document. The proposed constitution would become effective on ratification by nine states. The proponents were aware ratification by all states was an impossibility since Rhode Island did not participate in the convention and there was strong opposition to the document, particularly in several of the large states. The delegates did not want their work nullified by the refusal of two or three states and maintained ratification by nine states was in conformance with the Articles of Confederation and Perpetual Union that required the affirmative votes of nine states before Congress could act. It also was believed ratification by nine states would pressure the remaining states to approve the proposed fundamental law.

Opponents loudly objected that the convention was convened to revise the Articles of Confederation and Perpetual Union, and lacked authority to draft a new basic law. It also was maintained that since the articles had been ratified by state legislatures, only theses bodies possessed authority to supplant the articles by the proposed constitution and unanimous approval would be required. Whereas many opponents were convinced that the national government under the proposed constitution would be too strong, other opponents argued the proposed fundamental law would be too weak. Charges also were made the new government either would be too dependent on the states or would be too independent of the states.

The most major criticism levied against the proposed basic law was the lack of a bill of rights. This criticism was not surprising as the English had brought to the colonies and embodied in the colonial charters provisions against arrest and punishment except on the basis of a specific charges, and guarantees of due process of law, right to a trial by a jury of peers in the area where the accused lived, right to petition for redress of grievances, and taxation only by vote of elected representatives. Exaggerated fear was expressed the new proposed national government would be a monster above the states and might enslave the people.

It must be pointed out that Section 9 of Article I of the unamended constitution contains three civil liberty guarantees: prohibition of the enactment of a bill of attainder (legislative declaration of guilt and imposition of punishment) or an ex post facto (retroactive) law and prohibition of the suspension of the writ of habeas corpus, except "when in cases of rebellion or invasion the public safety may require it." Nevertheless, the document did not contain guarantees of freedom of the press, speech, assembly, petition, and religion that had been incorporated into most state constitutions. George Mason of Virginia, a convention delegate, opposed the document strenuously: "There is no declaration of rights; and the laws of the general government being paramount to the laws & constitutions of the several States, the declarations of rights in the separate States are no security. Nor are the people secured even in the enjoyment of the benefits of the common law; (which stands here upon no other foundation than its having been adopted by respective acts forming the constitutions of the several States)."[12]

Convention opponents of a bill of rights argued that Congress was a government of specifically delegated powers and would possess no powers to allow it to encroach on the liberties of the citizenry. Hence, a bill of rights would be unnecessary and would be superfluous.

Many issues debated in the constitutional convention were debated again in the states. In addition, a number of clergymen denounced the document as sacrilegious because God was omitted and there was no requirement that holders of federal offices must be Christians. Other critics were fearful that making the President commander-in-chief of the armed forces might produce another Cromwell and resented the fact that states were forbidden to coin money.

The opposition to the proposed constitution was strongest in the interior of the nation and in areas with a small population. Approximately 90 percent of the population was engaged in agriculture. Farmers and settlers favored state-issued cheap paper money as did debtors who were imprisoned and whose property often was seized by sheriffs. Furthermore, many citizens found it difficult to pay taxes. Citizens lacking the voting franchise because they did not own real property also opposed the proposed fundamental law.

Popular conventions in Delaware, New Jersey, and Pennsylvania quickly ratified the proposed constitution and were followed shortly thereafter by conventions in Connecticut and Georgia. Serious objections, however, emerged in Massachusetts, New York, and Virginia (the most populous state), and it was apparent failure of these states to ratify the proposed constitution would doom it. Opposition was especially strong in New York which occupied a strategic location between the Atlantic Ocean and the Great Lakes with four states to the east and eight states to the south.

The Federalist Papers

To convince New York, and by extension other states, to ratify the proposed basic law, Alexander Hamilton enlisted the cooperation of John Jay and James Madison in the writing of a series of eighty-five letters, during the winter and spring of 1787–1788, to editors of newspapers in New York City. In late March 1788, the first thirty-six letters were published in book form and letters thirty-seven through eighty-five were published on May 28, 1788, in a second volume. Proponents of the proposed constitution in New York and Virginia used these collections of letters effectively.

Each letter examined in detail a provision of the document and defended the provision. Each letter was signed by "Publius" and there is a dispute relative to the author of a few letters that subsequently were published in a single volume entitled *The Federalist Papers*. These papers are the best expositions on the unamended U.S. Constitution and merit serious reading today.

The terms "confederation" and "federation" were used interchangeably in the eighteenth century. Constitution proponents labeled themselves federalist, perhaps to appeal to citizens opposed to a strong national government. Madison in *The Federalist Number 39* conceded that the proposed constitution would establish a governance system that would be "neither wholly national nor wholly federal [confederate]."[13]

Madison wrote in *The Federalist Number 45* "the powers delegated by the proposed Constitution to the federal government are few and defined. Those which are to remain in the State governments are numerous and indefinite."[14] He added in *The Federalist Number 46* that "a local spirit will infallibly prevail much more in the members of Congress than a national spirit will prevail in the legislatures of the particular States."[15]

The supremacy of the laws clause of the proposed fundamental law was attacked as enabling Congress to convert the system into a unitary one. Hamilton responded in *The Federalist Number 33*: "If a number of political societies enter into a larger political society, the laws which the latter may enact, pursuant to the powers entrusted to it by its constitution, must necessarily be supreme over those societies and the individuals of whom they are composed. It would otherwise be a mere treaty, dependent on the good faith of the parties, and not a government, which is only another word for political power and supremacy."[16]

These letters had a great influence on the public in general and delegates to the New York State ratification convention in particular as the latter often lacked a full understanding of the nature of specific provisions of the proposed constitution. There is little doubt that these letters were responsible for the convention ratifying the proposed basic law by a margin of only three votes.

In Virginia, Patrick Henry led the opposition to the proposed fundamental document, but he was countered by the influence of Madison, George Washington, and John Marshall. The Virginia convention ratified the proposed constitution by a vote of 89 to 79.

Countering *The Federalist Papers* were a series of sixteen essays, signed "Brutus," which were published in the *New York Journal* between October 1787 and April 1788. These essays, however, were not reprinted as one document at the time. Evidence suggests that the author was Robert Yates, a delegate to the constitutional convention and an associate of Governor George Clinton of New York. "Brutus" objected in particular to the development of a unitary system, stressed the dangers in granting the taxing power to Congress, and warned the national judiciary would subvert the powers of the States.[17]

"Brutus" in an October 18, 1787 letter referred to the necessary and proper clause and the supremacy of the laws clause and concluded:

> It is true the government is limited to certain objects, or to speak more properly, some small degree of power is still left to the States, but a little attention to the powers vested in the general govern-ment, will convince every candid man, that if it is capable of being executed, all that is reserved for the individual States must very soon be annihilated, except so far as they are barely necessary to the organization of the government. The powers of the general legislature extend to every case that is of the least importance— there is nothing valuable to human nature, nothing dear to free men, but what is within its power. It has authority to make laws which will affect the lives, the liberty, and property of every man in the United States; nor can the constitution or laws of any State, in any way prevent or impede the full and complete execution of every power given.[18]

Final Ratification

By the summer of 1788, the required nine states (New Hampshire was the ninth) had ratified the proposed constitution and were joined shortly there-after by Virginia and New York. North Carolina did not ratify the document until the autumn of 1789 and Rhode Island withheld its ratification until the spring of 1790.

Would the U.S. Constitution have been approved if it had been sub-mitted to the voters for their verdict? The evidence suggests that the answer is no since the delegates to the state conventions, with the exception of New York, were required to meet property or taxpayer qualifications, and the propertied people generally favored the proposed constitution on the ground that it granted Congress sufficient powers to protect their interests, which Congress under the Articles of Confederation and Perpetual Union was unable to do. Available evidence reveals the proposed basic law was sup-ported strongly by businessmen, professionals including lawyers and clergy-men, and southern plantation owners.

The price of ratification in the key states included a promise by pro-ponents that the first action of the new Congress would be the proposal of a bill of rights as an amendment to the Constitution.

Motives of the Framers

A major debate over the motive of the framers of the Constitution erupted in 1913 on publication of a book by Professor Charles A. Beard based on the premise economics motivated most convention delegates.[19] He marshaled evidence demonstrating many delegates owned government bonds, land mortgages, and paper money that had lost most of their value. In other words, Beard suggested these delegates would benefit financially from the establishment of a strong national government.

Professor William B. Munro countered wealthy men also wrote the Declaration of Independence and that fact does not support the conclusion economic gain was the dominant motive for the issuance of the Declaration.[20] He added: "If men of wealth and influence had been kept out of the convention in 1787, the natural leaders of the people would have been absent."[21]

Robert E. Brown and other historians produced evidence that the wealthy citizens in several states opposed the proposed constitution, which was supported by poor citizens.[22] William H. Riker agreed with Brown and offered a military interpretation. Riker documented what he referred to as "a very uneasy peace with the imperial power, uneasy because significant politicians in Britain regretted the outcome and hoped to reopen the war," and "the threat from Spain in the Southwest."[23] He added the evidence suggests strongly "the primacy of the military motive in the adoption of centralized federalism. The suggestion is in fact so strong that one wonders how Beard and his followers could every have belied that the main issues at Philadelphia were domestic matters of the distribution of income."[24]

A review of the evidence leads to the conclusion the motives of the delegates in drafting specific provisions of the constitution were multiple, but the primary motives were economic and defense of the states. These two motives were intertwined since a strong defense force was dependent on a strong national economy.

SUMMARY

Each colony became an independent state, later formed a confederation, and subsequently abandoned the confederation for a federation. The confederation would have been formed at an earlier date but for the disputes over titles to territories. The strong fear of a more centralized government suggests the confederation might have continued if the Articles of Confederation and Perpetual Union had been easier to amend. The requirement for unanimous consent of the thirteen states for amendment precluded needed amendments during a period when interstate disputes over boundaries and trade were common.

Although the Articles of Confederation and Perpetual Union have been criticized strongly for their inadequacies, incorporation of several provisions from the articles in the U.S. Constitution is evidence the articles were not a total failure. With good faith on the part of all states, the confederation might have been able to continue to exist.

The Philadelphia Constitutional Convention assembled an unusually competent group of men who were able to forge compromises between large states and small states and between sections of the nation. Use of general terms by the framers of the Constitution in delegating powers to Congress and provision for a judicial system to interpret the respective powers of Congress and the states enable the Constitution to become a flexible document capable of adjustment to major economic, political, and social changes without the necessity for numerous constitutional amendments. It should be noted that relations between the national government and individual states are asymmetrical and continually changing.

Commencing in the 1930s, several observers predicted the death of the states and the development of a unitary system. Many of these observers held positions similar to the positions of antifederalists such as "Brutus." Similar statements about the demise of the states seldom appear today.

Chapter 3 examines in detail the constitutional distribution of powers between Congress and the states, prohibited powers, national guarantees to the states, federal dependence on the states, admission of new states, expansion of national powers, and national assistance to the states.

CHAPTER 3

The United States Constitution

The U.S. Constitution was the first written document in the world to provide for the distribution of significant powers between the national government and territorial governments. Although the Constitution might have delegated specific powers to Congress and other specific powers to the states, specific powers were delegated only to Congress, the President, and United States courts. All other powers, except prohibited ones, are reserved to the states. Whereas most delegated or enumerated powers are important ones, the unspecified reserved or residual powers are of great importance and indescribable except in the broadest of terms.

Powers delegated to Congress and powers reserved to the states are subject to interpretation by national courts and state courts; the former courts often give an expansive interpretation of the enumerated powers. The powers of Congress and states also have been affected by twenty-seven amendments to the fundamental document and innovative use of preemption powers by Congress to nullify state and local government regulatory laws and administrative regulations as explained in chapter 4.

Indian tribes occupy a special position in the governance system. Native Americans are citizens of the United States possessing all rights and privileges of other citizens. Treaties entered into between the United States and individual tribes govern Native Americans residing on reservations; several treaties predate the Constitution. Under various treaties, a Native American may be exempt from license requirements and paying state taxes and fees, and also may be permitted to engage in activities forbidden by state law. Numerous disputes have arisen relative to gambling activities on reservations that violate state laws and sale of tax-exempt products, primarily, alcoholic beverages and cigarettes, to nonresidents of the reservations.[1]

DISTRIBUTION OF POWERS

The U.S. Constitution delegates enumerated powers to Congress and reserves all other powers unless prohibited to states and citizens. Enumerated powers also are referred to as delegated or expressed powers and are subject to interpretation by Congress and state and U.S. courts. Flowing from the enumerated powers are implied powers necessary and proper for the implementation of the preceding powers, and resultant powers based on two or more enumerated powers. Concurrent powers are ones exercisable by Congress and state legislatures. Certain specified powers, known as prohibited ones, may not be exercised by Congress and/or state legislatures.

Enumerated Powers

Congress is a government of limited powers and in theory may exercise only powers specifically delegated to it or powers incidental to the enumerated ones. The expressed powers have led to development of implied powers and related resultant powers described in subsequent sections.

> Section 8 of Article I of the Constitution grants the following powers to Congress:
>
> To lay and collect taxes, duties, imposts and excises, to pay the debts and to provide for the common defence and general welfare of the United States, but all duties, imposts, and excises shall be uniform throughout the United States.
>
> To borrow money on the credit of the United States;
>
> To regulate commerce with foreign nations, and among the several States, and with the Indian Tribes;
>
> To establish an uniform rule of naturalization, and uniform laws on the subject of bankruptcies throughout the United States;
>
> To coin money, regulate the value thereof, and of foreign coin, and fix the standards of weights and measures;
>
> To provide for the punishment of counterfeiting the securities and current coin of the United States;
>
> To establish post offices and post roads;
>
> To promote the progress of sciences and useful arts, by securing for limited times to authors and inventors the exclusive right to their respective writings and discoveries;

To constitute tribunals inferior to the supreme court;

To define and punish piracies and felonies committed on the high seas, and offenses against the law of nations;

To declare war, grant letters of marque and reprisal [privateering], and make rules concerning captures on land and water;

To raise and support armies, but no appropriation of money to that use shall be for a longer term than two years;

To provide and maintain a navy;

To make rules for the government and regulation of the land and naval forces;

To provide for calling forth the militia to execute the laws of the Union, suppress insurrections, and repel invasions;

To provide for organizing, arming, and disciplining the militia, and for governing such part of them as may be employed in the service of the United States, reserving to the States respectively, the appointment of the officers, and the authority of training the militia according to the discipline prescribed by Congress;

To exercise exclusive legislation in all cases whatsoever, over such district (not exceeding ten miles square) as may, by cession of particular States, and the acceptance of Congress, become the seat of the government of the United States, and to exercise like authority over all places purchased by the consent of the legislature of the State in which the same shall be, for the erection of forts, magazines, arsenals, dock-yards, and other needful buildings;—and

To make all laws which shall be necessary and proper for carrying into execution the foregoing powers, and all other powers vested by this Constitution in the Government of the United States, or in any department or officer thereof.

Several of the above powers are exclusive ones since states are forbidden by Section 10 of Article I of the U.S. Constitution to exercise them. In theory, the reserved or residual powers of the states are exclusive powers, but many have been subject to congressional preemption statutes removing in part or completely regulatory powers in a field from subnational governments as described in chapter 4.

It is important to recognize that the grants of power have been modified over the years by constitutional amendments, judicial interpretation, and custom and tradition. These power grants are latent ones initiated only by Congress enacting a bill into law subject to a possible presidential veto and a veto override. No power is self-executing. Congress did not exercise its power to regulate interstate commerce or its power to regulate bankruptcies until 1887 and 1898, respectively. Congress found ways of indirectly exercising other powers via conditions attached to grants-in-aid to state and local governments, tax credits, and cross-cutting and cross-over sanctions explained in chapter 7.

Implied Powers

Immediately on establishment of the federal system, an argument developed between the loose and strict constructionists of the delegated powers. Alexander Hamilton, for example, argued that Congress possessed the power to charter a government-owned bank whereas Thomas Jefferson and other strict constructionists maintained that Congress lacked the power since authority to establish a bank was not one of the enumerated powers.

Jefferson and James Madison were disturbed greatly by congressional enactment of the *Alien and Sedition Acts*. Madison was the author of the "Address of the General Assembly to the People of the Commonwealth of Virginia" and registered his objection to the expansion of congressional powers in the following terms:

> The sedition act presents a scene which was never expected by the early friends of the Constitution. It was then admitted that the State sovereignties were only diminished by powers specifically enumerated, or necessary to carry the specific powers into effect. Now, Federal authority is deduced from implication; and from the existence of State law, it is inferred that Congress possesses a similar power of legislation; whence Congress will be endowed with a power of legislation in all cases whatsoever, and the States will be stripped of every right reserved, by the concurrent claims of a paramount legislature.[2]

Although not expressly listed in the constitution, implied powers exist because they are essential for implementation of the expressly granted powers. As noted, the "elastic clause" of the constitution grants Congress authority "to make all laws which shall be necessary and proper for carrying into operation the foregoing powers, and all other powers vested by this Constitution in the government of the United States or to any department of officer thereof."

This provision serves as the basis for the doctrine of implied powers, the liberal interpretation of which has resulted in greatly augmenting the powers of the national government. This judicial doctrine originated in *McCulloch v. Maryland* in which the U.S. Supreme Court in 1819 opined: "Let the end be legitimate, let it be within the scope of the Constitution, and all means which are appropriate which are plainly adapted to the end, which are not prohibited, but consistent with the letter and spirit of the Constitution, are constitutional."[3]

Appropriate means that Congress may employ vary widely and include establishment of national banks and other institutions not listed in the constitution; creation of agencies and departments to regulate agriculture, business, and labor; and initiation of almost innumerable other activities based on the authority to levy taxes to provide for the general welfare and national defense.

Whether Congress possesses an implied power based on an inference drawn from a delegated power is subject to judicial interpretation in the event there is a challenge to the exercise of an implied power. The key question is whether the delegated power is sufficiently encompassing to include exercise of a power implied from it.

Resultant Powers

Congress can infer it possesses a resultant power on the basis of two or more powers expressly delegated to it. Although Congress is authorized "to establish an uniform rule of naturalization," the Constitution does not delegate specifically to Congress power to control immigration. The Constitution, however, grants Congress power to regulate commerce with foreign nations and naturalization of aliens, and the Senate is granted power to confirm treaties with foreign nations negotiated by the President.

Similarly, Congress authorized the issue of paper money although the constitutional grant of authority refers only to coining and regulating the value of money. Authority for issuance of paper money stems from the power to borrow funds and to coin money.

The General Welfare Clause

Some observers misinterpreted this clause as allowing Congress to enact any law promoting the general welfare of the United States. If this interpretation was accurate, the governmental system would be a unitary rather than a federal one since such laws would be part of the supreme law of the land notwithstanding contrary provisions in the constitutions and statutes of the several states.

Congress lacks the power to enact laws regulating individuals and property in states in order to promote and protect the health, safety, morals, welfare, and convenience of the public in spite of the reference to promoting the general welfare of the United States. Congress, however, is able to influence the exercise of these powers by the states as explained in chapter 7.

POWERS OF THE STATES

By ratifying the proposed constitution providing for a federal governance system, states lost their status as sovereign units of government yet they theoretically possess complete power over matters not delegated to Congress with the exceptions of the prohibited powers. Although the media tends to focus attention on the exercise of powers by the national government, the reader should not overlook the great number and variety of fundamental powers reserved to the states.

The constitution's drafters assumed the residual powers would outweigh the delegated powers. Opponents of the proposed constitution did not share this assumption and were convinced Congress might encroach on the powers of the states. Their concern led to the proposal and ratification of the Tenth Amendment stipulating "the powers not delegated to the United States by the Constitution, nor prohibited by it to the States, are reserved to the States respectively, or to the people."

The reserved or residual powers of the states are inherent and important ones that are to a great extent undefined. It often is difficult to draw a sharp dividing line between the powers of Congress and the unsurrendered powers of the states, and the courts are called on to resolve disputes. The reservoir of state powers can be placed in four very broad categories: the police power, provision of services to citizens, taxation and borrowing, and creation and control of local governments.

The Police Power

This power is of great importance because it serves as the basis for a vast amount of social legislation. The power can be defined only in broad terms as the power to regulate personal and property rights in order to protect and promote public health, safety, morals, convenience, and welfare. Justice Oliver Wendell Holmes of the U.S. Supreme Court in 1911 in *Noble State*

Bank v. Haskell wrote "the police power extends to all great public needs. It may be put forth in aid of what is sanctioned by usage, or held by the prevailing morality or strong and preponderant opinion to be greatly and immediately necessary to the public welfare."[4] Exercise of the police power, however, must conform to the Fourteenth Amendment's requirement of due process of law and may not be arbitrary.

The police power has been devolved in broad terms by some state legislatures to general-purpose local governments and serves as the basis for building, electrical, plumbing, sanitary, zoning, and other local ordinances and regulations. A state or a general-purpose local government may exercise the power by enactment and enforcement of a law or public officers may exercise the power summarily to cope with emergencies, such as fires and riots.

The following state and local governmental activities are indicative of the wide scope of the police power: (1) Public safety—building construction standards, inspection of buildings, motor vehicle safety regulations, and destruction of buildings to prevent fires from spreading; (2) public health—the requirement of vaccination against specific diseases, quarantine laws, licensing of the medical profession, inspection of foods and drugs, draining of marshes where mosquitoes breed, destruction of diseased animals, maintenance of sewage and drinking water systems, and operation of public hospitals; (3) public morals—enactment of antifraud laws, prohibition of prostitution and the use of narcotics, suppression of obscene literature, and regulation of the sale of intoxicating beverages; (4) public convenience—zoning and other land use regulations, construction and maintenance of highways and parks, and regulation of private transportation companies; and (5) public welfare—enactment of laws prohibiting child labor and monopolies in restraint of intrastate commerce, and regulation of electric supply and natural gas companies, hours of work, and billboards and other outdoor signs. U.S. Supreme Court decisions, based on the First Amendment and the Fourteenth Amendment to the U.S. Constitution, in recent decades have made it difficult for subnational governments to suppress obscene literature, nude dancing, and pornographic films.

Public Services

State and local governments, under the authority of the reserved powers of the states, provide the bulk of the governmental services citizens receive directly. Six major types of services are described below.

With the exceptions of schools operated by religious institutions and other private bodies, schools ranging from kindergartens to secondary schools are operated by locally governed school districts or cities. Locally governed schools and privately operated schools, however, are subject to supervision by their respective state government. New York City operates the City University of New York including its graduate school. States operate universities and specialized schools such as maritime academies and schools for the developmentally handicapped.

The second type and one of the oldest governmental services is public protection. Although the national government has certain public protection responsibilities, policing is primarily a local government responsibility supplemented by the state police or state highway patrol. In some states including New York, the state-operated force is termed the state police and it has general statewide jurisdiction with perhaps the exception of a large city. The state highway patrol in California and other states, on the other hand, has authority over only state highways and does not patrol highways maintained by local governments.

The third category—public welfare services—dates to the Massachusetts Bay Colony in the third decade of the seventeenth century. These services have expanded greatly at the state and local governmental planes since the mid-1930s. Because of the sharply increased cost of providing these services in recent decades, Vermont in 1967 transferred responsibility for social welfare from cities, towns, and villages to the state.[5] Massachusetts and Delaware initiated similar actions in 1968 and 1970, respectively. In 1990, New Jersey assumed responsibility from counties for all general assistance costs and most of the other costs of providing welfare assistance.

The fourth major category is public health services that have undergone major expansion in the twentieth century. These services include mental health programs, assistance for crippled children, dental and maternity clinics, screening programs for various diseases, and inspection of restaurant and food-processing facilities. The 1966 Rhode Island State Legislature abolished city and town health departments and transferred their functions to the state department of health. Although most Vermont towns have a town health officer, the state department of health is responsible for nearly all health programs.

The fifth category is transportation services, ranging from construction and maintenance of highways to provision of public transportation in the form of bus and subway systems, and construction and operation of air and marine ports. Congress lacks authority to construct highways, with the exception of ones designed to transport the post. To date, Congress has not authorized construction of a post road within a state, but provides grants-in-aid to states for the construction and maintenance of post and other highways.

The sixth category includes agricultural and conservation services. All states operate agricultural research, water resources, reforestation, soil conservation, and fish and game conservation programs.

The Local Government System

A federal relationship exists between the national government and the states, but a unitary relationship originally existed between each state and its local governments (see chapter 8). The latter were viewed as creatures of the state possessing only the limited powers expressly delegated to them by the state legislature. Municipal charters were issued only by the state legislature and were subject to revocation or amendment by the legislature at will. No local government legally could initiate an action, no matter how minor, without explicit permission from the state government.

The unitary relationship between the state and its political subdivisions began to break down in the nineteenth century as state constitutions were amended to place restrictions on the power of the state legislature to control municipalities. Today, the relationship generally is similar to a federal relationship in several states as the state constitution divides power between the state and general-purpose local governments. In practice, however, the attempt to implement a modified federal system within a state has been hindered in several states by court decisions as explained in chapter 8.

Concurrent Powers

The delegation of specific powers to Congress by the national constitution does not necessarily prevent states from exercising the same powers since not all powers delegated to Congress are exclusive in nature. These concurrent powers include levying taxing, borrowing money, establishing courts, and constructing highways. Relative to taxation, Congress and state legislatures both impose levies on corporate and personal income, alcoholic beverages, petroleum products, and cigarettes and other tobacco products.

A state may exercise the police power in a field delegated to Congress if the latter has failed to legislate in that field or if the national law is inadequate to protect public health and safety. In the absence of a national law, the judicial function extends only to an inquiry relative to whether the state in enacting a law took action within its province and whether the regulations are reasonable.

If Congress decides to assume total responsibility for a regulatory function within its sphere of powers, the supremacy of the law clause of the U.S. Constitution (Article VI) automatically nullifies all major state constitutional provisions and statutes if a judicial challenge is brought. In effect, the supremacy of the laws clause makes Congress the judge of the extent of its powers subject to a judicial challenge. Bankruptcies, for example, were regulated primarily by states until 1898 when Congress assumed complete responsibility for the function and all state bankruptcy laws except the homestead provision immediately were nullified.[6] The ability of Congress to assume partial or complete regulatory in various fields automatically produces continuing changes in national-state relations as described in greater detail in chapter 4.

Congress often assumes only partial responsibility in a regulatory field and states are free to regulate in other parts of the field. Congressional regulation of interstate commerce is relatively extensive, yet states may regulate aspects of such commerce not requiring uniform regulation throughout the nation subject to a court challenge. Furthermore, Congress specifically can authorize states to regulate in a field, such as interstate commence, which the U.S. Constitution assigned to Congress. In 1945, for example, Congress devolved authority to regulate the business of insurance to states.[7]

Prohibited Powers

Section 9 of Article I of the U.S. Constitution contains a list of powers the national government may not exercise or may exercise only in special circumstances. In addition to the prohibition of the importation of slaves prior to 1808, the constitution stipulates:

> The privilege of the writ of *habeas corpus* shall not be suspended, unless when in cases of rebellion or invasion the public safety may require it.

> No bill of attainder [legislative declaration of guilt and imposition of punishment] or *ex post facto* [retroactive] law shall be passed.

> No capitation, or other direct, tax shall be laid, unless in proportion to the census or enumeration herein before directed to be taken.

> No tax or duty shall be laid on articles exported from any state.

> No preference shall be given by any regulation of commerce or revenue to the ports of one State over those of another; nor shall vessels bound to, or from, one State, be obliged to enter, clear, or pay duties in another.

> No money shall be drawn from the Treasury but in consequence of appropriations made by law; and a regular statement and

account of the receipts and expenditures of all public money shall be published from time to time.

No title of nobility shall be granted by the United States, and no person holding any office of profit or trust under them, shall, without the consent of the Congress, accept of any present, emolument, office, or title, of any kind whatever, from any king, prince, or foreign state.

The habeas corpus provision is derived from the Petition of Right, to which Charles I was required to assent in 1628, providing that "freemen be imprisoned or disseized only by the law of the land, or by due process of law, and not by the King's special command without any charge." The U.S. Supreme Court in 1798 in *Calder v. Bull* opined the prohibition of ex post facto laws applies only to criminal statutes.[8] The capitation tax provision has been changed by the Sixteenth Amendment which authorizes Congress to levy graduated income taxes "without apportionment among the several States, and without regard to any census or enumeration."

Section 10 of Article I of the Constitution prohibits state exercise of three of the above powers. A state legislature may not enact a bill of attainder or an ex post facto law, or grant titles of nobility. In order to prevent interference with national powers, states are forbidden to enter into a treaty, alliance, or confederation with foreign nations, grant letters of marque and reprisal to privateers, "coin money, emit bills of credit, make any thing but gold and silver coin a tender in payment of debts," or enact a law impairing the obligation of contract. Interestingly, there is no constitutional prohibition of congressional impairment of contracts. Of the various prohibitions of state actions, the only major litigations have involved the contract clause.

The prohibition of state impairment of contracts refers only to private contracts. The U.S. Supreme Court in *Dartmouth College v. Woodward* in 1819 opined that a Crown granted college charter was protected against impairment by the New Hampshire General Court (state legislature).[9] The U.S. Constitution, however, does not protect a local government charter issued by a state legislature against impairment by the legislature. However, state constitutions often forbid the state legislature to impair a municipal charter.

Constitutional Amendments

The Bill of Rights, the first ten amendments to the U.S. constitution, forbids Congress to abridge the liberties of citizens or encroach on the states' reserved powers. As explained in chapter 5, most prohibitions contained in the first eight amendments have been held by the U.S. Supreme Court to apply to states and their political subdivisions through the judicial doctrine of incorporation, which includes these prohibitions within the ambit of the Fourteen Amendment's prohibition against the states.

Six constitutional amendments specifically restrict the reserved powers of the states. The Fourteenth Amendment forbids states, and by extension local governments, to deny any citizen due process of law, equal protection of the laws, and privileges and immunities of citizens of the United States. The equal protection of the laws requirement does not mean that each individual must be treated in exactly the same manner as all other individuals. Legislation applying to a class of individuals, however, must be reasonable and justified on the basis of important differences between the classes, such as farmers and factory workers.

The Fifteenth Amendment prohibits state denial or abridgement of the rights of citizens to vote in any election. The U.S. Supreme Court interpreted this provision as applying only to black citizens.[10]

The Seventeenth Amendment changed the system for selecting U.S. senators from appointment by state legislatures to popular election. With ratification of this amendment, state legislatures no longer could direct their respective U.S. Senators to oppose preemption bills approved by the House of Representatives.

The Nineteenth Amendment forbids states to deny the right to vote because of sex, thereby providing for women's suffrage throughout the nation. Kentucky in 1838 allowed widows and unmarried women whose property was assessed for taxation to vote in school elections. In 1861, Kansas permitted all women to vote in school elections and its example was followed before 1880 by Colorado, Massachusetts, Michigan, Minnesota, and New Hampshire. The territory of Wyoming allowed women to vote in all elections in 1869 and continued the provision for universal suffrage when it was admitted as a state in 1890. Nevertheless, women in many states and local governments were not allowed to vote in all elections until the Nineteenth Amendment became effective in 1920.

The Twenty-fourth Amendment prohibits states from denying the right of citizens to vote in any election for presidential and vice-presidential electors, U.S. senator, and U.S. representative for failure to pay a poll or other direct tax levied by a state.

All states required an individual to be twenty-one years of age to be eligible to vote in a general election until Georgia lowered the age to eighteen in 1943. In 1970, Congress enacted a voting rights act lowering the voting age to eighteen in all elections. The U.S. Supreme Court, however, ruled in *Oregon v. Mitchell* that Congress lacked the power to lower the voting age for state and local elections.[11] This decision prompted congressional proposal and state ratification in 1971 of the Twenty-sixth Amendment lowing the voting age to eighteen in all elections.

Implied Prohibitions

In addition to the specific prohibitions of the exercise of powers by states contained in the U.S. Constitution, there are implied prohibitions. For example, delegation of the power to regulate interstate commerce to Congress implies a restriction on the taxing powers of a state.[12] In other words, a state may not levy a tax that places an undue burden on such commerce. Determining whether a state tax is a valid one is a difficult task since the point at which merchandise and raw materials lose their interstate character is not always clear. If the goods shipped in interstate commerce become commingled with intrastate goods, the former may be taxed by a state on the same basis as the latter goods.

Real property employed exclusively in interstate commerce located in a single state is not exempt from state and local government taxation. A warehouse used to store merchandise for shipment in interstate commerce may be taxed by subnational governments as may the income of firms engaged in interstate commerce located within the state.[13]

Although the U.S. Constitution does not specifically forbid states to tax instrumentalities of the national government, the U.S. Supreme Court in McCulloch v. Maryland in 1819 opined that the power to tax involves the power to destroy and struck down a Maryland tax on the circulation of notes issued by the United States Bank.[14] A state, nevertheless, may levy a nondiscriminatory tax, such as a real property tax, on banks chartered by the U.S. government since this type of tax does not interfere with the operations of the national instrumentality.

State and local governments may not levy taxes on national government properties, such as post offices and military bases. Congress, however, directed various officers in charge of national properties, including the Tennessee Valley Authority, to make payments in lieu of taxes to state and local governments, but these payments are less than the amounts that would be payable if the properties were subject to taxation.

Congress also authorized states to levy specific taxes on certain national government instrumentalities and national government employees. In 1923, Congress permitted states to levy a tax on the shares of national banking associations within the respective states.[15] And Congress in 1939 authorized states to levy a nondiscriminatory tax on the salaries and wages of national government employees.[16]

NATIONAL GUARANTEES TO THE STATES

The U.S. Constitution not only reserves vast powers to states, but also contains five provisions protecting the states and guaranteeing their integrity.

Territorial Integrity

Article IV of the U.S. Constitution mandates the national government to respect the territorial boundaries of each state. No territory may be taken from a state to form a new state without the consent of the state legislature and Congress, and the latter may not combine two or more states without their consent.

The territory of Vermont was admitted to the Union as the fourteenth state in 1791. New Hampshire and New York each claimed Vermont, but neither claim was maintained and hence admission of Vermont to the Union was not the creation of a state from territory taken from a state.

Maine, which was part of the Commonwealth of Massachusetts, was admitted to the Union with Massachusetts's consent as part of the famous Missouri Compromise of 1820 under which Maine entered the Union as a free state and Missouri entered the Union as a slave state.

The 1845 joint resolution of Congress annexing Texas authorizes the creation of "new States, of convenient size, not exceeding four in number, in addition to the said State of Texas."[17] Texas, however, has not been divided to form additional states.

The most controversial admission of a new state involved West Virginia in 1863. The ten western counties of Virginia remained loyal to the Union subsequent to the outbreak of the Civil War in 1861 and petitioned to be admitted to the Union as a state. Members of the Virginia State Legislature from these counties granted consent to the separation of the counties from Virginia and Congress admitted them to the Union as the State of West Virginia.

Foreign Invasion and Domestic Violence

Article IV of the constitution guarantees that the U.S. government will protect each state against foreign invasion and against domestic violence on application of the state legislature or the governor if the legislature cannot be convened. A national guarantee of protection against foreign invasion is essential since states are not allowed to maintain standing armed forces.

While invasion is a threat to a state or nation from without, domestic violence is a rebellion, or condition of riotous resistance, to state authority from within the state. When a state is unable to suppress domestic violence, the legislature or the governor may request that national troops be dispatched to help quell the uprising. The President may refuse to dispatch troops to the state if he or she concludes the situation does not warrant such action. On the other hand, if a federal function—such as interstate commerce—is interfered with, the President will send troops to the state even though the state legislature and the governor protest against the dispatch of the troops. During the nationwide railroad strike in 1894, President Grover Cleveland posted troops to Chicago to prevent interference with the mails without the request of the governor of Illinois and against his protests.

Republican Form of Government

Article IV also guarantees each state a republican or representative form of government. In 1842, two groups in Rhode Island during the Dorr "rebellion" each claimed to be the legitimate government of the state and appealed to the President for military assistance. President John Tyler responded that any action on his part would be to help the charter government and the "rebellion" collapsed. The national courts will not rule on the question of which of two or more groups is the legitimate government of a state on the ground the question is a political one to be settled by the political department of the government and not the judiciary. The courts will support decisions in such a controversy made by Congress and the President.

Although the term is not defined in the constitution, the U.S. Supreme Court in *Pacific State Telephone and Telegraph Company v. Oregon* in 1912 defined a "republican form of government as a representative government; *i.e.*, one in which the power rests with legislators chosen by the people."[18] The case involved the question of whether the provisions of the Oregon Constitution authorizing voters to employ the initiative to place a proposed law on the referendum ballot impaired a republican form of government.[19] The court upheld the state constitutional provision.

Equal State Representation

As noted, the Connecticut Compromise provides that each state would have equal representation in the U.S. Senate. In order to safeguard and perpetuate the original equality of the states, the U.S. Constitution specifically provides in Article V that "no State, without its consent, shall be deprived of its equal suffrage in the Senate." In other words, on this one point it is impossible to amend the constitution without the unanimous concurrence of all states, an impossible event, and this guarantee retains the principle of a confederacy that unanimous consent is required to initiate a change.

Immunity from Suits by Private Citizens

The original thirteen states continued to operate under the English Common Law and substituted the word State for the Crown in the doctrine the Crown can do no wrong and hence cannot be sued without its consent. The doctrine clearly prevents a citizen from suing his or her state in the courts of the state without permission of the state legislature.

To the surprise of the states, the U.S. Supreme Court in *Chisholm v. Georgia* in 1793 interpreted Section 2 of Article III—extending the judicial power of the United States to controversies between citizens of different states—to allow a citizen of one state to sue a second state.[20] This ruling, involving a suit in a federal court by a citizen of South Carolina against Georgia, shocked states which had been assured during the ratification campaign that no individual could sue a state without its consent. In fairness to the court, it must be explained it was following the literal wording of the Constitution.

Georgia and other states denounced the decision as an encroachment on their sovereignty and pressured Congress to propose the Eleventh Amendment to the Constitution prohibiting national courts from taking cognizance of any suit brought against a State "by citizens of another State, or by citizens or subjects of any foreign State." In the twentieth century, a number of states waived partially (completely in New York) their sovereign immunity from suit.

Federal Dependence on the States

The constitution's framers made the national government dependent on the states for initiation of four types of action. First, states are responsible for the conduct of all elections and originally possessed complete authority to determine the suffrage qualifications for voters who choose presidential and vice-presidential electors and members of Congress. Voters currently cast ballots for electors who vote for presidential and vice-presidential candidates. A proposed interstate compact, examined in chapter 7, would change the system and guarantee the election of the presidential-vice presidential slate receiving the most popular votes.

Commencing in 1868, constitutional amendments restricting the election responsibilities of the states were ratified as described in a subsequent section. In addition to suffrage qualifications, states determine the form of the ballot, conduct the elections, count the votes, conduct recounts if needed, and certify the results of the election. Neither house of Congress will utilize its Article I, Section 5 power to settle a disputed election unless the concerned states have failed to do so.

Second, affirmative state action is necessary before the U.S. Constitution can be amended. States have a duty to consider all amendments proposed by the two authorized methods. A decision to ratify a proposed amendment is irrevocable. Under the method employed to date, amendments are proposed by a two-thirds vote in each house of Congress. To become effective a proposed amendment must be ratified either by the state legislature or a specially chosen convention in each of three-fourths of the states.

The Constitution provides a second amendment method. At the request of memorials from two-thirds of the state legislatures, Congress must call a convention for the purpose of proposing amendments to the Constitution for submission for ratification to the state legislatures or state conventions. Although this method has not been employed, increasing state unhappiness with the expansion of the powers of the national government led to state legislatures approving numerous memorials for a convention. A number of state legislatures subsequently withdrew their memorials for the convening of a convention to propose a specific constitutional amendment, and it is unclear whether a state legislature may recall a memorial.

Opponents of a constitutional convention are concerned it might be a "runaway" one that would destroy much of the work of the framers of the fundamental law. To calm these fears, proposals have been made for a convention limited to specified subjects, but questions have been raised whether a convention can be a limited one similar to ones held occasionally by individual states. Proponents of an unlimited convention place their faith in the constitutional requirement of approval by three-fourths of the state legislatures or state conventions of proposed amendments before they become effective to ensure that an unlimited convention would do no serious harm to the Constitution.

Third, the national government is dependent on the states to fill vacancies in the U.S. House of Representatives and the Senate. In the event of a vacancy in the former, Section 2 of Article I of the Constitution requires the governor of the concerned state must issue writs of election to fill the vacancy. Should a vacancy occur in the Senate, the Seventeenth Amendment directs the governor to issue writs of elections unless the state legislature empowers the governor to make a temporary appointment until voters fill the vacancy.

Fourth, Congress is delegated power to organize, arm, and discipline the militia (renamed the National Guard in 1916), but officers are appointed by the state. Failure of a state to appoint officers would render the militia ineffectual since Congress and the President lack the power to appoint militia officers.

More important than the above constitutional provisions is the national government's reliance on states to implement national policies in areas outside of the enumerated powers of Congress. Lacking authority to exercise the reserved powers, Congress must persuade states to adopt national policies and relies heavily on conditional grants-in-aid, cross-cutting sanctions, and cross-over sanctions to convince states to implement the policies as described in chapter 7.

Admission of New States

Section 3 of Article IV of the U.S. Constitution grants Congress complete discretionary authority to admit territories to the Union as states subject to two restrictions. Without the consent of the concerned state legislature, a state may not be divided or two or more state may not be combined without the approval of the two state legislatures. Four states—Kentucky, Maine, Tennessee, and West Virginia—were formed from parts of existing states with the consent of the concerned state legislatures. As noted, the joint resolution annexing Texas authorizes the division of the state to form up to an additional four states. No states have been combined to form a new state and Texas had not been divided into new states.

Thirty-seven states have been admitted to the Union since the Constitution became effective in 1789. With the exceptions of Vermont in 1791, Texas in 1845, and California in 1850, the new states were required prior to admission to the Union to pass through a territorial stage. While Congress possesses authority to admit territories to the Union as states, Congress cannot be compelled to admit a territory as a state.

Congress established a relatively uniform procedure for the admission of new states. First, residents of a territory, through their legislature, petition Congress for admission to the Union. Second, if Congress favorably receives the petition, an "enabling act" is enacted specifying conditions for framing a proposed constitution.

Third, territorial voters elect a constitutional convention to draft a constitution for a new state. Fourth, the draft document is submitted to the territorial voters for approval.

Fifth, voter approval leads to submission of the Constitution to Congress, which may approve the document by enacting a joint resolution of admission. The Missouri territory was not allowed by Congress to enter the Union until the proposed constitution was amended to permit free blacks to enter the state. The Utah territory was refused admission to the Union until the territory agreed to abolish polygamy, which was allowed by the Church of the Latter Day Saints (Mormons) whose members controlled the territory. And Congress refused to approve the proposed Arizona constitution because it contained a provision for the recall of judges from office by the voters.[21] Arizona removed the provision, was admitted to the Union, and shortly thereafter amended the constitution to provide for the recall of judges.

Sixth, admission to the Union is followed by voters electing officers for the new state. When all arrangements have been made, the President of the United States issues a proclamation declaring the state is a member of the Union. The President, of course, could impose conditions on the territory by vetoing a statehood bill not containing the President's conditions, but no President has taken such action.

Congress occasionally imposes on a territory conditions with which it must comply prior to admission to the Union as a state. The U.S. Supreme Court in *Stearns v. Minnesota* in 1900 ruled conditions are judicially enforceable if they concern national property in the new state or land or money grants to the state for specific purposes.[22] Should the conditions restrict the state in its internal organization and government, the state may ignore the conditions after admission to the Union. Oklahoma, for example, transferred its capital from Guthrie to Oklahoma City following its admission to the Union even though one condition of admission was that the capital must be located in Guthrie for a decade. The U.S. Supreme Court in *Coyle v. Smith* in 1911 upheld the right of Oklahoma to move its capital.[23]

Based on its Article I, Section 8 power, Congress subsequent to the Civil War imposed conditions, including repudiation of the debt of the Confederate States of America and authorization for black adult males to vote, on the rebellious states before their senators and representatives would be seated in Congress.

Under the U.S. Constitution, every state is legally equal to every other state. The two newest states, Alaska and Hawaii, possess the identical Tenth Amendment reserved powers possessed by the original thirteen states. The only distinction between states authorized by the constitution is the number of members of the House of Representatives and the number of presidential and vice-presidential electors, distinctions based on the population of each state.

Interestingly, the constitution contains no provision for expelling a state from the Union. Whether a state could secede from the Union was debated prior to the Civil War, which established the principle that the Union is indissoluble and a state may not secede without the permission of the other states.

EXPANSION OF NATIONAL POWERS

The framers of the U.S. Constitution were aware that Congress would expand the powers of the national government as conditions necessitated exercise of the various enumerated powers. By providing two methods for the proposal of constitutional amendments and two methods for ratification of proposed amendments, the framers recognized the need for adjustments in the distribution of powers between Congress and the states that might be required to meet future challenges. When establishing a federal system retaining features of a confederate system, the framers foresaw the need for a referee in cases involving disputes between the national government and the states and between states, and created the U.S. Supreme Court as the ultimate arbiter.

The powers of Congress have been expanded by statutory elaboration, constitutional amendments, and judicial interpretation.

Statutory Elaboration

The delegated powers are latent ones capable of being exercised as a consensus to do so develops in Congress. A few powers were not exercised for decades or were exercised to a very limited extent leading to the term "the silence of Congress" relative to the power to regulate interstate commerce.[24] The latter power was not employed in a relatively comprehensive manner until 1887 and the power to assume complete responsibility for regulation of bankruptcies, except the homestead exemption, dates only to 1898.

The U.S. Constitution delegates specific powers to Congress in broad terms and Congress initially determines the scope of these powers subject to challenges in courts. There is little evidence suggesting what the framers meant by commerce among the several states. The scope of the interstate commerce power in practice is vast and has been employed in new fields and in innovative ways since 1965. This power serves as the basis for numerous environmental statutes and administrative regulations relative to air, land, and water pollution (see chapter 4).

Congress lacks authority to make regulations for the general welfare—a power that belongs to the states—but Congress possesses authority to "lay and collect taxes . . . for the general welfare." Utilizing this power, Congress has spent and is continuing to spend billions of dollars for agriculture, education, and other matters traditionally considered to be solely within the domain of the states. Similarly, this power justifies grants-in-aid to local governments for a wide variety of purposes, including housing and sewage treatment. These actions are examples of statutory enactments based on a power that came into existence through gradual development. The principal difference between the early grants and more recent grants is the addition of conditions, cross-cutting sanctions, and cross-over sanctions to grants (see chapter 6).

Constitutional Amendments

Formal amendment of the constitution increased the national government's power to protect individual rights and strengthened its potential revenue sources. The Fourteenth Amendment, a product of the Civil War, originally was designed to protect the rights of former slaves against infringement by state and local governments. The amendment extends the protection of Congress and the national courts to all persons denied due process of law, equal protection of the laws, and privileges and immunities of all citizens of the United States by subnational legislatures and courts. The wide scope of this amendment must be emphasized.

The Fifteenth Amendment served as the basis for the *Voting Rights Act of 1870* and the *Voting Rights Act of 1871*, but most provisions of these acts were invalidated by the U.S. Supreme Court in *State v. Reese* in 1875 on the ground they protected the voting rights of white citizens while the amendment authorizes Congress to protect the voting rights of only black citizens.[25] Congress repealed the remaining valid provisions of the acts in 1890 and its Fifteenth Amendment powers were not exercised again until the *Voting Rights Act of 1965* was enacted.[26] This act is a unique national suspensory law applicable to a state or a local government only if two conditions are present as explained in chapter 4.

The Sixteenth Amendment grants Congress power to levy income taxes without apportionment among the several states in accordance with their respective populations. In other words, Congress no longer is confined to levying a proportional tax on the income of corporations and individuals, and may levy a graduated income tax. The additional revenues produced by the graduated income taxes enable Congress to raise huge sums of money to finance grants-in-aid to state and local governments and the conditions attached to the grants allow Congress to influence significantly the exercise of reserved powers by the recipient governmental units.

The unamended constitution provided for the appointment of two U.S. senators by each state legislature. This constitutional provision was the product of the Connecticut Compromise that settled the dispute between the large and the small states relative to state representation in Congress. In theory, the Senate would be subject to control of state legislatures and would reject any bill approved by the House of Representatives that would encroach on the reserved powers of the states. A proposed amendment providing for the direct popular election of senators was introduced in Congress in 1826, but the required three-fourths of the states did not ratify a similar proposed amendment until 1913.

Prior to the ratification of the Seventeenth Amendment providing for the direct popular election of U.S. senators, there had been many protracted election contests in state legislatures that consumed a considerable amount of time and limited the amount of time available for addressing affairs of the state. Furthermore, there were instances when the election contests were stalemated and no Senators were elected, thereby depriving the concerned states of their full representation in the Senate. The famous Lincoln-Douglas debates in Illinois in 1858 involved a contest for a senatorship.

With ratification of the Seventeenth Amendment, members of both houses of Congress are elected directly by the voters in their respective states. Although the election method is the same for each house, the same political party does not always control the two houses and even when controlled by one party there often are disagreements over bills by the houses. Furthermore, voters in several states relatively often elect one Democratic senator and one Republican senator.

The Eighteenth Amendment granted Congress the power to prohibit "the manufacture, sale, or transportation of intoxicating liquors," but the Twenty-first Amendment repealed this power.

Judicial Interpretation

There is no provision in the U.S. Constitution specifically authorizing the U.S. Supreme Court to invalidate statutes enacted by Congress or presidential actions. The court, under Chief Justice John Marshall, in *Marbury v. Madison* in 1803 developed the doctrine of judicial review of laws enacted by Congress that subsequently was extended to executive orders issued by the President.[27] And in *Fletcher v. Peck* in 1810, the court invalidated for the first time a state law by striking down a statute enacted by the Georgia State Legislature impairing a contract entered into by a previous state legislature.[28]

It is important to note that most national and state laws are not tested in the national courts for their constitutionality. Major acts of Congress appearing to encroach on state prerogatives are litigated and the U.S. Supreme Court typically makes the final determination of their constitutionality.

James Madison in 1819 acknowledged the framers of the Constitution were aware there occasionally would be differences of opinion relative to the specific division of powers between Congress and the states, but added none of the framers anticipated a ruling as broad as the 1803 one. He stressed:

> Much of the error in expounding the Constitution has its origin in the use made of the species of sovereignty implied in the nature of government. The specified powers vested in the Congress, it is said, are sovereign powers, and that as such they carry with them an unlimited discretion as to the means of executing them. It may surely be remarked that a limited government may be limited in its sovereignty as well with respect to the means as to the objects of its powers; and that to give an extent to the former, superseding the limited to the latter, is in effect to convert a limited into an unlimited government.[29]

With the exception of the period 1835 to 1937, the trend in the court's decisions has been toward a broad interpretation of the powers delegated by the constitution to Congress. As noted, the court in *McCulloch v. Maryland* in 1819 held: "Let the end be legitimate, let it be within the scope of the Constitution, and all means which are not prohibited, but consistent with the letter and spirit of the Constitution are constitutional."[30]

The tendency of the U.S. Supreme Court to interpret the delegated powers of Congress broadly was stressed in 1885 by Professor Woodrow Wilson of Princeton University who subsequently became President of the United States: "Congress must wantonly go very far outside of the plain and unquestionable meaning of the Constitution, must bump its head directly against all right and precedent, must kick against the very pricks of all well-established rulings and interpretations, before the Supreme Court will offer its rebuke."[31]

Many of the court's decisions were rendered under special circumstances, such as those resulting from the nation's growth in area and population, and development of new technologies. As new modes of transportation and communications were developed, the court enlarged the meaning of the interstate commerce power to include railroads, telegraphs, telephones, airplanes, buses, radio, and television that were nonexistent in 1787 when the constitution was drafted. As large-scale manufacturing processes commenced to cross state and national boundaries, the court brought the processes within the scope of national control.

Moreover, the court interpreted the power to raise and support armies to include selective service for men of military age, and rationing and price controls for the civilian population during wartime. Under the treaty-making power, the court upheld an act of Congress preventing the shooting of migratory birds.[32]

Although often controversial, judicial interpretation of the respective powers of Congress and states has added flexibility to the U.S. Constitution and obviated the need for numerous formal amendments. By contrast, employment of specific provisions in a number of state constitutions has made necessary their frequent amendment since state courts lack flexibility in interpreting the provisions.

NATIONAL GOVERNMENT ASSISTANCE TO STATES

The national government has cooperated with the states since the shortly after establishment of the federal system.[33] The earliest forms of cooperation between the two planes of government involved the loan of personnel and equipment, such as surveying instruments. The minor types of cooperation grew into a major system of national government assistance to states in the twentieth century as Congress authorized and funded numerous grant-in-aid programs described in chapter 6.

The national governmental departments and agencies share much of the information and data they collect with the states and also provide various services for state and local governments without charge. The internal revenue service, for example, exchanges its computer tapes of federal income tax returns with states that levy an income tax to enable the states to determine whether a person who filed a federal return is required to file a state return and to ensure all income is reported on the state return. One of the best-known of such national services is the federal bureau of investigation's fingerprint service. Without it, state and local police agencies would not be as successful in their efforts to apprehend criminals and to prosecute individuals accused of crimes.

A large number of national departments and agencies provide technical assistance to subnational governments and conduct training programs for their employees. Relative to the latter, seven federal agencies—emergency management agency, environmental protection agency, national fire academy, coast guard, department of transportation, department of energy, and department of health and human services—provide funding for or conduct training programs for state and local government emergency response personnel whose need has increased with the advent of the war on terror.

Congress employed its power to regulate interstate commerce to assist states in enforcing their laws. The *Lacey Act of 1900*, for example, makes it a national government crime for any person to transport animals or birds killed in violation of the laws of a state across state boundary lines.[34] Similar statutes make it a national crime to transport persons for immoral purposes, stolen motor vehicles and parts, and stolen or counterfeit money or securities across state boundary lines.

To help states combat the loss of tax revenues resulting from the importation of cigarettes without payment of the state excise tax, Congress enacted the *Contraband Cigarette Act of 1978* making it "unlawful for any person knowingly to ship, transport, receive, possess, sell, distribute, or purchase contraband cigarettes.[35]

Illegal gambling is a major problem for many states. To assist them in apprehending gamblers, Congress enacted the *Revenue Act of 1951* levying a $50 tax on persons engaged in the business of accepting wagers, and requiring such persons to register with the collector of internal revenue.[36] The tax obviously was not levied for the purpose of raising revenue. The collection of the tax allows the transfer of details of the registrants to state and local police agencies as *prima facie* evidence the persons are violating state laws against gambling. The U.S. Supreme Court in *States v. Kahriger* in 1953 upheld the constitutionality of the act.[37]

SUMMARY

The U.S. Constitution grants specific powers to Congress and reserves all other powers with the exception of prohibited ones to the states and the people. Several powers are exclusive national powers since states are forbidden to exercise them. Similarly, many of the reserved powers of the states are exclusive ones Congress may not exercise. Other powers are concurrent ones capable of being exercised by either Congress or the states. In the event of a conflict between a congressional statute based on a delegated power and a state statute, the supremacy of the law clause of the U.S. Constitution provides for the prevalence of the national law unless the conflict is incidental.

The reserved powers of the states are undefinable except in broad terms and may be placed in four general categories: the police power, provision of numerous services to citizens, creation and control of local governments, and taxation and borrowing.

The U.S. Constitution contains five national guarantees to the states: territorial integrity, protection against foreign invasion and domestic violence, a republican form of government, equal representation in the U.S. Senate, and immunity from suits by private citizens of other states.

The national government is a partial government heavily dependent on the states. The constitution assigns several duties to the states to assist the national government, including conduct of elections for national offices, consideration of constitutional amendments proposed by Congress, filing of vacancies in the U.S. House of Representatives and Senate, and appointment of National Guard officers. To achieve national goals, Congress must rely on the cooperation of the states in the implementation of national policies in jurisdictional areas reserved to the states.

Congress has complete control over admission of new states to the Union and occasionally placed conditions on the admission of a territory to the Union. On receiving statehood, the former territory can ignore the congressional conditions. The newest state is equal under the constitution to each of the original states.

If the framers of the U.S. Constitution returned to life in the early twenty-first century, they would recognize their handiwork but probably would be surprised by the great expansion of the powers of the national government. The power expansion is attributable to increasing and innovate use of latent powers by Congress, expansive judicial interpretation of the enumerated powers of Congress, and certain constitutional amendments.

The national government, states, and local governments generally cooperate with each other in many functional fields. The national government in particular has been helpful to subnational governments by providing grants-in-aid and other types of financial assistance, sharing information and equipment, and furnishing technical assistance. In addition, Congress has enacted laws to assist states in solving particular problems including loss of tax revenue from the sale of contraband cigarettes.

Although national-state relations in general are governed by comity, disputes occur. The number of disputes has increased since 1965 when Congress began to employ its powers of partial and complete preemption more frequently and in innovative ways, as explained in chapter 4.

CHAPTER 4

Congressional Preemption
of State Regulatory Authority

The U.S. federal system has become a dynamic and flexible one characterized by fluidity in the distribution of formal political powers between Congress and states over time. The framers of the U.S. Constitution, as noted, recognized the undesirability of a static distribution of political powers between the two planes of government by providing a procedures for amendment of the fundamental law and including the supremacy of the law clause to permit Congress to employ its enumerated powers to remove partially or completely state concurrent and reserved regulatory powers to respond to changing conditions. In other words, Congress was designed, through its authority to propose constitutional amendments and to preempt state regulatory powers, to be the principal architect for the restructuring aspects of the federal system on a continuing basis.

The drafters of the U.S. Constitution, by employing general terms and phrases, ensured the metamorphic nature of the federal system as it adjusted to dramatic changes in the means of production, globalization of the economy, population growth, transportation systems, technology, and degree of urbanization over a period of more than two centuries.

Congress enacted in 1790 its first preemption acts, *Copyright Act* and *Patent Act*, but did not enact another one until 1800.[1] Only 29 such statutes were enacted prior to 1900. The enactment rate increased sharply during the decade of the 1970s and the total number of preemption statutes was 589 on March1, 2008 (see table 4.1). Commencing in 1986, Congress began to include one or two preemption acts in many consolidated and other appropriations acts that are hundreds of pages in length. The *Satellite Home Viewer Extension and Reorganization Act of 2004*, for example, is included in the 657–page *Consolidated Appropriations Act for Fiscal Year 2005*.[2]

TABLE 4.1
Congressional Preemption Statutes, 1789–2007*

Prior to 1900	29
1900–1909	14
1910–1919	22
1920–1929	17
1930–1939	31
1940–1949	16
1950–1959	24
1960–1969	47
1970–1979	102
1980–1989	93
1990–1999	87
2000–2007	106

*Compiled by author.

The vast accretion of powers in Washington, DC, is attributable primarily to Congress exercising more frequently and extensively a number of major supersession powers in the period 1964–1880.[3] The revolution in national-state-local relations produced by congressional preemption has not been recognized as widely or analyzed in detail as was the early intergovernmental revolution flowing from the sharp increase in the number of national conditional grant-in-aid programs with their attached conditions, a subject explored in chapter 6. Establishing responsibility for governmental action, inaction, or both has become a difficult task in several important functional areas where Congress has assumed partial responsibility for traditional state and/or local governmental regulatory functions. The current complexity of the federal system baffles the general public, thereby making it nearly impossible for dissatisfied citizens to fix responsibility with certainty for failure to attain certain stated public goals. The Daedalian nature of the legal mosaic is revealed immediately by even a cursory examination of the thousands of pages of preemption statutes in the *United States Code* and the more numerous implementing regulations in the *Code of Federal Regulations*.

The initial centralizing tendencies resulted from Congress authorizing numerous conditional grants-in-aid for state and local governments. The sharp increase in the number of and variety of preemption statutes, particularly in the period 1964–1980, reduced substantially the discretionary authority of states and their political subdivisions; promoted additional interest group lobbying in Congress and national regulatory agencies; and affected the power relationships between the governor and the state legislature in each state. A significant number of congressional statutes remove all regulatory authority from states in certain fields and other statutes only partially preempt state regulatory authority. A small number of supersession statutes contain both complete and partial preemption provisions.

Interestingly, Alexander Hamilton in *The Federalist Number 17* assured readers that "it will always be far more easy for the State government to encroach upon the national authorities than for the national government to encroach upon the State authorities."[4] Compare Hamilton's statement with one of the declared purposes of the *Americans with Disabilities Act of 1990*: "To invoke the sweep of congressional authority, including the power to enforce the Fourteenth Amendment and to regulate commerce, in order to address the major areas of discrimination faced day-to-day by people with disabilities."[5]

The broad power potential of Congress was not recognized fully by most observers at the time of the drafting of the U.S. Constitution although a few antifederalists appreciated the potential scope of congressional preemption powers should Congress decide to employ them fully. Antifederalist delegates to the 1788 Pennsylvania Convention considering the ratification of the proposed U.S. Constitution argued aggressive employment of delegated powers would "produce . . . one, consolidated government."[6]

Although Congress employed its complete preemption powers as early as 1790 and various observers expressed concern about the growing national governmental powers, the exercise of preemption powers had a relatively limited impact on national-state relations until 1965 when the powers were employed in traditional state government regulatory fields and in innovative manners.[7] A 1940 issue of a major journal was devoted to intergovernmental relations, yet no reference was made to formal national governmental preemption powers.[8] In 1974, however, several references to such preemptions were contained in an issue of the same journal devoted to intergovernmental relations.[9] A 1990 issue of this journal featured a major article devoted to the subject of congressional supersession of state and local governmental authority.[10]

States on occasions attempted to forestall enactment of a preemption statute by promoting adoption of a uniform state law and/or entering into an interstate compact, described in chapter 7, creating agencies with regulatory authority to solve specific problems. An example of an unsuccessful effort of the latter type is the Mid-Atlantic States Air Pollution Control Compact entered into by Connecticut, New Jersey, and New York subsequent to President Lyndon B. Johnson's 1967 message to Congress recommending national government assumption of responsibility for air pollution abatement. Congress did not grant its consent to the proposed compact and enacted the *Air Quality Act of 1967*, preempting completely responsibility for regulating emissions from new motor vehicles and assuming partial responsibility for regulation of other sources of air pollutants.[11]

CONGRESSIONAL RESTRAINT OF STATE POWER EXERCISE

All observers recognized Congress may exercise its delegated powers, reinforced by the supremacy of the law clause, to nullify concurrent powers of a state when the U.S. Constitution became effective in 1789. Time revealed that Congress also can nullify a state law based on a nonconcurrent reserved power of the states if the state law conflicts with a congressional act based on a delegated power. The antifederalist feared the U.S. Constitution would allow Congress to preempt most reserved powers of the states. The national legislature, for example, can employ the power to regulate commerce among the states to invalidate a state law, based on the reserved police power, requiring the inspection of concrete imported into the state if an undue burden is placed by the inspection requirement on interstate commerce. Congress also can employ a delegated power to preempt the English Common Law followed by all states except Louisiana.

Preemption statutes may be classified as complete or partial depending on whether Congress permits states to exercise any independent regulatory power in the fields preempted.[12] In addition to restraining exercise of powers by states, a preemption statute may mandate that states initiate a specific action or meet minimum national standards. Federal mandates are major irritants in national-state relations, particularly because many mandates are expensive to implement, a subject examined in a subsequent section.

Galloping Preemption

The dramatic increase in the number of preemption statutes may be traced to seven major developments. First, powerful economic interests, major contributors to the election campaigns of many members of Congress, have been able to augment their influence as the cost of election campaigns grew sharply with candidates relying more heavily on expensive television advertisements.

Second, influential congressional leaders desire to become President or vice president and need the electoral and other support of important interest groups often favoring national preemption of particular state powers. Somewhat surprisingly, members of Congress who formerly were state government officers often support preemption bills. And notwithstanding their rhetoric, Presidents since 1965 generally supported preemption statutes or offered only mild opposition to preemption bills in Congress.

Third, the general failure of states to initiate effective corrective action individually or collectively to solve several critical problems generated public support for national government action. Individual states failed to solve environmental problems, particularly air and water pollution, which had adverse spill-over effects on sister states. Television must be credited with generating public pressure on Congress to enact preemption statutes as news and documentary programs often highlight environmental degradation. And the shipping industry was burdened by different state truck weight and size limits impeding the free flow of highway transported materials and goods across state boundary lines, thereby adding to costs.

Felix Morley in 1959 explained the drift of political power to the national government in the following terms: "State governments, with a few honorable exceptions, are both ill-designed and ill-equipped to cope with the problems which a dynamic society cannot, or will not, solve for itself. State constitutions are in many cases unduly restrictive. Their legislatures meet too briefly and have most meager technical assistance. Governors generally have inadequate executive control over a pattern of local governments unnecessarily complex and confusing."[13]

The shift of power to the national government could be described accurately in 1959 as a drift, but must be described as a gallop since 1965. Morley's comments on the states generally were accurate in 1959, but there have been major changes in many states in subsequent years, including provision of additional professional staff for state legislators.

Fourth, Congress became convinced in 1965 conditional grants-in-aid for state and local governments failed to solve several critical national problems, particularly air and water pollution. Many members viewed complete preemption, partial preemption, or both as the only alternative approach with potential for solving national problems.

Fifth, pertinacious public interest groups lobbied Congress successfully to assume complete responsibility for solving particular regulatory problems, such as environmental pollution. These groups also mobilize citizen support for enactment of preemption statutes and apply pressure on national and state administrative agencies responsible for promulgating implementing rules and regulations. There are, of course, other interest groups, including associations of state and local officers, which lobby against certain preemption bills in Congress.

Edward I. Koch, a former U.S. Representative and a former mayor of New York City, explained congressional enactment of preemption statutes:

> As a member of Congress I voted for many of the laws, . . . and did so with every confidence that we were enacting sensible permanent solutions to critical problems. It took a plunge into the

Mayor's job to drive home how misguided my congressional out-
look had been. The bills I voted for in Washington came to the
floor in the form that compelled approval. After all, who can vote
against clean air and water, or better access and education for the
handicapped. But as I look back it is hard to believe I could have
been taken in by the simplicity of what the Congress was doing
and the flimsy empirical support—often no more than a carefully
orchestrated hearing record or a single consultant's report—
offered to persuade the members that the proposed solution could
work throughout the country.[14]

Sixth, a related development—the large and increasing national budgetary deficit—reduced the amount of funds available for use as conditional
grants-in-aid to encourage states to adopt and implement national policies.

Seventh, many state government officers recognized there are critical
interstate problems incapable of solution by states acting individually or by
interstate cooperation. Brevard Crihfield and H. Clyde Reeves of the Council of State Governments in 1974, while not maintaining that all preemptive actions by Congress are wrong, were highly critical of indiscriminate
supersession of state laws:

> Regulation of everybody and everything is not necessarily the
> *Summum Bonum* of a legislative assembly, be it state or national.
> Legislative forbearance, like judicial restraint, has its place in the
> body politics. Congress is often urged to supersede state law as a
> means of promoting uniform applications throughout the nation,
> and on occasion the need will be manifest. On the other hand,
> interstate cooperative devices have shown their ability to achieve
> necessary uniformity and coordination in many areas of public
> concern. A federal system of government, by definition, envisions
> finer intergovernmental tuning devices than a central doctrine.[15]

By 1980, state government views had begun to change dramatically as
illustrated by the following policy position of the National Governors Association: "The Association is concerned with increasing costs to truckers as
well as consumers resulting from the lack of uniformity in allowable vehicle weights and dimensions which still exists among many States. . . .
    The Association urges that Congress immediately enact legislation
establishing national standards for weight (980,000 gross; 20,000 per single
axle; 34,000 for tandem) and length (60 ft.)."[16] In response, Congress
enacted the *Surface Transportation Assistance Act of 1982* and the *Motor
Vehicle Width Regulations of 1983.*[17]

State government officers generally supported enactment of the *Commercial Motor Vehicle Safety Act of 1986* because states were unable to solve the problem resulting from truck drivers holding operator licenses issued by more than one state. If a driver was convicted of a serious driving offense and his or her operator's license was revoked, the driver might continue to operate a truck by utilizing an operator's license issued by a sister state.[18] This act makes it a federal crime for a motorist to have more than one commercial driver's license.

Court Interpretation

A number of congressional statutes contain an expressed provision for complete preemption. The *Flammable Fabrics Act of 1967*, for example, declares "this Act is intended to supersede any law, of any State or political subdivisions thereof inconsistent with its provision."[19] The *Gun Control Act of 1968*, however, limits the scope of its preemption in the following terms: "No provision . . . shall be construed as indicating an intent on the part of the Congress to occupy the field in which such provision operates to the exclusion of the law of any State on the same subject matter unless there is a direct and positive conflict between such provision and the law of the State so that the two can not be reconciled or consistently stand together."[20] The "direct and positive conflict" phrase is a "savings" clause preventing complete preemption of state regulatory authority relative to all aspects of gun control.

States specifically are authorized by the *Federal Railroad Safety Act of 1970* to enact laws and promulgate regulations, orders, and standards with respect to railroad safety more stringent than the counterpart federal ones "when necessary to eliminate or reduce an essential local safety hazard, and when not incompatible with either any federal law, rule, regulation, or order, or standard, and when not creating an undue burden on interstate commerce."[21]

Many congressional regulatory acts do not contain an explicit preemption section, but have been held to be preemptive by the courts. In several decisions, the U.S. Supreme Court emphasized it lacks precise criteria for determining whether Congress intended to exercise its preemption powers if a statute does not contain an explicit preemption statement. Among other things, the court examines congressional debates and reports of hearings and congressional committees in an effort to determine the intent of Congress, a subject examined in greater detail in chapter 5.

The court in *Rice v. Santa Fe Elevator Corporation* in 1947 stressed that the first key question is What was the purpose of Congress in enacting the statute?; the second key question is whether the statute is in "a field in which the federal interest is so dominant that the federal system will be assumed to preclude enforcement of state laws on the same subject."[22] On occasion, the court agreed with the plaintiff that a state law violates the supremacy of the law clause of the U.S. Constitution by conflicting with an act of Congress, but opined that the conflict is a minor one and does not confer jurisdiction on the national courts.

Not surprisingly, the Supreme Court occasionally invalidated only one section of a multisection state law on preemption grounds. A three-section State of Washington law, pertaining only to Puget Sound, requires oil tankers to be guided by state-licensed pilots, specifies oil tanker design standards, and prohibits tankers over 125,000 deadweight tons from entering the Sound. The court upheld the constitutionality of the first section in *Ray v. Atlantic Richfield Company* in 1978, but invalided the other two sections on preemption grounds.[23]

The Supreme Court on rare occasions invalidates an act of Congress on the ground Congress exercised an *ultra vires* power; that is, exceeded its constitutionally delegated powers. The 1970 Congress lowered the voting age in all elections to eighteen, but the court ruled the following year in *Oregon v. Mitchell* that Congress lacks the power to lower the voting age for state and local government elections.[24] In *National League of Cities v. Usery*, the court in 1976 similarly invalidated the *Fair Labor Standards Amendments of 1974* extending minimum wage and overtime pay provisions to non-supervisory employees of subnational governments.[25] The court, however, in *Garcia v. San Antonio Metropolitan Transit Authority* in 1985 reversed the *Usery* decision.[26]

Rules Precluding Preemption

Although the *Voting Rights Act of 1965* is a national law, it does not apply to a state or a local government unless two conditions prevail: A voting device—such as a literacy test—had been employed in 1964 and less than 50 percent of the electorate cast ballots in the preceding presidential election.[27]

Amendments enacted in 1975 expanded the act's coverage to include language minorities defined as "persons who are American-Indian, Asian American, Alaska Natives, or of Spanish heritage."[28] The language minority "triggers" applying the act to a state or a local government are (1) members of one language group constituting in excess of 5 percent of the unit's population and (2) fewer than one-half of these voters cast ballots in the preceding presidential election. The act also is applied if more than 5 percent of the citizens are members of one language minority group and the group's illiteracy rate exceeds the national illiteracy rate.

State and local governments subject to the act may make no change in their electoral system, no matter how minor, unless the U.S. attorney general fails to register an objection to the proposed change within sixty days of its submission to him or her or the U.S. District Court for the District of Columbia issues a declaratory judgment that the proposed change would not abridge the right to vote of citizens protected by the act.

The *Hazardous Materials Transportation Uniform Safety Act of 1990* also authorizes administrative rulings precluding federal preemption.[29] The U.S. Department of Transportation can issue rulings addressing the question whether a state law or rule is preempted by the act. State or local government requirements are not preempted provided they afford an equal or greater level of safety protection than the national requirements and do not burden unreasonably interstate commerce. The department must make a determination within 180 days of receipt of an application for a determination. The concerned governments also are authorized to seek a determination of preemption in a court of competent jurisdiction in lieu of applying to the department for a determination.

Complete Preemption

There are seventeen types of complete preemption statutes enacted by Congress, ranging from ones prohibiting all state exercise of regulatory power in a field to ones authorizing states to cooperate in enforcing a congressional preemption statute.[30] States have been stripped of their powers to engage in the economic regulation of airlines, bus, and trucking companies, establish a compulsory retirement age for their employees other than judges, or regulate bankruptcies other than the homestead exemption and ionizing radiation.

The national government can exercise exclusive regulatory powers successfully in several fields as illustrated by the *Copyright Act of 1790* and the *Patent Act of 1790*. In other functional areas, however, the limited resources of the national government and lack of complementary powers make successful regulation dependent on state government, local government, or both assistance. Incidents necessitating a prompt emergency response, such as a transportation accident involving hazardous materials, are beyond the capabilities of the national government and it assumes state and local government will respond in an emergency situation.

Complete preemption statutes until the late 1950s vested all regulatory powers in the national government. By 1959, Congress determined that states could play a role, although a limited one, in administering several complete preemption statutes. Four such statutes currently authorize states to enter into agreements with national agencies to perform inspections in accordance with national standards—grain quality and weighing, hazardous and solid waste materials, railroad safety, and specified types of low-level ionizing radiation. States performing these inspections are not reimbursed by the national government for incurred expenses, but user charges finance state grain inspection. The *Safe Drinking Water Act Amendments of 1986*— banning use of lead pipes, solder, and flux in public water systems—implicitly recognizes the need for subnational governmental assistance by mandating that these governments enforce the ban.[31]

Congress employed its powers of complete preemption to require state legislatures to enact statutes. The framers of the U.S. Constitution did not contemplate such a coercion of the states. The *Equal Employment Opportunity Act of 1972, Fair Labor Standards Amendments of 1974, Safe Drinking Water Act Amendments of 1986,* and *Federal Mine and Health Act of 1977* are examples of national laws requiring state legislatures to enact compliance laws under the threat of civil or criminal penalties.[32] And the *Low-Level Radioactive Waste Policy Act of 1980* makes states responsible for disposal of low-level radioactive wastes generated within their respective boundaries in conformance with national standards and encourages formation of interstate compacts.[33] Ten such compacts, encompassing forty-four states, have received congressional consent (see chapter 7).

Three complete preemption statutes are contingent ones. As noted, the *Voting Rights Act of 1965* applies only to a state or a local government if two conditions exist. The *Atlantic Striped Bass Conservation Act Amendments of 1986* requires individual states to comply with the management plan developed by the Atlantic States Marine Fisheries Commission, which otherwise lacks enforcement powers, or be subject to a striped bass fishing moratorium imposed by the U.S. Fish and Wildlife Service and the Marine Fisheries Services in the coastal waters of a noncomplying state.[34] And the *Gramm-Leach-Bliley Act of 1999* threaten to establish a national licensing insurance system for insurance agents if twenty-six state legislatures did not enact by November 12, 2002, harmonious licensing statutes as determined by the National Association of Insurance Commissioners.[35] The association on September 10, 2002, certified thirty-five states had enacted such statutes.

One complete preemption statutes is designed to assist coastal states. The *Abandoned Shipwreck Act of 1987* asserts a national government title to abandoned historic shipwrecks and subsequently transfers the title to the state within whose coastal waters the ship is located.[36]

The *Nuclear Waste Policy Act of 1982* is an unusual complete preemption statute because it authorizes a state veto of a federal administrative decision.[37] The act directs the secretary of energy to select a site for a new high-level radioactive waste facility subject to the site being vetoed by the concerned state legislature or governor. The veto is a conditional one and may be overridden by Congress. In 1987, Congress included an amendment to the 1982 act in the *Omnibus Budget Reconciliation Act of 1988* removing sites for the facility in Texas and Washington and in effect selecting the Yucca Mountain site in Nevada.[38] On April 8, 2002, Congress formally overrode the notice of disapproval of the site submitted by the governor of Nevada.[39]

Partial Preemption

Important changes in the federal system have been produced by complete preemption of the regulatory authority of the states in a number of functional fields. Nevertheless, partial preemption—removal of some but not all state political powers in a regulatory area—has had more important consequences for the system in terms of its increasing complexity. This type of preemption assumes two general forms. The first form involves Congress enacting a statute assuming complete responsibility for only a portion of a regulatory field. The second form is the product of Congress enacting a law and/or federal administrative agencies, as authorized by law, promulgating rules and regulations establishing minimum national standards and authorizing states to exercise regulatory primacy provided state standards are as stringent as the national ones and are enforced.

Congressional statutes partially assuming regulatory authority can be placed in eight categories.[40]

1. *Minimum Standards Preemption.* Congress initiated a revolution in national-state relations by enacting the *Water Quality Act of 1965* (now *Clean Water Act*), a contingent complete preemption statutes, based upon the "gun-behind-the-door" theory that states have to be pressured to initiate action in a functional area meeting minimum national standards under the threat of losing regulatory authority in the field.[41]

   The act authorizes the secretary of the interior, now environmental protection agency administrator, to establish national water quality standards and to delegate "regulatory primacy" to any state submitting a plan with standards meeting or exceeding national standards and guaranteeing enforcement of state standards. Other major minimum standards preemption acts are the *Air Quality Act of 1967* (now *Clean Air Act*), *Safe*

Drinking Water Act of 1974, and *Surface Mining Control and Reclamation Act of 1977.*[42]

This type of partial preemption is designed to foster formation of a national-state partnership with states assuming regulatory responsibilities delegated by a federal department or agency and enforcing standards equal to or exceeding national standards. Only if a state fails to apply for and accept "regulatory primacy" or returns it will the concerned federal department or agency assume complete responsibility for the function within the state.

An advantage of this type of partial preemption is the ability of a state to tailor regulatory programs to meet special conditions and needs in the state, provided the supervising federal agency certifies the state's program. It is important to note state regulation is at the sufferance of Congress, which at any time may preempt completely the responsibility for the regulatory function or change the minimum standards.

States are not required to apply for "regulatory primacy." Nine states with coal-mined land decided not to seek primacy under the *Surface Mining Control and Reclamation Act of 1977,* twenty-four states have been delegated regulatory primacy, and Tennessee in 1984 returned primacy to the office of surface mining of the U.S. Department of the Interior.[43]

To date, the U.S. Environmental Protection Agency (EPA) has not revoked the delegation of "regulatory primacy" under the *Clean Water Act.* On rare occasions, a state has returned "regulatory primacy." Iowa, for example, was granted primacy under the *Safe Drinking Water Act of 1974* but state financial problems led to the return of primacy to the agency in 1981. When the financial problems were solved, primacy was redelegated by the agency to the state in 1982. California in 1983 returned its primacy for the construction grant program of the *Clean Water Act* to the agency "because state officials believed the EPA required more of primacy States than it did of its own regional officers who served as implementers in States that did not accept primacy."[44]

2. *Stricter State Controls.* The *Port and Tanker Safety Act of 1978* and the *National Gas Policy Act of 1978* permit states to impose controls provided that they are more stringent than the federal ones. This type differs from the first type because there is no requirement that states must submit a plan for approval to a national regulatory agency prior to exercising a power.[45]

3. *Combined Minimum Standards Preemption and Dual Sovereignty.*
The *Occupational Safety and Health Act of 1970* establishes minimum national standards to protect workers and authorizes delegation of "regulatory primacy" to a state, but also empowers a state to regulate an activity if there are no applicable federal standards.[46]

4. *Regulatory Authority Transfer.* The *Wholesome Meat Act of 1967* authorizes the secretary of agriculture to inspect meat and to transfer responsibility for intrastate meat inspection to a state provided its inspection law is consistent with national standards. In addition, a state is authorized to transfer the responsibility for intrastate meat inspection to the secretary.[47] Similar transfer provisions are contained in the *Poultry Products Inspection Act of 1968.*[48]

5. *Administrative Rule Preemption.* The *Toxic Substances Control Act of 1976* permits a state or local government to regulate a chemical substance or mixture until the EPA administrator promulgates a rule applicable to that substance or mixture.[49] A section in the act permits regulatory flexibility by allowing the administrator to exempt a substance or mixture from the national standards if the state standards offer a higher degree of protection to citizens and the environment.

6. *Additional Uses for a Nationally Controlled Product.* The *Environmental Pesticide Control Act of 1972* authorizes states to register pesticides formulated for use within the state to meet local needs if the EPA administrator certifies the states as being capable of exercising proper controls over the product.[50] The act also permits states to cooperate in the enforcement of the national standards.

7. *Franchise Renewal Preemption.* The *Cable Communications Policy Act of 1984* empowers states and their political subdivisions to issue and renew cable television franchises consistent with national standards that make it exceedingly difficult for a subnational government legally to refuse a renewal application.[51]

8. *Reverse Preemption.* The *Coastal Zone Management Act of 1972* forbids national governmental departments and agencies to issue licenses or permits to private party applicants in the coastal zone of a state with a nationally approved land and water management program if the state objects to the application.[52] The secretary of commerce, however, can override a state's objection.

The Reagan Preemption Legacy

"The Reagan Revolution" was a well-publicized one relative to the President's political decentralization efforts, particularly his proposal of block grants-in-aid. There also was a "Silent Reagan Revolution" as Congress continued to enact many preemption statutes often with the President's quiet and full support. He approved 106 preemption bills, more than any other President, during his 8 years in office, including ones amending earlier preemption statutes.[53] Only three acts have a major impact on state regulatory powers: *Bus Regulatory Reform Act of 1982, Fair Credit and Charge Card Disclosure Act of 1988*, and *Ocean Dumping Ban Act of 1988*.[54]

He vetoed only two preemption bills, and his disallowance of the congressionally enacted *Water Quality Act of 1986* was based on what he considered to be excessive spending authorization for sewage treatment construction grants and rather than on preemption grounds.

In general, President Reagan favored complete preemption statutes granting greater freedom of action to the banking, communications, and transportation industries. In part, these preemption statutes respond to technological developments or the need to stimulate economic growth at the time the economy was experiencing a mild recession.

President Reagan also was a strong supporter of preemption and crossover sanction statutes (see chapter 6) designed to protect and promote the environment, public health, and public safety. Most of these statutes permit states to play major roles in the implementation of national policies.

Subsequent Presidential Actions

President George H. W. Bush (1989–1993) approved thirty-four preemption bills, but only one—*Clean Air Act Amendments of 1991*—had a major impact on the regulatory powers of the states.[55]

President William J. Clinton (1993–2001) approved sixty-four preemption bills, but only three had a major impact on state regulatory powers: *Riegle-Neal Interstate Banking and Branching Efficiency Act of 1994, Telecommunications Act of 1996*, and *Gramm-Leach-Bliley Financial Modernization Act of 1999*.[56]

President George W. Bush approved eighty-seven preemption bills into law during the period 2001–2007 and vetoed no preemption bill. These statutes removed relatively little power from states with the exception of two acts extending the sunset clause of the *Internet Tax Freedom Act of 1998* prohibiting subnational governments to tax access to the Internet.[57]

Most preemption bills approved by the President in the period 1989–2007 were minor ones on the periphery of state exercised powers when compared to acts enacted in the period 1964–1980 striking at the core of state regulatory powers.[58]

PREEMPTION RELIEF

If states are unsuccessful in blocking enactment of a preemption statute, they often pressure Congress to provide relief from the costs associated with mandates imposed by the statute. Similarly, states lobby Congress to reverse burdensome preemption decisions of the U.S. Supreme Court.

The broad reach of the power of Congress to regulate commerce among the states was recognized at an early date and questions were raised relative to restraining Congress from using this power to encroach on traditional state governmental responsibilities. In 1824, Chief Justice John Marshall of the U.S. Supreme Court wrote in *Gibbons v. Ogden* that "the wisdom and the discretion of Congress, their identify with the people, and the influence which their constituents possess at elections, are . . . the sole restraints on which they have relied to secure them from its abuse."[59]

Herbert Wechsler in 1953 expanded Marshall's conclusion and developed the political safeguards theory of federalism, explaining state officers can employ the political process to defeat bills in Congress designed to remove their regulatory powers.[60]

In 1985, Justice Harry A. Blackmun of the U.S. Supreme Court was inspired by the Wechsler theory and wrote in *Garcia v. San Antonio Metropolitan Transit Authority*: "[T]he principal and basic limit on the federal commerce power is inherent in all state participation in federal government action."[61] Blackmun was referring to state officers employing the political process to ensure that Congress does not use the interstate commerce power to place undue burdens on states.

Another thesis can be added to the Marshall, Wechsler, and Blackmun theses: Congress will respond favorably to strong state pressure for relief from preemption statutes. Experience reveals that if the number of states petitioning is small—licensing nuclear power plants is an example—Congress may provide no relief. On the other hand, if all or a sizable number of states seek relief from a preemption statute, the *Safe Drinking Water Act* is an example, or preemption decision of the U.S. Supreme Court, Congress may provide a degree of relief.

In effect, Congress employs its preemption powers on the basis of a leadership-feedback model with Congress leading by enacting preemption statutes establishing new national policies and amending the statutes on the basis of feedback from states, local governments, or both. Subnational governments, of course, also attempt to block enactment of certain preemption bills in Congress or seek to have the bills amended before they become law.

To date, Congress has enacted ten preemption relief laws and all were enacted during the presidency of Ronald Reagan who did not sponsor or promote the bills although he publicly favored devolution of certain national powers to states.

Vigorous state opposition on safety grounds to the *Surface Transportation Assistance Act of 1982*, which authorized very large and heavy trucks to operate on most major state highways, led to congressional enactment of the *Tandem Truck Safety Act of 1984* and the *Motor Carrier Safety Act of 1984* responding to many of the states' safety concerns.[62]

Six additional laws grant relief from earlier enacted preemption statutes:

1. The *Nuclear Waste Policy Act of 1982* authorizes a state to veto a site for a high-level radioactive waste facility selected by the secretary of energy subject to an override of the veto by Congress.

2. The *Tax Reform Act of 1984* exempts refunds to nonitemizing taxpayers from the national requirement that state and local governments making income tax refunds to their respective taxpayers must report information on the refunds to the national Internal Revenue Service.

3. The *Virus, Serum, and Toxin Act Amendments of 1985* direct the U.S. department of agriculture to exempt from national licensing requirements any animal geologic prepared solely for distribution within a state or produced and licensed by the states under a state regulatory program determined by the secretary of agriculture to meet specified criteria.

4. The *Competitive Equality Banking Act of 1987* exempts state-chartered banks not controlled by bank holding companies from the prohibition of banks engaging in insurance activities.

5. The *Marine Plastic Pollution Research and Control Act of 1987* provides for nonpreemption of state laws relating to vessel source garbage.

6. The *Age Discrimination in Employment Amendments of 1986* repealed in part the provision of the 1982 amendments to the *Employment Act of 1967* prohibiting public and private employers requiring employees to retire because of age. Strong opposition from subnational governments to the 1982 amendments induced Congress to enact the 1986 amendments stipulating it is not

unlawful for a state or a local government to refuse to hire or to discharge an individual because of age if the individual is seeking employment as a firefighter or a law enforcement officer.[63]

Two statutes provide relief from preemption decisions of the U.S. Supreme Court. In 1943, the court in *Parker v. Brown* developed the state-action doctrine holding that the national antitrust laws were not designed "to restrain a State or its officers or agents from activities directed by its legislature."[64] The court retreated from this ruling in *City of Lafayette v. Louisiana Power and Light Company* by concluding "when the State itself has not directed or authorized an anticompetitive practice, the State's subdivisions in exercising their delegated power must obey the antitrust laws."[65] In *Community Communications Corporation v. City of Boulder*, the court in 1982 opined that local governments and their officers could be held liable under the antitrust laws and be subject to triple damages.[66] Reacting to pressures from local governments and states, Congress enacted the *Local Government Antitrust Act of 1984* stipulating that damages cannot be recovered under the national antitrust laws from a local government or employee acting in an official capacity.[67]

The national *Fair Labor Standards Act Amendments of 1974* extend minimum wage and overtime provisions to nonsupervisory state and local government employees. In 1975, the U.S. Supreme Court, by a five to four vote in *National League of Cities v. Usery*, opined Congress exercised an *ultra vires* power violating the Tenth Amendment to the U.S. Constitution.[68] The court, however, in *Garcia v. San Antonio Metropolitan Transit Authority* in 1985 reversed itself in a five to four ruling.[69]

State and local government officers were appalled by the ruling and estimated the decision would necessitate annual compliance costs ranging from one-half to one-and-one-half billion dollars. Congress reacted to complaints of subnational governments by amending the *Fair Labor Standards Act* in 1985 to authorize these governments to offer their employees compensatory time off at the rate of one and one-half hours for each hour of overtime work in lieu of overtime compensation, clarifying the labor standards do not apply to volunteers, and granting legislative employees of subnational governments identical exemption from the standards as apply to congressional employees.[70]

THE CONFUSED RESPONSIBILITY PROBLEM

The theory of dual federalism postulates the national government and a state each has autonomous political powers and there is no interaction between the two planes of government. To a great extent, this theory possessed considerable validity in the period 1789 to the late nineteenth century as the two planes of government tended to act independently of each other and one plane generally did not encroach on the other plane. Hence, it was possible during this time period to determine whether the national government or a state(s) was responsible for solving a given public problem. With the development of congressional conditional grants-in-aid, the separation between purely national functions and purely subnational functions broke down and fixing responsibility for solving problems became a more difficult task.

Extensive use of congressional preemption powers since 1965 has made it extremely difficult to determine which plane of government is responsible for actions initiated or not initiated to solve many major public problems. Citizens, according to a central premise of democratic theory, should be able to fix governmental and public officer responsibility in order to hold governments and their officers accountable for implementing their assignments in an effective manner. In a unitary system, citizens readily can determine responsibilities for governmental failures. In a federal system today, uncertainty regarding responsibility for certain actions is an inherent problem.

Intergovernmental problems can be created and responsibility clouded by the wording of preemption statutes. Senator Howard H. Baker Jr. of Tennessee in 1967 recognized this problem: "But I respectfully suggest that we ought to give very close attention to the language that we adopt so that this question of preemption or non-preemption or every personal legislative preemption is clearly spelled out, so that we do not hinder the efforts of local authorities to respond to local circumstances."[71]

Congress generally ignores Senator Baker's advice and numerous preemption statutes enacted since 1967 fail to establish clearly the respective responsibilities of the national government and the states. In these instances, the courts are called on to decide if Congress intended the statutes to preempt completely or partially the regulatory authority of the states.

Congress often avoids precise language in a preemption statute since more precise language could generate additional opposition of sufficient strength to prevent enactment of the bill into law. A second reason for avoidance of such language is the complexity of the activities being regulated. It is apparent that a body with general legislative responsibilities and lacking functional expertise is incapable of developing a more precise statute. Hence, Congress typically enacts a skeleton or outline law establishing general policies and authorizing administrative agencies to draft and promulgate regulations containing specific provisions and standards.

Congress enacted two preemption statutes recognizing the need for a clarification mechanism by authorizing a court to issue a declaratory judgment regarding the rights and responsibilities of the concerned parties and/or authorizing a national executive agency to make an administrative determination whether a statute preempts subnational government action. The *Voting Rights Act of 1965* and the *Hazardous Materials Transportation Uniform Safety Act of 1990* provide for both types of determination.[72]

Congressional exercise of a complete preemption power suggests Congress and appropriate national administrative agencies would be completely responsible for the preempted function. Responsibility, however, often becomes clouded because Congress is a government of enumerated powers and may lack essential complementary powers to ensure it is able to exercise a preempted function successfully. Hence, Congress relies on subnational governments for assistance in implementing national policies. The result may be confusion in the minds of citizens with respect to which government is responsible for the regulatory function.

Governor Mario M. Cuomo of New York in 1983 posted a letter to U.S. Senator Daniel P. Moynihan of New York requesting assistance in sorting out governmental responsibilities:

> I am writing to request that you initiate a hearing process to: (1) achieve a clarification and a precise specification of the respective responsibilities of local, state, and federal governments for off-site emergency plans at our nation's nuclear plants, (2) devise a federal system for the administration and funding of extensive activities undertaken by all three levels of government in the implementation, and (3) examine the consequences of decisions required by this off-site emergency planning process.[73]

The governor was referring specifically to plans for the evacuation of all residents within a ten-mile radius of the Shoreham nuclear power plant, under construction on Long Island, in the event of a release of radioactive materials. The national government clearly lacks the resources to ensure the safe evacuation of all residents and assumes the State of New York and local governments will assist in the event an evacuation is ordered.

Confusion relative to which plane of government is responsible for solving a problem also is a product of minimum standards preemption statutes authorizing concerned federal government agencies to delegate "regulatory primacy" to states which, in turn, are free to return the primacy to the concerned federal agency. Furthermore, a state is not required to apply for "regulatory primacy" and the federal agencies on receipt of an application will delegate primacy only if state standards are as high as national ones and the state has the capability to enforce the standards.

NATIONALLY DELEGATED GUBERNATORIAL POWERS

The formal constitutional powers of a governor vary greatly from state to state. In the so-called strong governor states, the state constitution grants the governor broad executive powers, including appointment and removal of officers (usually subject to confirmation by the state senate or governor's council), supervision of the entire executive branch, preparation of the state's budget and implementation of appropriation acts, and military powers. In addition, the governor is granted important legislative powers, including the call of special sessions of the state legislature, veto of bills enacted by the legislature, and veto of items in appropriations.

A so-called weak governor, on the other hand, lacks a number of these powers. Typically, the governor's powers of appointment and removal are limited, the entire executive branch is not under the governor's supervision, a number of executive officers are elected rather than appointed by the governor, and the governor lacks the item veto power. In four states, the governor is not responsible for preparing the budget.

An examination of major preemption acts and presidential executive orders reveals that thirteen acts and one executive order devolve powers to governors they have not received from their respective state constitution and statutes.

The *Tandem Truck Safety Act of 1984* authorizes a governor, after consulting concerned municipalities, to notify the secretary of transportation that the governor has concluded named segments of the interstate highway system cannot accommodate in a safe manner the longer commercial vehicles authorized by the *Surface Transportation Assistance Act of 1982*.[74]

Several preemption statutes authorize a governor to submit a plan to a national agency for the assumption of responsibility for implementing a national preemptive statute as illustrated by the *Environmental Pesticide Control Act of 1972*.[75]

The *National Health Planning and Resources Development Act of 1974* stipulates that the members of the Statewide Health Coordinating Council are to be appointed by the governor.[76]

The *Safe Drinking Water Act of 1974* authorizes the EPA administrator to issue temporary permits for injection wells and underground injection of a particular fluid on application of a governor.[77]

Many national statutes stipulate that a single state agency must be responsible for administering a given program. State officers often object to such a requirement on the ground other organizational arrangements are more economical and/or efficient. The *Metal and Nonmetallic Mine Safety Act* empowers the secretary of labor to waive the single agency requirement on the request of a governor.[78]

Another power granted to the governor is authorization to request that the state assume responsibility for a federally preempted function. Such an authorization is contained in the *Wholesome Meat Act of 1967.*[79]

The *Water Pollution Control Act Amendments of 1972* authorize the governor to delineate areas with major water quality problems and to designate an organization to develop areawide treatment management plans for the areas and agencies to be responsible for waste treatment.[80]

A significant delegated power, contained in the *Highway Safety Act of 1966*, stipulates that the Secretary of Transportation may not approve a state highway safety program if it does not provide for the governor to be responsible for administration of the program. In other words, the state legislature cannot place responsibility for some highway safety programs in an agency independent of the governor.

During a petroleum shortage, the governor is delegated authority, by presidential executive order 12140, "to establish a system of end-user allocation of motor gasoline."

The *Clean Air Act Amendments of 1977* establish three air zones. New sulfur dioxide and suspended particulates are not allowed in a Class I zone, a limited amount of development is allowed in Class II zones if it would not cause "significant deterioration of air quality," and deterioration up to secondary standards is allowed in Class III zones. Primary ambient air quality standards are designed to protect the health of susceptible persons. Secondary standards generally are more stringent and are designed to prevent adverse environmental effects such as damage to animals, climate, vegetation, or water quality.

The amendments authorize the governor to redesignate areas from Class I to Class III with specific exceptions provided the governor consults with the concerned committees of the state legislature if it is in session or with the leaders of the legislature if it is not in session.

FEDERALLY INDUCED COSTS

Enactment of several congressional partial preemption statutes has imposed substantial costs on state and local governments. In examining federally induced subnational governmental costs, it is essential to distinguish a mandate from a restraint.[81] The former is a legal order—constitutional provision, statute, or administrative rule—requiring a state and/or its local governments to undertake a specified activity or to provide a service meeting minimum national standards. The latter prevents completely or partially an action contemplated by a subnational government. The national government provides no direct reimbursement for mandated costs incurred by state and local governments. Restraints may impose significant costs on these governments.

Mandated Costs

An examination of nationally mandated costs that must be financed by state and local government is confused by the tendency of many state subnational governmental officers to identify conditions attached to grant-in-aid programs as federal mandates. Such conditions, examined in chapter 6, must be distinguished from genuine mandates, as a state or a local government can avoid the former by failing to apply for and accepting grants-in-aid.

A small number of federal grant-in-aid programs in effect have "mandates" when the conditions are changed subsequent to a subnational government opting to participate in the program, and the new conditions are expensive but the recipient unit is unable to withdraw from the program because of "sunk" economic costs and/or dependence on the large sum of money flowing from Washington, DC. The federal-aid highway and Medicaid programs are examples.

Determining the costs of genuine federal mandates is difficult because of lack of data on compliance, inadequate state and local cost accounting systems, and failure of various national departments and agencies to promulgate all rules and regulations authorized by law. EPA in particular has been slow in promulgating implementing rules and regulations.

Nevertheless, studies have been conducted to estimate costs of complying with various mandates. When EPA was created by executive order in 1970 municipalities were affected primarily by mandates relating to water quality—sewer and waste-water treatment. Today, municipalities are affected also by major mandates relating to drinking water supply and solid waste disposal. In 1986 alone, Congress mandated that general-purpose local governments control an additional eighty-three drinking water contaminants.[82]

In 1988, EPA estimated user charges and fees per household would increase by an average of an additional $100 annually by 1996.[83] The increase, however, would be $160 per household annually for municipalities under 2,500 population and $170 per household for municipalities over 250,000 population. The study estimated that between 21 and 30 percent of municipalities under 2,500 population would experience financial difficulties in attempting to comply with the mandates and fiscally strained larger municipalities also would experience difficulties. Faced with the prospect of many small municipalities either abandoning their public water systems or filing for bankruptcy protection because of the mandate, Congress enacted the *Safe Drinking Water Act Amendments of 1996*, providing municipalities with relief from the burdensome mandates.[84]

The congressional budget office in 1985 estimated the initial annual compliance costs for state and local governments as the result of the U.S. Supreme Court decision extending federal fair labor standards to these units would be between one-half and one-and-one-half billion dollars.[85] The estimated costs were reduced to an extent by the *Fair Labor Standards Amendments of 1985*, authorizing subnational governments to offer compensatory time off at a rate of one and one-half hours for each overtime work hour in lieu of overtime compensation.[86]

A particularly expensive mandate is the requirement in the *Asbestos Hazard Emergency Response Act of 1986* requiring removal of asbestos from all public buildings.[87]

Not all national mandates have high compliance costs. The *Tax Equity and Fiscal Responsibility Act of 1982*, for example, requires subnational governments to submit reports on remuneration for services and direct sales to the internal revenue service.[88] Compliance costs are not large since such information typically is available in computer files.

Congress increased costs financed by states and generated sharp internal conflict within many states by mandating they are responsible for a function that previously had been an exclusive responsibility of the federal government. The *Low-Level Radioactive Policy Act of 1980* contains such a mandate and urges states to enter into interstate compacts providing for regional radioactive disposal facilities.[89]

Restraints

In contrast to a mandate, a restraint forbids a state or a local government to exercise a specific regulatory power. In the area of transportation, preemption statutes stripped subnational governments of authority to engage in economic regulation of airline, bus, and motor carrier firms.

A restraint may necessitate state and/or local government expenditures and Congress recognized this fact in the *Airline Deregulation Act of 1978* by authorizing grants to subnational governments for "essential" air service to small municipalities that lost scheduled air service because of deregulation.[90] A similar restraint in the *Bus Regulatory Reform Act of 1982* forbids states to condition issuance of a franchise to operate buses between two major cities on agreement by the carrier to provide service to small communities.[91] To ensure bus service to these communities, many states today subside the carriers.

A restraint may contribute to loss of revenue for a subnational government and create other problems. U.S. Representative Guy V. Molinari of Staten Island, New York, added a rider to the *Omnibus Budget Reconciliation Act for Fiscal Year 1986*, for example, stipulating tolls for motor vehicles on any bridge connecting Brooklyn and Staten Island may be collected only as vehicles exit the bridge in Staten Island.[92] The rider results in the loss of significant toll revenues, increased congestion at the eastern entrance to the Holland Tunnel under the Hudson River, and enables motorists to cross the Verrazano bridge to Brooklyn without paying a toll and to return to Staten Island via a bridge from New Jersey.

The *Social Security Act of 1935* did not mandate state and local governments to provide coverage under the act to their employees, but a number of state and local legislative bodies decided to provide such coverage.[93] The act was amended in 1983 to prevent states and their political subdivisions from terminating participation in the social security program and increased the old-age, survivors, and disability insurance contribution rate in 1984, 1988, and 1989 over the scheduled rates.[94] These changes cost subnational governments an estimated $470 million in 1984, $750 million in 1988, and $810 million in 1989. In addition, the amendments accelerated the times that subnational governments are required to deposit in the U.S. Treasury withheld employee and employer taxes to twice a month from once a month.

Congress enacted the *Age Discrimination in Employment Act of 1967* and amended it in 1982 to prohibit employers from requiring employees to retire because of age.[95] Congress responded in 1986 to subnational governmental complaints that older employees lack the required physical strength and stamina for certain positions by amending the act to stipulate it is not unlawful for a state or a political subdivisions "to fail or refuse to hire or to discharge any individual because such individual's age if such action is taken—(1) with respect to the employment of an individual as a firefighter or as a law enforcement officer and the individual has attained the age of hiring or retirement in effect under applicable State or local law on March 3, 1983, and (2) pursuant to a bonafide hiring or retirement plan that is not a subterfuge to evade the purpose of this Act."[96] This amendment expired automatically on December 31, 1993.

The *Marine Protection Research and Sanctuaries Act of 1972* restricts subnational governments by requiring them to obtain permits from the U.S. army corps of engineers prior to dumping dredged materials in an ocean.[97] While this act increased disposal costs to limited extent, the *Ocean Dumping Ban Act of 1988*, prohibiting the dumping of sewage sludge in oceans, imposed major costs for coastal municipalities that had been dumping the sludge in the ocean.[98]

The Moral Obligation to Respond

A small number of complete preemption statutes removing regulatory authority in a given field from states and their political subdivisions induce spending by these units. While the *Atomic Energy Act of 1954* assigns exclusive responsibility for regulation of nuclear power generating plants to the U.S. nuclear regulatory commission, the lack of resources makes it dependent on subnational governments for emergency response personnel and equipment to protect public health and safety in the event of a radioactive discharge at a nuclear generating station.[99]

Similarly, the federal government is completely responsible for regulating transportation of radioactive and other hazardous materials, yet lacks the personnel to respond promptly to transportation accidents. Although they lack authority to regulate such transportation, subnational governments are under a moral obligation to respond to emergencies resulting from transportation activities involving these materials.

SUMMARY

The federal invention of 1789 has proved to be highly adaptable to vastly different economic, political, and social conditions in the twenty-first century, and this ability to adapt is reflected in systemic instability, a feature of federalism in the United States.

The unamended constitution implied, without expressly stipulating, the existence of dual sovereignty and the Tenth Amendment to the U.S. Constitution was drafted and ratified to incorporate dual sovereignty expressly in the Constitution. Under this constitutional conception, Congress and national courts were powerless to regulate states and local governments in their capacities as sovereign polities.

National-state relations, however, were not frozen by the amendment. Ratification of the Fourteenth and Fifteenth Amendments devolving powers on Congress and the U.S. Supreme Court's broad interpretation of the delegated powers of Congress have made state regulatory sovereignty to a significant extent largely symbolic with real sovereignty residing in Congress with its nearly plenipotentiary preemption powers.

In 1982, Congress commenced to become more responsive to subnational governmental complaints and enacted ten statutes granting a degree of relief to these governments from certain provisions of earlier preemption laws and two U.S. Supreme Court decisions viewed as burdensome, unwise, or both by states and their political subdivisions.

Recognition must be accorded to the fact Congress, despite its strong preemption powers, is a government of constitutionally delegated powers and lacks complementary powers to implement fully certain expressed powers. In addition, the large national budgetary deficit is forcing Congress to rely more heavily on the states for effective implementation of national policies.

With respect to preemption issues, the interests of the various states are both common and diverse as illustrated by the acid rain controversy. The northeastern states are pressuring Congress to lower the permissible amount of sulfuric pollutants emitted by coal-fired electric generating stations in the Midwest and are opposed by the midwestern states.

Local governments are excluded by preemption statutes from exercising regulatory powers with a few exceptions such as the *Cable Communications Policy Act of 1984*. Other than lobbying Congress and national administrative agencies preparing to promulgate new or revised rules and regulations, local governments must pressure their state legislatures and state administrative agencies with respect to the "regulatory primacy" devolved on states by national administrative agencies.

The most major changes in national-state relations since 1965 have been produced by minimum standards preemption under which Congress removes regulatory authority of the states and authorizes the concerned national agency to devolve broad regulatory powers to the states developing standards and an enforcement plan approved by the agency, thereby allowing states to play an important ancillary role in national policy implementation.

Minimum standards preemption and delegation of "regulatory primacy" are compromises between the Scylla of complete centralization and the Charybdis of complete decentralization of political power. This type of national preemption relieves states of responsibility for solving difficult problems if they so choose and also affords a state the opportunity to register a complaint with the concerned national agency that a sister state is not in compliance with a preemption statute and/or implementing rules, or regulations, or alternatively to bring a court suit.

Fortunately, Congress has become more innovative in its use of preemption powers by enlisting the resources of states and allowing them a degree of discretionary flexibility by statutes and administrative regulations, thereby permitting state adaptive and experimental regulatory responses to local conditions. Congress recognized complete preemption without a provision for state administrative involvement, with a few exceptions, cannot be successful throughout the nation because of the wide diversity of local and regional conditions.

The induced costs associated with federal mandates and restraints reduce the discretionary authority of state and local governments and impose severe burdens on small local governments and fiscally distressed cities. In effect, the national government since 1965 has changed from a generous supplier of funds to subnational governments to a preemptor imposing major costs.

In sum, intergovernmental relations have increased greatly in complexity since the mid-1960s when Congress commenced to exercise its complete and partial preemption powers more frequently. In general, national-state relations today exhibit elements of conflict, coercion, and cooperation with the latter more common than the other two elements. Chapter 9 examines the adequacy of the dual theory and cooperative theory of federalism and offers postulates of a broader theory encompassing national-state, state-local, and state-local relations.

Chapter 5 describes the dual judicial system in the United States and examines the roles of courts in determining whether the states and their political subdivisions are completely or partially forbidden to exercise certain regulatory powers because of conflicts with provisions of the U.S. Constitution, preemption statutes, or both.

CHAPTER 5

Federalism and the Judiciary

Laws and courts are essential to the existence of organized society. Through a well-developed legal system the rights, privileges, and duties of individuals are established and controversies are settled authoritatively.

The United States is distinguished by a dual judicial system—one national and one state. The state courts constitute an independent judicial system and are in no way dependent on the federal court system. Whether there was a need for a national court system was a subject of debate at the 1789 Philadelphia constitutional convention.

THE NATIONAL JUDICIARY

There were only state courts under the Articles of Confederation and Perpetual Union. Experience with total reliance on state courts during the confederacy convinced delegates to the constitutional convention there must be a national judiciary since disputes between states would become more common in the future and an impartial judicial forum would be essential. Furthermore, suits between citizens of different states also would become more frequent and experience revealed a tendency for state courts to favor citizens of their state.

The strongest argument for a national judiciary was the need for an impartial tribunal to resolve disputes over the meaning of the various provisions of the proposed constitution and statutes enacted by Congress. Legal chaos would result if the adjudication were the responsibility of the courts of the various states, which might issue different decisions on the same provision, whereby a constitutional or statutory provision would have a given meaning in one state and a different meaning in a sister state.

Alexander Hamilton justified the need for a national judiciary in *The Federalist Number 80*: "If there are such things as political axioms, the propriety of the judicial power of a government being coextensive with its legislative may be ranked among the number. The mere necessity of uniformity in the interpretation of national laws decides the question. Thirteen independent courts of final jurisdiction over the same causes, arising upon the same laws, is a hydra in government from which nothing but contradiction and confusion can proceed."[1]

The convention agreed there was a need for a national supreme court, but opinions differed as to whether other national courts should be established and how they should be organized if established. Hamilton in *The Federalist Number 81* emphasized: "The power of constituting inferior courts is evidently calculated to obviate the necessity of having recourse to the Supreme Court in every case of federal cognizance. It is intended to enable the national government to institute or *authorize*, in each State or district of the United States, a tribunal competent to the determination of matters of national jurisdiction within its limits."[2]

The U.S. Constitution contains only a brief reference to the structure of the national courts. Section 1 of Article III simply stipulates that "the judicial power of the United States shall be vested in one Supreme Court and in such inferior courts as the Congress may from time to time ordain and establish." The Constitution does not establish the number of members of the Supreme Court, and the number has varied from six members provided for in a 1789 congressional statute to five members in 1801, to seven in 1802, to nine in 1837, to ten in 1861, to seven in 1866, and to nine in 1869. Currently, the court consists of the chief justice and eight associate justices. Six justices constitute a quorum and the approval of four is required for the issuance of a writ of certiorari directing a lower court to send records of a specified case to the Supreme Court. Section 2 of Article II of the Constitution authorizes the President to appoint justices of the Supreme Court and judges of other national courts with the advice and consent of the Senate.

Section 2 also grants the Supreme Court original or trial jurisdiction only in cases involving ambassadors, public ministers, and consuls, and cases in which a state is a party. In all other cases, the "Court shall have appellate jurisdiction, both as to law and fact, with such exceptions, and under such regulations as the Congress shall make." Congress in the *Judiciary Act of 1789* made the court's jurisdiction over interstate controversies exclusive.[3]

The convention's decision that the national government potentially should have a complete system of courts rather than rely on state courts proved to be a wise one since the U.S. Supreme Court in *Houston v. Moore* in 1820 ruled that Congress lacked authority to confer jurisdiction on courts not created by Congress.[4]

State courts have exclusive jurisdiction over all cases other than the classes of controversies listed in Section 2 of Article III of the U.S. Constitution:

> The judicial power shall extend to all cases, in law and equity, arising under the Constitution, the laws of the United States, and treaties made, or which shall be made, under their authority;—to all cases affecting ambassadors, other public ministers and consuls;—to all cases of admiralty and maritime jurisdiction;—to controversies to which the United States shall be a party;—to controversies between two or more states; [between a State and citizens of another state;—] between citizens of different states— between citizens of the same State claiming lands under grants of different States; [and between a State, or the citizens thereof, and foreign states, citizens, or subjects].

The sections in brackets have been modified by the Eleventh Amendment, which Congress proposed and the states ratified following the U.S. Supreme Court's 1793 decision in *Chisholm v. Georgia* opining that a citizen of South Carolina could sue the State of Georgia in a federal court.[5] The amendment expressly prohibits such suits.

The reference to cases arising under the constitution, laws, and treaties is to cases of a justiciable character involving civil and criminal proceedings. Controversies relate only to civil matters involving parties such as states. Courts lack authority to decide legislative or executive questions labeled "political questions." Only Congress, for example, can declare war.

It is apparent the jurisdiction of national courts is limited by the U.S. Constitution and covers only cases arising under the constitution, laws, and treaties: cases involving ambassadors, other public ministers, and consuls; cases involving admiralty; and cases in which the United States or a state is a party. Furthermore, congressional statutes often define narrowly the jurisdiction of federal courts. Until 1916, a decision of the highest state court holding a state law violated the U.S. Constitution could not be appealed to the U.S. Supreme Court.

Determining the line marking the jurisdiction of national courts is a difficult task. James Madison in *The Federalist Number 37* referred to the general problem of "marking the proper line of partition between the authority of the general and that of state governments" and added: "Perspicuity . . . requires not only that the ideas should be distinctly formed, but that they should be expressed by words distinctly and exclusively appropriate to them. But no language is so copious as to supply words and phrases for every complex idea, or so correct not to include many equivocally denoting different ideas."[6]

William B. Munro in 1937 wrote "the division of jurisdiction between the two sets of courts is in fact so indistinct at some points that even good lawyers are not always sure of their ground. And as for the ordinary layman he is often quite bewildered by the strange things which result from the divided judicial authority."[7]

In terms of the number of courts and the number of cases adjudicated, the court systems of the fifty states are more important than the federal court system. There are more than 14,000 state courts with many carrying the names of local governments. These courts handle more than 98 percent of all litigation in the United States. There is one U.S. Supreme Court, eleven numbered and the District of Columbia Circuit Courts of Appeal, one or more U.S. District Courts in each state, and several specialized courts including the U.S. Claims Court, U.S. Court of International Trade, and the U.S. Tax Court.

Most common crimes—assault, burglary, murder, and robbery—are violations of state laws and hence are triable in state courts. Civil law—relating to contracts, damages to persons and property, commercial and personal relations, inheritances, and wills—similarly is state law and, for the greater part, is enforced by state courts.

In stipulating the judicial power of the United States extends to the various classes of controversies listed, the constitution does not mandate that the national courts must assume exclusive jurisdiction in all such cases. Congress determines the extent of exclusive national court jurisdiction and may assign an entire field or only part of a field to national courts. Furthermore, Congress granted national courts exclusive jurisdiction over all suits to which the United States is a party, controversies between states, controversies between a state and a foreign nation, and specified civil suits arising under congressional statutes. Congress authorized state courts in all other cases and controversies to exercise concurrent jurisdiction.

CONCURRENT JUDICIAL JURISDICTION

In contrast to a unitary nation, a federal nation with a dual court system offers litigants in many types of cases the option to bring a suit in a national court or in a state court and forum shopping has become relatively common. In general, litigants select state courts. Attorney Morris Dees reported in 1991 that he decided to bring his civil law suit against white supremacist Tom Metzger in an Oregon court rather than in the U.S. District Court: "We chose state court because Oregon discovery rules are quite different than the federal rules. You can do trial by ambush in Oregon. You have no interrogatories, no production of evidence; you don't have to give the names of witnesses or give the other side your documents."[8]

Fear that state courts may reflect local prejudice induced many litigants to file suit in the allegedly more impartial U.S. District Court. Many black defendants during the 1960s often sought to have their cases removed from a state court to the U.S. District Court under the *Removal of Causes Act of 1920* on the ground that courts in southern states were prejudiced against blacks.[9] John W. Winkle III explained that "imprecise residency requirements for diversity plaintiffs have permitted large corporations, foreign entrepreneurs, and even commuters more flexibility in their selections."[10]

If cases are transferred, they usually go from state to national courts. However, transfers from national courts to state courts are not uncommon because of national court docket congestion, attorney's familiarity with state court procedures, different court rules, and geographical convenience of a state court's location.

A dual court system involving concurrent jurisdiction over certain types of cases affords plaintiffs the opportunity to commence an action in a state court and to appeal an adverse decision of the highest state court to the U.S. Supreme Court for review if a federal question is involved. In addition, a litigant may seek a U.S. District Court injunction to stop a state prosecution and state prisoners whose conviction has been upheld by the highest state court may seek federal habeas corpus relief. If an action is initiated in the U.S. District Court, it may seek a ruling by means of a certified question from the state's highest court if a state law is involved. In effect, the highest state court is requested to offer an advisory opinion to the federal court.

The U.S. Supreme may hear an appeal only from a decision of the highest state court with jurisdiction over the subject if a federal question is involved. The U.S. Supreme Court has final authority to determine the constitutionality of a state law under the U.S. Constitution, but the court will refuse to accept a case for review until all state judicial remedies have been exhausted. The state supreme court is the final arbiter if a law is alleged to be repugnant to the provisions of the state constitution.

A litigant has the right to appeal to U.S. Supreme Court if the highest state court upheld the validity of a state law alleged to be a violation of the U.S. Constitution, a congressional statute, or a treaty, or the highest state court ruled a national law or treaty to be invalid. Most cases adjudicated by the U.S. Supreme Court are the result of appeals of lower federal court decisions and not appeals of decisions of state supreme courts.

In contrast to ten states whose constitutions authorize the state supreme court to issue advisory opinions, the U.S. Supreme Court does not issue such opinions. In 1796, George Washington submitted twenty-nine questions relating to a proposed treaty to the court, but it refused to answer them.

CONGRESSIONAL INTENT TO PREEMPT

The supremacy of the laws clause of the U.S. Constitution was designed to preempt completely or partially regulatory state constitutional provisions and statutes, based on reserved and concurrent powers, if Congress enacts a conflicting regulatory statute based on a delegated power. As noted in chapter 4, many congressional statutes do not contain an explicit preemption section and the U.S. Supreme Court has not developed precise criteria for determining whether Congress in enacting a statute intended to preempt if the statute lacks an explicit preemption statement.

James T. Young in 1935 referred to members of Congress lacking "backbone" when subject to pressure by interest groups and members resort to use of "weasel words" in statutes.[11] The courts are left with the problem of determining what the words mean. The suggestion has been advanced a state law should remain valid unless explicitly prohibited by a congressional statute. George B. Braden in 1942 rejected such a proposal as "intolerable" since Congress could not be expected to anticipate all future state laws that might conflict with a congressional statute.[12]

The U.S. Supreme Court in *Hines v. Davidowitz*, in 1941 emphasized the particular facts of a case determine whether a state law is inconsistent with a congressional statute and the key question is whether the state law in question "stands as an obstacle to the accomplishment and execution of the full purposes and objectives of Congress."[13]

The justices in 1947 enunciated two tests of federal preemption in *Rice v. Santa Fe Elevator Corporation*.[14] First, "the question in each case is what the purpose of Congress was?" Second, does the congressional statute involve "a field in which the federal interest is so dominant that the federal system will be assumed to preclude enforcement of state laws on the same subject?" In 1973, the court in *City of Burbank v. Lockheed Air Terminal Incorporated* opined that control of noises is "deep-seated in the police power of the States," but added that the federal *Noise Control Act of 1972* leaves "no room for local curfews or other local controls."[15]

The court occasionally concedes a conflict between a state law and a federal law violates the supremacy of the law clause of the U.S. Constitution, yet holds the conflict is not the type that confers jurisdiction upon the national courts. In addition, the court on occasion invalidates only one or two sections of a state law conflicting with a federal law.

In 1978, the justices in *Hodel v. Virginia Surface Mining and Reclamation Association* listed three tests to determine whether state laws were preempted by the national *Surface Mining and Reclamation Act of 1977*: "First, there must be a showing that the challenged statute regulates the 'States as States' . . . Second, the federal regulation must address matters that are indisputably 'attributes of state sovereignty.' And third, it must be apparent that the states' compliance with the federal law would directly impair their ability 'to structure internal operations in areas of traditional functions.'"[16]

The statute in question was a minimum standards preemption one. The court ruled that the law did not regulate "states as states" by noting that the Virginia law did not require the state to enforce the standards contained in the law and "the regulatory burden" falls on the U.S. Department of the Interior in the event that a state does not seek regulatory primacy.

In the event that the court misinterprets congressional intent, Congress is free to repeal the court's interpretation. Congress, for example, enacted the *Older Workers Benefit Protection Act of 1990* reversing the court's 1989 decision in *Public Employee Retirement System of Ohio v. Betts*.[17]

MAJOR FEDERALISM DECISION

Alexander Hamilton in *The Federalist Number 78* suggested it was the duty of the courts "to declare all acts contrary to the manifest tenor of the Constitution void. Without this, all the reservations of particular rights or privileges would amount to nothing."[18] Nevertheless, the U.S. Constitution is silent relative to whether the U.S. Supreme Court possesses the authority to declare congressional acts, state statutes, or both unconstitutional. The constitution's framers were aware the Privy Council in England declared laws enacted by colonial legislatures to be void and state courts had declared state laws unconstitutional. Available evidence suggests the framers would have included in the constitution a provision prohibiting judicial review if they were opposed to such review.

The Marshall Court

Organized in 1790, the U.S. Supreme Court during its initial decade decided only six cases raising questions of constitutional law and its most controversial decision, *Chisholm v. Georgia*, was reversed by adoption of the Eleventh Amendment. The position of the court grew stronger with the accession of John Marshall to the post of Chief Justice in 1801. He was a supporter of a strong national government and exerted great influence on the development of the national governance system during his more than thirty-four years as Chief Justice. His opinions addressed thirty-six important constitutional law questions.[19]

Hamilton in *The Federalist Number 78* wrote "the judiciary is beyond comparison the weakest of the three departments of power."[20] Marshall in effect challenged that conclusion. In his decisions, he emphasized two major principles of constitutional construction. First, every power exercised by Congress must be based on a constitutional provision and can be an expressed or an implied grant of power. Second, every grant of power should be interpreted broadly, thereby allowing Congress discretion as to the manner of exercising the power.

One of the major achievements of the Marshall Court was the establishment in *Marbury v. Madison* in 1803 of the right of the U.S. Supreme Court to invalidate a congressional statute if it conflicts with the U.S. Constitution.[21] In other words, the final referee would be the court under this doctrine of judicial supremacy that continues to be accepted to this day. As noted, article III of the U.S. Constitution grants original jurisdiction to the U.S. Supreme Court in cases involving a state or a foreign minister or a consul as a party. The *Judiciary Act of 1789* empowered the court to issue a writ of *mandamus* to other public officers in specified cases directing them to perform a nondiscretionary duty(ies). Marshall wrote a congressional statute could not change the court's original jurisdiction from that provided in the constitution. The decisions in this case and in *Fletcher v. Peck* in 1810 established a firm constitutional principle that the federal courts may invalidate an act of Congress or an act of a state legislature.[22]

In 1819, the court enunciated in *McCulloch v. Maryland* the famous doctrine of implied powers interpreting the "necessary and proper" or coefficient clause of the constitution contained in Section 8 of Article I of the Constitution: "Let the end be legitimate, let it be within the scope of the Constitution, and all means which are not prohibited, but consistent with the letter and spirit of the Constitution are constitutional."[23]

One of the Marshall court's most expansive opinions is *Gibbons v. Ogden* in which the court in 1824 developed the doctrine of the continuous journey.[24] The court held that the interstate commerce power of Congress applies to every aspect of commercial intercourse, including navigation, and the power of Congress to regulate interstate commerce is applicable within a state. Under the doctrine, the commerce power extends to a steamship company operating solely within a state if some of the passengers and goods carried on the ship continue their journeys into a sister state. In 1827, the Marshall Court in *Brown v. Maryland* struck down a state law levying a $50 business tax on importers on the ground that the license interfered with foreign commerce.[25]

William B. Munro summarized Marshal's contributions to constitutional law in the following terms:

> Marshall's starting point was provided by the silences of the Constitution. This taciturnity was largely due to two practical considerations—the fact the Constitution was virtually without precedent, and, second, the desire of its framers to avoid a four-square decision on various controversial matters. Now one of the functions of a judge is to supply the incidental omissions of a statute, to bridge the gaps which the legislators leave. That must necessarily be a duty of the courts so long as lawmakers are forgetful, careless, or otherwise human. Marshall pressed the idea a step further. He found the organic law, the Constitution, full of silences which had to be made articulate. And his initial task was to assert the right of the Supreme Court to the exercise of this function.[26]

Although Marshall in general was a champion of a strong national government, he did not view the powers of Congress as plenary. In *Cohens v. Virginia*, the court expressed a dual federalism viewpoint by opining the general government, though limited as to its objects, is supreme with respect to those objects.[27]

Dual Federalism

Marshall's successor as Chief Justice in 1835 was Roger B. Taney, a strong proponent of the rights of the states. Under his leadership, there was a reaction against the centralization of powers in Congress expressed in decisions that can be labeled dual federalism ones. The court in *Briscoe v. Bank of the Commonwealth of Kentucky* upheld the creation of a state-owned bank authorized to issue and circulate notes by opining that "the notes issued by the bank are not bills of credit within the meaning of the federal constitution."[28] Similarly, the court in *Charles River Bridge v. Warren Bridge* in the same year gave an expansive reading to the police power of the states.[29]

The Taney Court provided a new interpretation of the interstate commerce clause of the U.S. Constitution in 1851 in *Cooley v. The Board of Wardens of the Port of Philadelphia*.[30] The court pointed out Congress has plenary power to regulate interstate and foreign commerce, but there were details of commerce of such a local nature that Congress might allow them to be regulated by the states. In this case, Pennsylvania required all ships coming into a harbor must take on a pilot, who must be paid at a fixed rate, to ensure the safe entry of the ships into the harbor. To this date, Congress allows states to regulate harbor pilots.[31] Other examples of a local nature subject to state regulation until Congress enacts a statute are anchorage rules, harbor buoys and lights, and erection of docks, piers, and wharves. Relative to matters requiring uniform regulation, such as the transport of goods into and out of states, only Congress may regulate. If Congress is silent, the commerce is free to move without hindrance by states.

Chief Justice Taney's most famous decision was issued in 1857 in *Dred Scott v. Sanford* and held Congress has no right to prohibit any citizen from owning slaves and the grant of citizenship by a state to a Negro would not make him a citizen of the United States:

> It does not by any means follow, because he [Dred Scott] has all the rights and privileges of a citizen of a State, that he must be a citizen of the United States. . . . Each State may still confer them [rights and privileges of citizenship] upon an alien, or anyone it thinks proper, or upon any class or description of persons; yet he would not be a citizen in the sense in which that word is used in the Constitution of the United States. . . . The rights which he would acquire would be restricted to the State which gave them.[32]

Since the slave states did not accord citizenship to Negro slaves, the court's decision meant they had no citizenship. Congress enacted the *Civil Rights Act of 1866* stipulating that all persons born in the United States and not subject to a foreign nation were deemed citizens.[33] In 1868, the Fourteenth Amendment to the U.S. Constitution was ratified, which declared "all persons born or naturalized in the United States, and subject to the jurisdiction thereof, are citizens of the United States and of the State wherein they reside." This Amendment has a major impact upon states and their political subdivisions as explained in a subsequent section.

The question of whether a state may secede from the Union was answered by the defeat of the Confederate States of America in the Civil War. In *Texas v. White*, Chief Justice Salmon P. Chase of the U.S. Supreme Court in 1869 declared that "the Constitution . . . looks to an indestructible Union, composed of indestructible States."[34]

Subsequently, the major federalism issues until the 1930s involved the state's use of the police power to regulate commerce, labor relations, manufacturing, and welfare. In an era of laissez-faire, the court ruled production, including agriculture and manufacturing, and relations between employers and employees were beyond national regulation and subject to state regulation. In 1918, Congress enacted a statute prohibiting interstate transportation of goods made by child labor, but the Court in 1918 in *Hammer v. Dagenhart* held the statute invaded "the reserved powers of the States."[35]

Prior to 1937, the court opined the due process of law guarantee of liberty includes freedom to contract and governmental regulation of economic relations abridged that liberty. In 1936, the court majority opined in *Carter v. Carter Coal Company* that "the relation of employer and employee is a local relation" over which Congress has no control.[36]

By enunciating its famous "Separate but Equal" Doctrine in *Plessy v. Ferguson* in 1896, the court effectively withdrew itself from the field of civil rights until the 1950s although the court declared unconstitutional several state laws excluding Negroes from participating in the primary elections of the Democratic party.[37]

The End of Dual Federalism

President Franklin D. Roosevelt, frustrated by decisions of the U.S. Supreme Court striking down statutes, by a vote of 5 to 4, as unconstitutional statutes that were part of his New Deal, recommended in 1937 congressional enactment of a bill authorizing the President to appoint a new justice to the Supreme Court for every justice over the age of seventy. If enacted by Congress, the bill would have allowed for the appointment of six additional justices. The proposal generated a major political controversy and was not enacted into law. Nevertheless, the court in 1937 commenced to uphold the constitutionality of the New Deal statutes by a 5 to 4 vote and shortly thereafter two of the four justices opposed to the New Deal retired.

In *West Coast Hotel Company v. Parrish*, the court in 1937 by a vote of 5 to 4 validated a State of Washington minimum wage law.[38] The court on the same day in *Virginian Railway v. System Federation No. 40* upheld the *Railway Labor Act*, mandating that employers must bargain exclusively with a union selected by a majority of the employees, as not violating the due process of law clause.[39] The court two weeks later rendered a similar decision in *National Labor Relations Board v. Jones & Laughlin Steel Corporation*.[40]

In 1938, the justices in *United States v. Carolene Products Company* opined that statutory regulation of commercial transactions will not be declared "unconstitutional unless in the light of the facts made known or generally assumed it is of such a character as to preclude the assumption that it rests upon some rational basis within the knowledge and experience of the legislators."[41] Between 1939 and 1944, the court rejected challenges to congressional laws fixing the price of milk and coal, minimum wage provisions of the *Fair Labor Standards Act of 1938*, and general price and rent controls.[42]

The Warren Court Revolution

President Dwight D. Eisenhower in 1953 appointed Earl Warren Chief Justice of the U.S. Supreme Court and under his leadership until retirement in 1969 what can be described accurately as a revolution occurred with respect to the rights of black citizens, the criminal justice system, and the political process. The court was labeled by its critics as activist and condemned for ignoring the intent of the drafters of the U.S. Constitution, a topic examined in a subsequent section.

Under the Warren Court rulings, the powers of Congress expanded as well as the powers of the national judiciary. The court rendered a blockbuster decision in *Brown v. Board of Education* in 1954 by reversing the court's decision in *Plessy v. Ferguson* which established the "separate but equal doctrine" holding separate public facilities for black citizens were constitutional provided the facilities were equal to ones provided for white citizens.[43] Whereas the 1896 decision involved transportation, the 1954 decision involved segregated publicly operated schools.

Ten years later, the court upheld in *Katzenback v. McClung* the prohibition in the *Civil Rights Act of 1964* of racial segregation in places of public accommodations by applying the act to a restaurant that had no known out-of-state customers.[44]

In a related civil rights case, the court in *South Carolina v. Katzenbach* in 1966 upheld the constitutionality of the *Voting Rights Act of 1965*, based on the Fifteenth Amendment, and its requirement that a state or local government covered by the act must obtain approval of the U.S. Attorney General or the U.S. District Court for the District of Columbia prior to implementing any change in election laws, no matter how minor.[45] The act was amended in 1975 to cover language minorities defined as Alaskan Natives, Asiatic Americans, American Indians, and persons of Spanish heritage if a minority constitutes five percent or more of the voting-age population of the subnational unit.[46] The U.S. Supreme Court in 1875 interpreted the Fifteenth Amendment as protecting only the voting rights of black citizens.[47] Consequently, Congress based its authority to enact the provision protecting the voting rights of designated language minorities on the Fourteenth Amendment.

Criminal procedure was governed by the U.S. Supreme Court's decision in *Palko v. Connecticut*.[48] This 1937 decision specifically held the Fourteenth Amendment did not incorporate against the states certain guarantees contained in the first eight amendments of the U.S. Constitution; that is, indictment by a grand jury, trial by a petit jury, and the double jeopardy prohibition.[49] In 1964, the court in *Malloy v. Hogan* adopted a policy of selective incorporation of criminal provisions of the Bill of Rights into the Fourteenth Amendment.[50]

The famous Miranda rights of arrested persons date to the court's 1966 decision in *Miranda v. Arizona* in which the court established rules for the guidance of police and courts.[51] A prosecutor may not use a statement obtained from police questioning of a person in custody as evidence unless the person has been informed that he or she has the right to refuse to answer questions, any statement the person makes may be used as evidence against him or her, and the person has the right to have an attorney present during interrogation. The person in custody may retain an attorney or have one appointed at government expense. Furthermore, a defendant who waived these rights may at any time reinvoke them.

The Political Process

The Warren Court had a major impact on the political process of state and local governments. The court exhibited relatively little interest in the elec-toral process prior to 1960. State constitutional requirements for periodic reapportionment of state legislatures following the decennial national cen-suses of population were ignored in a number of states; the state legislature in Alabama and Tennessee had not been reapportioned for sixty years. The result, in view of continuing urbanization and suburbanization, was increas-ing overrepresentation of rural areas. In 1962, a majority of state legislators represented as few as 12 percent of the voters in the lower house in three states and 8 percent in the Senate in one state.

The U.S. Supreme Court until 1962 refused to hear malapportionment appeals on the ground that they involve political questions. In that year, however, the court in *Baker v. Carr* ruled that the U.S. District Court had jurisdiction in such cases, but did not mandate population as the basis for apportionment of legislative seats.[52] In 1963, the court in *Gray v. Sanders* developed its "one-person, one-vote" dictum holding that the vote cast by a voter must be equal in weight to the vote cast by any other voter.[53]

The U.S. Constitution provides each state with equal representation in the Senate and representation in the House of Representatives based on population, with the exception that each state has at least one Representa-tive. A number of state constitutions in 1964 contained similar provisions for representation of counties in the state Senate; that is, one senator would be elected in each county regardless of its population. The federal analogy was an argument used by a number of states to justify the apportionment of their Senate seats.

In 1964, the court in *Reynolds v. Sims* rejected the analogy and opined both houses of a state legislature must be apportioned on the basis of "one-person, one-vote."[54] In *Chapman v. Meiers*, the court in 1975 provided rough guidelines as to what constitutes "substantial" population equality by opining "a variation of 10.14 percent cannot be deemed *de minimus*."[55] In general, the court has upheld population variations of up to 10 percent and occasionally larger variations because of special state conditions.

The justices in 1968 addressed the question of whether its "one-person, one-vote" dictum applied to general purpose local governments in *Avery v. Midland County* and ruled in the affirmative.[56]

The court's decisions necessitated reapportionment of seats in all state legislatures during the 1960s. Furthermore, a state legislature must be redistricted in accordance with the "one-person, one-vote" dictum every ten years when the results of the national decennial census of population become available. If a local governing body is elected at-large (by all the voters), the government is unaffected by the court's rulings. However, many local governments elect some or all members of the governing body by districts and hence are subject to the court's rulings.

State legislatures traditionally redistricted congressional and state legislative districts in the year ending in 2 after the federal decennial census of population. In 2002 state elections, Republicans captured control of the Texas State Legislature effective in 2003 when the legislature discarded the 2002 redistricting plan drafted by the former Democratic majority and replaced it with a new gerrymandered plan drafted by the Republican majority. A challenge to the constitutionality of the action by the Republican-controlled state legislature reached the U.S. Supreme Court which in 2006 upheld the action, thereby allowing the state legislature to redistrict at-will provided each district complies with the court's "one-person, one-vote" doctrine.[57] The court, however, struck down a southwestern Texas district, removing 100,000 Mexican-Americans and adding a white population to strengthen the Republican U.S. Representative, as violative of the *Voting Rights Act*.

Post-Warren Developments

Observers anticipated the court's "one-person, one-vote" doctrine would be employed by the court to invalidate state constitutional requirements for an extramajority affirmative vote in a referendum for the initiation of specific actions such as borrowing money since a negative vote carries more weight than a positive vote in the decision-making process. However, the court in 1971, under the chief justiceship of Warren Burger, in *Gordon v. Lance* upheld a West Virginia constitutional requirement of an affirmative majority of 60 percent of the voters casting ballots in a referendum before political subdivisions could incur bonded indebtedness or increase tax rates beyond the constitutional limits.[58] The court did not find a section of the population that would be "fenced out" from the franchise by the votes they cast in such a referendum, and decided the extramajority affirmative vote requirement was reasonable relative to bond issues since the taxes on and credit of unborn generations, as well as children, would be affected.

The justices limited the freedom of state legislatures to regulate effectively election campaign finance by enactment of corrupt practices to maintain the confidence of citizens in the integrity of the electoral processes. In 1976, the court in *Buckley v. Valeo*—a case involving the *Federal Election Campaign Act of 1971* and its amendments in 1974—upheld the individual contribution limits and disclosure, public financing, and reporting provisions, but opined on First Amendment grounds "the limitations on campaign expenditures, on independent expenditures by individual and groups, and on expenditures by a candidate from his personal funds are constitutionally infirm."[59]

Specifically, the court ruled "the Act's expenditure ceilings impose direct and substantial restraints on the quantity of political speech."[60] Relative to the limitations on personal expenditures by candidates, the court opined the limitation "imposes a substantial restraint on the ability of persons to engage in protected First Amendment expression."[61] The decision also emphasized: "The candidate, no less than any other person, has a First Amendment right to engage in the discussion of public issues and vigorously and tirelessly to advocate his own election and the election of other candidates. Indeed, it of particular importance that candidates have the unfettered opportunity to make their views known so that the electorate may intelligently evaluate the candidates' personal qualities and their positions on vital public issues before choosing among them on election day."[62]

This decision was extended in 1978 with the court's invalidation of a Massachusetts corrupt practices law restricting corporate contributions to issue campaigns "that materially affect its business, property, or assets" by holding a corporation under the First Amendment could spend funds to publicize its views in opposition to a proposed constitutional amendment authorizing the General Court (state legislature) to levy a graduated income tax.[63]

Subsequently, the court continued its policy of invalidating what the court conceives as overly restrictive state corrupt practices acts. In *Randall v. Sorrell* in 2006, the court in a 6 to 3 decision invalidated Vermont's campaign contribution limit of $400 by an individual or a political party to a statewide office candidate over a two-year period.[64] This decision is the first one based on a finding a state limit on campaign contributions was too low.

The Voting Rights Act

Under provisions of the national Voting Rights Act of 1965 as amended, no state or local government subject to the act (see chapter 4) may make a change in its electoral system without the permission of the U.S. Attorney General or the U.S. District Court for the District of Columbia.[65] In 1971, the Supreme Court in Perkins v. Matthew held an annexation enlarging a city's number of voters constituted a change within the meaning of the act.[66] Although the court's decision requires a city engaging in annexation to protect the voting rights interests of its racial and language minorities, the ruling does not prohibit that mode of municipal expansion. Nevertheless, virtually every annexation significantly contributing to a city's population could be rejected, regardless of the municipality's precautionary measures, because annexation would decrease the proportion of a city's voters belonging to a protected racial or language minority group.

The City of Richmond, Virginia, in 1970 annexed territory to increase its tax base and the amount of land available for industrial development. The U.S. Department of Justice denied approval of the annexation by stressing that, under Richmond's at-large electoral system, the annexation transformed the black population from a majority to a potentially powerless minority. Richmond decided to substitute a single-member district plan for its at-large electoral plan as promoted by the department. The U.S. District Court rejected the city's proposed solution, but the U.S. Supreme Court reversed the District Court's decision in City of Richmond v. United States.[67]

The Voting Rights Act of 1965 applies only to proposed changes to the electoral system of a state or a local government. Furthermore, the U.S. Supreme Court refused to invalidate an at-large electoral system unless the plaintiffs could prove in court that the system was adopted with the intent to discriminate against a protected minority group. In 1982, Congress amended and extended the act, and included as a ground for a challenge of an electoral system the results produced by the system. Whereas it is extremely difficult to prove discriminatory intent, it is much easier to prove discriminatory results. The U.S. Department of Justice commenced to pursue energetically court challenges of at-large electoral systems in southern states, and a large number of local governments replaced their at-large electoral systems with the single-member district system that is subject to potential gerrymandering. In 1991, the court opined the Voting Rights Act applies to election of state judges in states covered by the act.[68]

The Fourteenth Amendment

Ratification of this amendment with its broad provisions and authorization for Congress to enforce the guarantees made possible extensive congressional and judicial supervision of state and local governments. As noted, several U.S. Supreme Court decisions invalidating state constitutional provisions and statutes were based on the amendment's privileges and immunities of citizens, due process of law, and equal protection of the laws guarantees against abridgement by states and their local governments.

A major twentieth-century constitutional development was the selective incorporation by the U.S. Supreme Court into the due process of law clause of the Fourteenth Amendment of many of the rights contained in the Bill of Rights. The latter specifically forbids Congress to abridge enumerated rights, including freedom of speech and indictment by a grand jury. The due process clause is vague and the Supreme Court refuses to define the clause in precise terms. In effect, a majority of the court's members may declare invalid a state or local government law if it violates what the majority considers is a constitutional guarantee.

The justices in *Gitlow v. New York* in 1925 opined that "For present purposes we may and do assume the freedom of speech and of the press—which are protected by the First Amendment from abridgement by Congress—are among the fundamental personal rights and liberties protected by the due process clause of the Fourteenth Amendment from impairment by the States."[69]

The court in *Palko v. Connecticut* in 1937 emphasized: "In these and other situations immunities that are valid against the federal government by force of the specific pledges of particular amendments have been found to be implicit in the concept of ordered liberty, and thus, through the Fourteenth Amendment, become valid as against the States."[70]

Nevertheless, the court has not incorporated all guarantees contained in the Bill of Rights into the Fourteenth Amendment. In *Palko v. Connecticut*, the court opined that the Fifth Amendment's prohibition of double jeopardy does not apply to the states. The Seventh Amendment's guarantee of the right of trial by jury in common law suits if the amount exceeds $20 applies only to federal court proceedings, according to the court's 1964 decision in *Malloy v. Hogan*.[71] Similarly, the court ruled in *Duncan v. Louisiana* in 1968 a grand jury indictment was not necessary for due process of law under the Fourteenth Amendment.[72]

This amendment, as interpreted by the Warren Court, increased significantly the workload of the U.S. District Courts, which supervise state and local government institutions found to be in violation of the equal protection of the laws clause.

No state or national court can initiate action as courts are reactors to suits filed by individuals or corporations. If a suit is filed in the U.S. District Court, the judge possesses broad and flexible powers to order defendants to remedy a wrong. After declaring racially segregated public schools unconstitutional in 1954, the U.S. Supreme Court in *Brown v. Board of Education* in 1955 authorized the U.S. District Court to develop a program to desegregate the schools.[73]

The recalcitrance of the Boston School Committee to implement court-ordered remedies for segregated schools led to U.S. District Court Judge W. Arthur Garrity Jr. assuming complete control of the school system in 1974. He issued approximately 240 court orders affecting the schools and determined such miniscule issues as to whether a ceiling in a particular school should be repaired. In 1985, the judge returned control of the school system to the elected school committee. His final orders required the committee to assign students on the basis of prescribed ratios reflecting the racial composition of the student body, adopt a school building rehabilitation plan to promote desegregation, and finance for at least three years a parent's council.[74]

In 1988, the U.S. District Court imposed fines on the City of Yonkers, New York, and four members of its city council for failing to approve a court-ordered housing desegregation plan. The city was fined $100 for the first day in contempt, with the fines doubling each day it remained in contempt. Each defiant councilman was fined $500 a day and threatened with imprisonment if the housing plan was not enacted by August 10, 1988.

This complex case raised important issues involving federalism, separation of powers, legislative immunity, the First Amendment and the Eighth Amendment to the U.S. Constitution, citizen control of a city government, and state-city relations.[75] Whether the U.S. District Court possesses the power to order elected officers to vote for a particular ordinance under the threat of contempt of court was the key issue in the case.

Council members claimed legislative immunity based on the speech and debate clause of the U.S. Constitution providing that members of Congress "for any speech or debate . . . shall not be questioned in any other place."[76] In 1951, the U.S. Supreme Court extended immunity to members of state legislatures in *Tenney et al. v. Bandhove*, and in 1979 extended legislative immunity to members of a regional planning commission in *Lake County Estates, Incorporated v. Tahoe Regional Planning Agency*.[77] The U.S. Supreme Court was not presented with a case involving such immunity for members of a city council until 1990.

The court in *Spallone v. United States* avoided the constitutional issues of whether the U.S. District Court abridged the First Amendment rights of the councilmen and whether legislative immunity extends to them. The court issued a limited decision opining that the contempt sanctions were "an abuse of discretion under traditional equitable principles" and did not conform to the doctrine that a judge should exercise "the least possible power adequate to the end proposed."[78]

The U.S. Supreme Court in particular emphasized the District Court initially should have imposed contempt sanctions only on the City of Yonkers and not on council members and added: "Only if that approach failed to produce compliance within a reasonable time should the question of imposing contempt sanctions against petitioners even have been considered."[79] The court was convinced the threat of municipal bankruptcy would lead to voters pressuring the council to vote in favor of the proposed ordinance.

The Tenth and Eleventh Amendments

Earlier sections explained the U.S. Supreme Court invalidated congressional statutes on the ground Congress exercised *ultra vires* powers; that is, exceeded the scope of its delegated powers. The constitutional revolution produced by the court's decisions commencing with the upholding of New Deal statutes in 1937 suggested that the Tenth Amendment offers states little protection against congressional encroachment on their powers.

The justices, by a 5 to 4 vote in *National League of Cities v. Usery*, in 1976 struck down the *Fair Labor Standards Amendments of 1974* extending minimum wage and overtime pay provisions to nonsupervisory employees of subnational governments on the ground the amendments violated the Tenth Amendment and were a threat to the "separate and independent existence" of these governments.[80]

In the same year, the court ruled in *Washington v. Davis* a written examination for applicants for police officers did not violate the U.S. Constitution because a "substantially disproportionate" burden is placed on black applicants.[81] The court in 1977 extended this decision to school and housing desegregation cases in *Village of Arlington Heights et al. v. Metropolitan Housing Development Corporation*.[82]

Many state and local government officers interpreted these decisions as recognition by the court that states were sovereign relative to certain matters reserved to them by the Tenth Amendment. In 1980, however, the court commenced to limit the sovereign immunity of subnational governments. In *Maine v. Thiboutot* and *Owen v. City of Independence*, the court removed immunity from subnational governments for actions of their employees.[83] And in 1982, the court in *Federal Energy Regulatory Commission v. Mississippi* upheld the constitutionality of a 1978 congressional statute directing state public utility commissions to consider established rate-making standards.[84] The evidence was mounting that the court would reverse its *National League of Cities v. Usery* decision.

The court's 1985 decision in *Garcia v. San Antonio Metropolitan Transit Authority*, reversing the *National League of Cities* decision, sent shock waves through the states and local governments.[85] The court abandoned the traditional governmental functional standard and stressed attempts to draw lines between state and national governmental responsibility as unworkable. Although the *Garcia* decision has a major impact on States and their political subdivisions, the court subsequently issued a number of decisions upholding the constitutionality of state and local government laws and regulations. In 1978, for example, the court in *Foley v. Connelie* validated a New York State law limiting appointment of members of the state police to U.S. citizens.[86]

In 1990, the justices upheld (1) in *Michigan Department of State Police v. Sitz* the right of the police to operate a highway sobriety checkpoint program against the argument that stopping a vehicle at a checkpoint violates the Fourth Amendment's guarantee against seizure, (2) in *Oregon Department of Human Resources v. Smith* the authority of the department to deny claimants unemployment compensation benefits because of their religious use of peyote (a hallucinogenic drug), and (3) in *North Dakota v. United States* state laws regulating liquor sold to U.S. military bases located in the state.[87]

In 1991, the court ruled (1) in *Gregory v. Ashcroft* the Missouri Constitution's mandatory retirement age for judges does not violate the Fourteenth Amendment's guarantee of equal protection of the laws, (2) in *Barnes v. Glen Theatre* the First Amendment was not violated by the Indiana public indecency statute requiring female dancers to wear panties and a G-string; and (3) in *Wisconsin Public Intervenor v. Mortier* the federal *Insecticide, Fungicide, and Rodenticide Act* does not preempt regulation of pesticide use by local governments.[88]

A most important decision was rendered in 1995 when the justices in *United States v. Lopez* invalidated a provision of the *Gun-Free School Zones Act of 1990* prohibiting possession of a firearm within a school zone as exceeding the delegated powers of Congress.[89] Similarly, the court in *Prinz v. United States* in 1997 struck down a provision in the *Brady Handgun Violence Prevention Act of 1993* charging the chief law enforcement officer of a local government with responsibility for conducting a background check on any individual seeking to purchase a handgun in a state lacking a state law requiring an instant background check or a statute allowing a dealer to sell a handgun immediately if the intended purchaser possessed a state handgun permit issued after a background check.[90]

The court's decision in *Seminole Tribe of Florida v. Florida* was a victory for states with the invalidation of a section of the *Indian Gaming Regulatory Act of 1988* allowing Indian tribes to sue a state in the U.S. District Court if the state did not negotiate in good faith a tribal-state gambling regulatory compact.[91]

The U.S. Court of Appeals for the 1st Circuit in 2002 opined that the Eleventh Amendment protected Rhode Island against a suit asserting whistleblower claims under the *Solid Waste Disposal Act.*[92] In the same year, the U.S. Supreme Court issued two decisions involving the amendment. The court in *Federal Maritime Commission v. South Carolina State Ports Authority* ruled state sovereign immunity forbids the commission to adjudicate a private party's suit against the state.[93] The court's second decision held a state waives its Eleventh Amendment immunity from suit upon removing a case to the U.S. District Court under the *Removal of Causes Act of 1920.*[94]

In 2000, the court in *United States v. Morrison* examined the scope the *Civil Rights Remedies for Gender-Motivated Violence Act of 1994* and the interstate commerce clause and rejected "the argument that Congress may regulate noneconomic, violent criminal conduct based solely on the conduct's aggregate effect on interstate commerce. The Constitution requires a distinction between what is truly national and what is truly local. . . . The regulation and punishment of intrastate violence that is not directed at the instrumentalities, channels, or goods involved in interstate commerce has always been the province of the states."[95]

In 2006, the court issued two decisions involving the Eleventh Amendment. The first decision, by a vote of 6 to 3, held the bankruptcy clause of the U.S. Constitution abrogates the Eleventh Amendment's guarantee of the sovereign immunity of a state.[96] The second case involved a paraplegic prisoner who brought a per se action against the State of Georgia. The court opined that title II of the *Americans with Disability Act* abrogates a state's Eleventh Amendment immunity by creating a private cause of action for damages for conduct violating the Fourteenth Amendment.[97]

The reader should not underestimate the importance of the U.S. Supreme Court's validation of congressional preemption acts removing regulatory powers from subnational governments, but should note that most preemption lawsuits are litigated in the U.S. District Courts and often appealed to the U.S. Courts of Appeal, which make a final determination.

ORIGINAL INTENT OF THE FRAMERS

The sharp increase in the number of complete and partial preemption statutes enacted by Congress in the post-1965 period and the preemption decisions of the U.S. Supreme Court generated a major debate relative to the intent of the drafters of the U.S. Constitution and whether Congress and the courts were bound by the intent.

U.S. Attorney General Edwin Meese, III, a leading critic of the Supreme Court, in 1985 wrote "a jurisprudence seriously aimed at the explication of original intention would produce defensible principles of government that would not be tainted by ideological predilection. . . . To allow the Court to govern simply by what it views at the time as fair and decent is a scheme of government no longer popular, the idea of democracy has suffered . . . A constitution that is viewed only what the judges say it is no longer a constitution in the true sense."[98]

The Meese statement drew an unusual and strong rejoinder from Associate Justice William J. Brennan Jr. of the U.S. Supreme Court: "It is arrogant to pretend that from our vantage we can gauge accurately the intent of the Framers on application of principle to specific, contemporary questions. . . . Typically, all that can be gleaned is that the Framers themselves did not agree about the applications or meaning of particular constitutional provisions, and hid their differences in cloaks of generality."[99]

Agreeing in part with Justice Brennan, Judge Robert H. Bork of the U.S. Court of Appeals stressed the history of the development of the Constitution and the wording of the text provides a judge with "a core value that the framers intended to protect."[100] Under his intentionalist view, "entire ranges of problems will be placed off-limits to judges, thus preserving democracy in those areas where the framers intended democratic government. That is better than any non-intentionalist theory can do."[101]

Judicial interpretation of the U.S. Constitution is unavoidable since it contains many general grants of power to Congress and general guarantees of individual rights. In most instances, evidence relative to specific intent, if any, of the framers is not available. The Constitution, however, provides evidence of the core values it seeks to protect, as Judge Bork suggests. Applying these values to specific cases is a difficult task and individuals will continue to hold different views regarding the extent to which the court faithfully applied the values.

Similarly, judicial interpretation of congressional statutes is unavoidable since Congress often expresses its intent to preempt in vague terms as explained in chapter 4. In contrast to a decision involving constitutional intent, Congress can reverse a decision of the court involving congressional intent expressed in a statute if the national legislature concludes the court misinterpreted congressional intent.

SUMMARY

This chapter explains in abbreviated form the nature of the dual judicial system in the United States, the respective exclusive jurisdiction of national courts and state courts, and concurrent jurisdiction. Determining the boundary line between the jurisdiction of the national courts and state courts often is a difficult task.

The supremacy of the law clause of the U.S. Constitution allows Congress to preempt completely or partially concurrent and reserved powers of the states by enacting a statute based on a power delegated to Congress by the Constitution. The frequent failure of Congress to express clearly its intent to preempt state laws results in the national judiciary playing a major role in determining congressional intent. The court, however, has provided only three general tests to determine whether a congressional statute preempts state laws.

The U.S. Supreme Court under the leadership of Chief Justice John Marshall in the early part of the nineteenth century assumed the power to declare national and state laws unconstitutional, and rendered opinions interpreting broadly contested delegated powers of Congress. Commencing in 1835 and continuing for approximately 100 years, the court's decisions generally were based on a dual federalism theory and many congressional statutes were ruled unconstitutional on the ground they encroached on the powers reserved to the states by the Tenth Amendment. In 1937, the court reversed a number of its earlier decisions, thereby authenticating expanded national powers.

Following his appointment as Chief Justice in 1953, Earl Warren presided over a Supreme Court that issued revolutionary decisions involving the rights of black citizens, the criminal justice system, and the political process. Although the court as recently as 1976 rendered a dual federalism decision in *National League of Cities v. Usery*, the court reversed this decision in its *Garcia* opinion in 1985. The majority in the latter case gave a very broad reading to the power of Congress to regulate interstate commerce and suggested states unhappy with the decision should employ the political process to obtain preemption relief from Congress and to convince it not to enact preemption statutes. In the 1990s, however, the court rendered several decisions protecting the rights of states.

Chapters 4 and 5 focused on the loss of political power by states and their political subdivisions because of the exercise by Congress of its preemption powers and U.S. Supreme Court decisions generally interpreting the powers broadly. Chapter 6 examines congressional use of its fiscal powers to persuade subnational governments to implement its policies.

CHAPTER 6

Intergovernmental Fiscal Relations

Fiscal relations between the national government, states, and local governments in the United States are extremely complex, and the courts often are called on to resolve important legal disputes involving the power to tax. The huge sums of money involved in intergovernmental finance attract interest groups to the national capitol and state capitols in a manner similar to the attraction of bears to honey.

This chapter examines the power to levy taxes, governmental tax immunity, state taxation of nonresidents and foreign and alien corporations, various types of national government financial assistance to subnational governments, and congressional use of it fiscal powers to persuade these governments to implement national policies. The centralization of political power in Congress in the twentieth century is attributable in large measure to Congress's use of its fiscal powers.

THE POWER TO TAX

The national graduated individual income tax and corporation income tax produce 59 percent of the national government's revenue (see figure 6.1). Social security taxes and the income base on which they are levied have been increasing with the result these taxes provide the national government with 34 percent of its income.

Business, excise, and property taxes provided most of the revenues of state and local governments until the Great Depression of the 1930s. With the national government relying chiefly on the individual and corporate income taxes for revenue, the general sales tax in the 1930s was the logical new tax for states to levy. The three most important state taxes in fiscal year

FIGURE 6.1
Federal Government Revenue by Major Financial Source Fiscal Year 2007

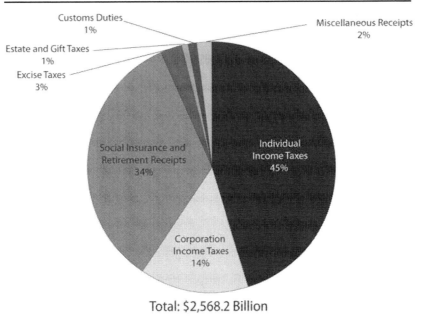

Total: $2,568.2 Billion

Source: Fiscal Year 2009 Budget (Washington, DC: U.S. Government Printing Office, 2008).

2005 produced revenues as follows: (1) Sales taxes $188,829 million, (2) personal income taxes $218,400 million, and (3) corporate income taxes $34,217 million.

Although the property tax and excise taxes on individual products are levied in all states, not all states levy a sales tax or income tax. Nevertheless, sales and gross receipts taxes today account for more than one-sixth of the revenues of state and local governments and are followed in importance by property taxes that only local governments generally levy.

The individual income tax is the largest revenue producer in California, Maryland, and New York. New Hampshire is the only state that does not levy either a general personal income tax or a sales tax.

State and local governments receive 17 percent of their revenues from the national government compared to 41 percent raised by taxes. The average percentage of state revenues received from the national government masks the amount of aid received for specific governmental functions. States

FIGURE 6.2
State and Local Government Revenue by Major Financial Sector: Fiscal Year 2004

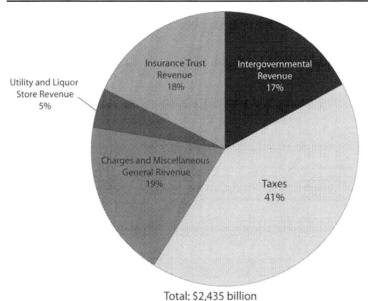

Total: $2,435 billion

Source: United States Bureau of the Census, *Compendium of Government Finances: 2004* (Washington, DC: U.S. Government Printing Office, 2006).

are heavily dependent on the national government for highway construction and maintenance grants, but receive relatively little national fiscal aid for state police forces. Similarly, local governments receive large amounts of national financial aid for education and social welfare programs, but only small amounts of aid for police and fire protection.

Although there generally has been an increase in federal financial grants to subnational governments since 1950, a decline in the amount of the grants as a percentage of total state and local government revenue has occurred. Nevertheless, the national government remains an important source of subnational governmental revenue with federal grants-in-aid alone totaling approximately $425 billion in fiscal year 2004.[1]

The potential exists in a federal system for more than one government levying the same type of tax (tax overlapping or multiple taxation) in the absence of constitutional provisions regulating or prohibiting such taxation. The national government and individual states rely on excise taxes— beer, distilled spirits, motor fuel, tobacco, distilled spirits—for revenue.

Because increases in federal excise taxes decrease consumption, states suffer a decline in excise tax revenue.

Constitutional Provisions

Section 8 of Article I of the U.S. Constitution grants Congress the broad power "to lay and collect taxes, duties, imposts, and excises," but Section 9 stipulates "all duties, imposts, and excise shall be uniform throughout the United States." This grant of power is not exclusive and state legislatures possess a similar broad power to levy taxes under their reserved powers subject to restrictions and prohibitions in the U.S. Constitution and state constitutions.

The U.S. Supreme Court has interpreted the taxing powers of Congress broadly, yet a federal tax levied without due process of law, as required by the Fifth Amendment to the U.S. Constitution, would be invalid. Similarly, a state tax levied without due process of law or equal protection of the laws required by the Fourteenth Amendment would be invalid.

Section 10 of Article I of the U.S. Constitution forbids states, unless authorized by Congress, to lay any duty on tonnage or export or import duties except to finance their inspection laws with any surplus revenue reverting automatically to the U.S. Treasury. The grant of power to Congress to regulate interstate and foreign commerce has restricted the ability of states to levy taxes imposing an undue burden on such commerce.[2]

Many state constitutions contain restrictions on the power of state and local governments to levy taxes.[3] The bulk of these restrictions apply to local governments and include tax and deficit limits and exemption of religious, eleemosynary, private educational, federal government, and state government property from taxation. Most constitutional restrictions are supplemented by statutory restrictions enacted by state legislatures.

Governmental Tax Immunity

The U.S. Supreme Court first was called on to address the issue of intergovernmental taxation in 1819. Although the U.S. Constitution does not contain a provision prohibiting state taxation of national government instrumentalities, the court in *McCulloch v. Maryland* ruled that the state could not tax notes issued by the United States Bank because such a tax would interfere with one of the delegated powers of Congress.[4] Ten years later, the court extended the doctrine of intergovernmental tax immunity in

Weston v. Charleston by opining the supremacy of the law clause of the U.S. Constitution prohibits state taxation of obligations of the U.S. Government.[5]

In 1870, the court in *Collector v. Day* made the tax immunity reciprocal by holding Congress could not tax the instrumentalities of a state, including the salary of a state judge, because "the tax exemption rests upon necessary implication, and is upheld by the great law of self-preservation."[6] The court in 1895 extended this ruling in *Pollock v. Farmers Loan and Trust Company* to holders of bonds issued by states and their local governments by declaring Congress could not levy an income tax on the interest received by bondholders.[7]

Ratification by states in 1913 of the Sixteenth Amendment authorizing Congress to levy a graduated income tax led observers to conclude the exemption granted in the *Pollack* decision no longer was valid. However, the court in 1916 in *Brushaber v. Union Pacific Rail Road Company* continued the exemption.[8]

The court in the twentieth century commenced to narrow the doctrine of intergovernmental tax immunity by distinguishing between governmental and proprietary functions of state and local governments. The former functions are traditional ones such as police and fire protection, and the latter are newer functions that could be performed by private business firms such as rubbish collection and disposal. In *South Carolina v. United States*, the court in 1965 opined that a state-owned system of stores for dispensing liquor was subject to national taxation since the state was operating an "ordinary private business."[9] The justices subsequently ruled Congress could tax a state-owned bank, a city-owned street railway, public wharfs, and state college football games. In 1946, the court in *New York v. United States* upheld the levy of a national excise tax on mineral water bottled by the State of New York on the ground the state enterprise competes with private mineral water firms, and Congress had decided mineral water should be taxed to provide revenue for the national government.[10]

The justices nevertheless continued to rule in favor of intergovernmental tax immunity in specific cases. In 1922, the court in *Gillespie v. Oklahoma* held a state could not levy its income tax on profits earned by a private firm on Indian lands leased from the national government.[11] In *Panhandle Oil Company v. Knox*, the court in 1928 opined that a state may not tax sales made by a private firm to the national government and issued a similar ruling in 1931 in *Indian Motorcycle Company v. United States* by holding a national tax cannot be applied to the sale by a private firm to a state government.[12]

In the late 1920s and early 1930s, the justices began to reduce the scope of intergovernmental tax immunities by sustaining in 1926 a state tax on the income of firms holding contracts with the national government and in 1931 a state income tax on capital gains made from the sales of federal government bonds.[13] In 1937, the court in *James v. Dravo Contracting Company* upheld a state gross receipts tax on a firm's contracts with the federal government.[14]

The court in *Helvering v. Gerhardt* in 1938 narrowed further intergovernmental tax immunity by allowing the federal income tax to be applied to the salaries of employees of the Port of New York Authority, created by an interstate compact entered into by New Jersey and New York, by ruling their activities were similar to activities of private firms.[15]

In 1939, the justices in *Graves v. New York* overruled its earlier decisions "so far as they recognize an implied constitutional immunity from income taxation of the salaries of officers or employees of the national or a State government or their instrumentalities."[16] In the same year, Congress enacted the *Public Salary Act* expressly providing for taxation of the salaries of subnational government officers and employees, and expressly authorizing subnational governments to tax in a nondiscriminatory manner the salaries of national government officers and employees.[17] The *Buck Act of 1940* authorizes states to extend sales, use, and income taxes to persons residing or doing business on federal properties.[18]

The *Graves* decision by extension suggests the court would uphold imposition of the national income tax on interest received by holders of bonds issued by state and local governments. This tax exemption permits subnational governments to borrow funds at lower than the market rate of interest and in effect is a very valuable national government subsidy, a controversial subject examined in greater detail in a subsequent section.

In spite of the cited Supreme Courts decisions, a state or a local government may tax a federal instrumentality if authorized to do so by Congress. The court in 1866 in *Van Allen v. Assessors* and in 1926 in *First National Bank v. Anderson* upheld as constitutional congressional acts allowing states to tax in a nondiscriminatory manner the shares of national banks.[19] Similarly, it is clear that if Congress specifically grants an exemption from subnational governmental taxation to a federal instrumentality, no state or local government may tax the instrumentality.

Although the U.S. Supreme Court made distinctions between governmental and proprietary functions of a state in determining whether a national tax could be constitutional, such distinctions do not apply to federal governmental activities. The court in *Graves v. New York* opined in 1939 that since the national government "derives its authority wholly from powers delegated to it by the Constitution, its every action within its constitutional power is governmental action."[20] This opinion does not mean a nationally chartered corporation automatically is exempt from subnational taxation. Such a corporation has tax immunity only if Congress expressly grants such immunity.

State Taxation of Nonresident Income

Adoption of a federal system automatically presents the possibility a state would attempt to tax the income of nonresidents. In *Shaffer v. Carter*, the U.S. Supreme Court in 1920 ruled Oklahoma could tax the net income of a nonresident derived from sources within the state and dismissed summarily the argument the tax imposes an undue burden on interstate commerce.[21] In the same year, the court in *Travis v. Yale & Towne Manufacturing Company* issued a similar ruling by opining that a state may tax nonresidents and may limit deductions for nonresidents to ones related to the production of income subject to the tax.[22]

The problem of multistate taxation of an individual or a firm is compounded if two or more states levy a personal income tax, a corporate income tax, or both. To prevent undue double taxation, many states entered into reciprocal income tax agreements exempting nonresidents from paying the tax. Other states lightened the burden on their taxpayers by allowing them a credit for income taxes paid to sister states.

State taxation of nonresident income is subject to the equal protection of the law clause of the Fourteenth Amendment to the U.S. Constitution. New Hampshire levied an income tax on nonresidents who work in the state. The U.S. Supreme Court in *Austin v. New Hampshire* invalidated the tax because it did not apply to New Hampshire residents and hence deprived nonresidents of equal protection of the laws.[23]

With a multitude of business firms operating in several or all states, developing a fair system of taxation is a complex task. To determine its share of a multistate firm's income to tax, states utilize separate accounting, specific allocation, and formula apportionment. The first method has limited applicability because of the difficulty of separating income earned in a state from income earned in sister states or abroad. The second method, also of limited applicability, provides that certain types of income, such as interest, must be allocated to a single state and cannot be divided among states.

States rely principally on formula apportionment; that is, a method employing a formula to determine a firm's income earned within a state. The formula typically utilizes payrolls, property, and sales within the state to determine a ratio between a firm's income earned in the state versus its multistate income. Since states employ different apportionment formulas, definition of taxable income varies from state to state.

State taxation of the worldwide operations of multinational corporations has generated strong protests by the British, Japanese, and other governments. California levies a franchise tax on corporations based on the worldwide earnings of multinational corporations, instead of their earnings within the state, by utilizing a unitary business formula apportionment method. The state determines the total earnings of the corporation, including its California operations, and develops an allocation fraction for the corporation by taking an unweighted average of three ratios: California payroll to worldwide payroll, California property value to total property value, and California sales to total sales. To determine the corporation's taxable income allocable to California, the state multiplies the taxpayer's allocation fraction by the total income of the unitary business.

Alcan Aluminum Limited, a Canadian company, and Imperial Chemical Industries PLC, a British company, brought a constitutional challenge in the U.S. District Court for the Northern District of Illinois to California's franchise tax, but the challenge was dismissed.[24] On appeal, the U.S. Court of Appeals for the 7th Circuit reversed the decision.[25] The U.S. Supreme Court, on appeal, opined that the corporations had standing to bring suit under Article III of the U.S. Constitution, but such suits were barred by the *Tax Injunction Act of 1937*.[26]

Prior to the court's decision validating the franchise tax, the 1986 California State Legislature enacted a law modifying the system of taxation by allowing multinational corporations to change from the worldwide taxation system to a "water's edge" taxation method. Under the latter, only the United States earnings of a corporation are taxed and the tax is based on the size of the corporation's operations in California. The British Government objects to the this system because restrictions of the law and the election fee of 0.03 percent of the corporation's payroll, property, and sales make it difficult for many corporations to shift to the new system.

New Jersey employed the unitary tax system to assess the Bendix Corporation for taxes on income derived from a gain from the sale of stock in another corporation. The U.S. Supreme Court in 1992 upheld the constitutionality of the system, but directed the state to refund the tax on the capital gain on the ground that a state may not tax a nondomicilliary corporation's income derived from an unrelated business activity including stock sales.[27]

NATIONAL FINANCIAL ASSISTANCE

National-state-local relations generally have been cooperative and are epitomized today by extensive direct and indirect financial assistance the national government provides to states and their political subdivisions and similar provision of financial and other assistance by most states to their local governments. Congress in fiscal year 2006 appropriated $450 billions in grants to state and local governments.

With the exceptions of war periods, national government receipts and expenditures historically were only a fraction of the revenues and expenditures of subnational governments. As late as 1929, federal expenditures were only 35 percent of the combined state and local government expenditures and federal tax receipts were only slightly higher. With the exception of highway aid, federal grants were relatively unimportant in 1929. The Great Depression of the 1930s produced a dramatic change in the nature of the intergovernmental fiscal system.

National assistance to local governments dates to the *Land Ordinance of 1785*, popularly known as the Northwest Ordinance, enacted by the unicameral Congress under the Articles of Confederation and Perpetual Union.[28] This ordinance reserved one square mile in each township for educational purposes in the area covered by the ordinance.

The original thirteen states incurred substantial debts in financing the Revolutionary War. The Constitutional Convention of 1787 considered a proposal to have the new national government assume the debts of the states, but the proposal was rejected. In 1790, however, Congress enacted a statute providing for assumption of state debts by the national government.[29]

In 1808, Congress appropriated $200,000 annually to help finance the cost of arming and equipping state militias.[30] Congress subsequently provided financial assistance to states for construction of post roads and canals, but Presidents, commencing with James Madison, vetoed bills providing such assistance. In 1837, Congress enacted a statute distributing the national government's surplus funds to states in the form of unconditional cash grants.[31]

The 1803 enabling act admitting the Ohio territory into the Union as a state granted land to the state and stipulated one section of land in each local government must be reserved for school purposes.[32] A similar act, admitting the Illinois territory into the Union as a state, provided that 5 percent of the net proceeds of lands sold by Congress within the state must be dedicated to the construction of roads and "encouragement of learning."[33] After 1848, Congress commenced to reserve two sections of land for schools and subsequently reserved four sections of land in admitting Arizona, New Mexico, and Utah as states into the Union. In 1850, Congress granted swamplands to states and in 1862 enacted the *Morrill Act* granting lands to states for the purpose of establishing colleges of agriculture and mechanical arts.[34]

Conditional Grants-in-Aid

Congress today influences greatly the exercise of many reserved powers by state and local governments through conditions attached to national grants-in-aid. Whether Congress could attach conditions to grants to states was a controversial issue. The U.S. Supreme Court in *McGee v. Mathias* in 1866 opined that the acceptance of a grant with conditions by a state is a binding contract that cannot be violated by state law.[35] The controversy over attached grant conditions continued until 1923 when the court in *Massachusetts v. Mellon* upheld as constitutional the conditions attached by Congress to a 1921 maternity act requiring states accepting a grant to exercise their reserved powers to comply with the conditions.[36]

The origin of continuing national grants-in-aid with conditions to states is the *Hatch Act of 1887* authorizing grants to establish agricultural experiment stations at state colleges of agriculture.[37] The first condition, other than a purpose, is the requirement in the *Carey Act of 1894* of the preparation of a comprehensive plan for irrigation of arid land.[38] Most grants-in-aid require the recipient state or local government to provide matching funds, typically on a two-thirds national and one-third state or local government basis. The matching fund requirement dates to the *Weeks Act of 1911* authorizing grants for state forestry programs.[39] This act also is the first one containing the condition that national government officers have authority to inspect state programs financed in part with national funds.

The "single state agency" requirement—each grant-in-aid must be administered by only one state agency—originated in the *Federal Road Aid Act of 1916*.[40] This requirement has proven to be a controversial one with many states maintaining it limits their ability to organize the state governments in the most economical and efficient manner. Amendments to the 1921 act broadened the influence of the national government by authorizing the secretary of agriculture to evaluate the competence of state highway departments receiving federal grants.[41]

With the growing amount of federal grants for highway construction, Congress became concerned states would divert revenue produced by their highway user taxes to other purposes. To prevent such a diversion, the *Hayden-Cartwright Act of 1934* contains a maintenance-of-effort provision and penalizes a state for such diversions by withholding one-third of the federal highway aid a diverting state was eligible to receive.

Selection of state and local government personnel historically was based in most instances on political patronage rather than competence. With the sharp increase in federal grants-in-aid in the 1930s during the Great Depression, Congress concluded competent and politically neutral employees did not always administer subnational programs financed in part with national funds. As a result, Congress included a provision in the *Social Security Act of 1935* stipulating state and local government employees administering programs with funds provided by the act must be selected and promoted on the basis of merit.[42] In 1939 and 1940, Congress enacted statutes prohibiting employees of subnational governments to engage in partisan political activities if national funds finance any part of their salaries.[43]

Most conditions-of-aid, however, are programmatic in nature and relate to specific programs in contrast to conditions referred to above that generally apply to all or most national grant-in-aid programs. Not surprisingly, many programmatic conditions attached to grants are controversial.

The Federal Grants-in-Aid Explosion

There are two types of national categorical grants-in-aid. Formula grants provide for distribution of funds to state and local governments by means of a formula containing several factors, such as population, urban population, and per capita income. Project grants, in contrast, are designed to aid capital construction projects such as sewage treatment plants and light rail systems.

National cash grants-in-aid to states were not an important source of state revenue prior to 1916. All national financial assistance to states totaled less than $5 million in 1915.[44] Federal grants to states increased sharply with the enactment of the *Federal Road Aid Act of 1916* and averaged $100 million annually between 1918 and 1930, or approximately 3 percent of national appropriations.[45]

The serious economic and social problems associated with the Great Depression induced Congress to authorize a relatively large number of new grant-in-aid programs during the 1930s and the amount of aid increased to nearly 10 percent of annual congressional appropriations. The new programs focused on social welfare and were successful in persuading most states and most local governments to administer national programs. World War II consumed national revenues that otherwise might have been distributed to states and their political subdivisions.

The *United States Housing Act of 1937* represented a new departure in intergovernmental relations by authorizing direct federal grants-in-aid to local governments.[46] The trend toward establishment of direct national-local fiscal relations became more pronounced when twenty-three of thirty-eight federal grant programs enacted between 1961 and 1967 bypassed states. Several observers attributed establishment of such direct relations to the failure of state governments to assume their responsibilities and to play a major partnership role in the federal system. It must be pointed out, however, the charge does not apply to all states, and progressive states, such as California and New York, launched urban programs subsequently adopted by Congress.

To counter threatened diminution of state government significance in the federal system caused by establishment of direct federal-local fiscal relations, the U.S. Advisory Commission on Intergovernmental Relations recommended that the states create appropriate administrative machinery and "buy into" federal-local programs by providing at least one-half of the nonfederal share of the funds.[47] This recommendation is based on the belief the administration of intergovernmental programs can be improved by state participation that, in turn, would strengthen states as partners in the federal system. Most states adopted the recommendation and provide one-half of the nonfederal share of the funds for many federal grant programs.

Congress authorized nineteen new programmatic categories of aid between 1946 and 1960. An explosion in such grant programs commenced in fiscal year 1960 as the total amount of grants increased annually by 15 percent from $7 billion to $91 billion in fiscal year 1980. Of the ninety-five programmatic categories authorized between 1950 and 1979, thirty-nine were authorized between 1961 and 1966. Congress in particular was very responsive to pressure from special interest groups with narrow goals.

Classifying federal financial aid by function reveals significant shifts in the nature of the aid over time. The early cash grants were designed primarily to promote agriculture and include the *Federal Road Aid Act of 1916*, popularly known as the farm to market road act. During the 1920s, there was a sharp increase in grants for highways. A new program—social services—was established by the *Social Security Act of 1935* and grew rapidly in importance. Between 1950 and 1955, for example, approximately 60 to 65 percent of all grants were for health, labor, and welfare. The *National Interstate and Defense Highways Act of 1956* resulted in the largest amount of funds being granted for highways.[48]

The emphasis shifted during the administration of President Lyndon B. Johnson in the 1960s as his "Great Society" programs concentrated on health, labor, and social welfare. More recently, Congress increased sharply grants for public education and the War on Terrorism prompted Congress to appropriate grant funds to assist state and local governments to counter the threat of terrorists.

An examination of federal grants-in-aid by administering agencies reveals similar grants are administered by more than one agency. Carl W. Stenberg, former executive director of the council of state governments, attributed "the presence of so many separate or functionally related programs administered by various agencies" to "differences in individual missions and clienteles."[49] The overlapping grant programs have been subjected to considerable criticism.

THE GRANTS-IN-AID CONTROVERSY

As noted, opposition to grants-in-aid dates to the nineteenth century. The proliferation of grant programs in the twentieth century generated major controversies. As late as 1947, the Indiana State Legislature declared "we propose henceforward to tax ourselves and take care of ourselves. We are fed up with subsidies, doles, and paternalism. We are no one's stepchild. We have grown up. We serve notice that we will resist Washington, D.C. adopting us."[50]

Opposition to federal grants in the 1920s focused on charges that unelected national bureaucrats were dictating what the sovereign states must do, grants are a type of bribe to induce subnational governments to execute national policies, the spending power was divorced from the taxing power, and grants are a mechanism by which money is extracted through taxation from rich states to subsidize poor states.

Not unexpectedly, these charges were rejected by proponents of national grants who maintained grants and associated conditions improve administration of state and local government programs, promote tax equity by redistributing national tax resources in part on a need basis, help subnational governments to finance programs they otherwise could not finance, and foster intergovernmental cooperation in service provision.

The early arguments against national grants tended to be ideological in nature whereas the more recent arguments emphasize reduction in the discretionary authority of subnational governments, less economy and efficiency in the provisions of the aided services, problems with programmatic accountability, lack of citizen understanding of the responsibilities of the various involved governments, and failure of many grant programs to achieve their stated goals.

Newer Criticisms

The explosion in the number of grant programs and new conditions attached to grants in the 1960s led to a new period of criticisms of the programs. The changed nature of such programs was highlighted by the U.S. Advisory Commission on Intergovernmental Relations, which in 1978 noted that "at least through the 1950s, federal assistance activities were confined by an effort to restrict aid to fields clearly involving the national interest or an important national purpose."[51] Subsequent to 1965, the commission explained national interest no longer was the basis for grants with "any action passed by both legislative chambers and signed by the president being accepted as appropriate."[52]

Major criticisms of national grant-in-aid programs included (1) reduction in the discretionary authority of subnational governments, (2) program dominance by national bureaucrats, (3) strengthening the position of the state governor versus the state legislature, (4) greater independence of subnational bureaucrats from control by elected officers, (5) distortions of subnational government budgets as nonfederal funds are employed to match federal grants, (6) promotion of additional spending by state and local governments as a result of the matching requirements, (7) ineffective congressional review of proposed grant programs supported by politically strong interest groups, (8) conflicting objectives of various grant programs, (9) duplicative and overlapping grants-in-aid, (10) voluminous national rules and regulations, (11) inadequate opportunity for state and local governments to influence the drafting of national grant-in-aid regulations, (12) complex and costly grant applications procedures, (13) inflexible programmatic conditions preventing needed adjustment of programs to changed circumstances, (14) the "single agency" requirement, (15) expensive changes in the conditions-of-aid after subnational governments opt to apply for and accept grants-in-aid, and (16) a serious accountability problem.

Relative to the latter criticism, Stenberg noted that "the highly fragmented intergovernmental assistance program provides many buck-passing opportunities. Local officials can always blame the 'feds' for unpopular actions or policy decisions such as fair share housing programs or community-based corrections projects. Both can criticize the insensitivity, unwillingness, or inability of some States to provide needed assistance or authority to their local governments."[53]

The conflicting goal objectives of grant programs are highlighted by the interstate highway grant program promotion of suburban development and the need for suburban residents to travel by private motor vehicles, and the mass transit system program seeking to encourage travel by bus and subway systems.

Subnational government officers object strongly to Congress changing conditions-of-aid after their governments accepted grants-in-aid. In 1990, for example, Congress expanded the coverage of the Medicaid program, thereby sharply increasing costs states must finance.

W. Brooke Graves, a leading federalism expert, acknowledged in 1964 the grant-in-aid programs have disadvantages, yet added:

The impartial observer must admit that grant funds have helped many states both to inaugurate many new programs and to expand existing programs which would not otherwise have been undertaken. He must admit also that the grant system has had a centralizing influence, which may be good or bad according to one's point of view, and that it has tended to promote uniformity among the States. National grants have established national programs which have to be administered in accordance with national standards, which are to a large extent determined and agreed upon by a process of mutual accommodation. Even so, administrative responsibility has remained, to a considerable extent, in the hands of State and local officials.[54]

A second federalism expert, David B. Walker, drew different conclusions in 1981 and maintained the servicing system is overloaded and dysfunctional: "In broadly systemic terms, this has arisen because of the ever-expanding role of the national government in regulatory, promotional, and aided program undertakings of both a major and minor nature, because subnational governments and other intermediate instrumentalities are relied upon to implement many of the national government's regulatory policies and practically all of its service-related programs."[55]

In addition to the above criticisms, subnational government officers objected to the thirty-one cross-cutting conditions attached to all programs by 1980. These conditions—such as affirmative action promoting the hiring of members of specified minority groups and women as employees, citizen participation, payment of prevailing wages in an area on grant-aided projects, and environmental protection—are designed to promote achievement of social goals and are not related directly to the specific purpose of a categorical grant, and reduce significantly the discretionary authority of recipient governmental units.

National Administrative Responses to the Criticisms

President Johnson heard the criticisms of state and local government officers of the grant-in-aid system and sponsored new organizations and procedures as positive responses. To improve communications between the subnational planes and the national plane, he designated in 1965 the office of the vice president as the contact point for officers of local governments and the office of emergency preparedness in the executive office of the President to perform a similar function for governors. Four years later, President

Richard M. Nixon by executive order established an office for intergovernmental relations under the vice president's supervision to assist state and
local governments.

To improve coordination between federal administrative departments
and agencies, interagency agreements were signed outlining the respective
responsibilities of each signatory and providing for ongoing consultation.
The confusion generated by hundreds of grant-in-aid programs resulted in
the office of economic opportunity in 1967 being made responsible for publishing a consolidated catalog of all grant programs; the responsibility subsequently was shifted to the office of management and budget. In addition,
the *Vice-President's Handbook for Local Officials* was prepared and distributed throughout the nation.

President Johnson in 1967 directed the bureau of the budget (now
Office of Management and Budget) to study the possibility of consolidating
categorical grant programs, simplifying grant application procedures and
financial accounting, and changing the location and structure of federal
regional offices.

President Nixon assumed office in 1969 and initiated several administrative actions to solve problems identified by critics of the national grant-
in-aid system. He promoted decentralization of decision-making by field
units of national departments and establishment of ten standard national
regions and federal regional councils composed of national officers administering grant programs in each region. He also had his office of management
and budget issue circular A-102 to improve the grant application process and
management of grants-in-aid. His major federalism initiatives, however,
were his special revenue sharing and general revenue-sharing proposals that
are examined in the next two sections.

President James E. Carter (1977–1981), a former governor of Georgia,
expressed interest in improving intergovernmental relations, yet his administrative actions had little impact. David B. Walker concluded in 1981 that
"the confused and conflicting effects of Carter's managerialism, procedural-
ism, fiscal conservatism, and program flexibility underscore the absence of
any consistent theory of federalism or approach to intergovernmental relations in his administration."[56]

Ronald Reagan, a former governor of California, in his 1980 presidential election campaign stressed the overcentralization of political power in
the national government and his desire to return power to the states. He also
was disturbed greatly by what he perceived to be excessive national governmental regulation.

One of his first administrative initiatives was the appointment in 1981
of the presidential task force on regulatory relief, which issued its report in
1983. On February 17, 1981, he issued executive order number 12291

requiring all proposed and final regulations be submitted to the Office of Management and Budget for review prior to publication in the *Federal Register*.

President Reagan also issued in 1981 executive order number 12303 establishing the presidential advisory committee on federalism and directed it to advise him relative to federalism policy. His third federalism executive order, number 12372, was issued in 1982 and designed to provide state and local governments with additional opportunities to influence the federal administrative decision-making process.

In 1983, the office of management and budget released a revised circular A-102 establishing uniform requirements for grants to subnational governments and reducing the burden of federal government audits on these governments. Two years later, President Reagan issued executive order number 12498 establishing a regulatory planning process by directing each national department and agency to submit to the office of management and budget a statement listing goals and policies for the forthcoming year to assist the office in developing a regulatory program on an annual basis.

In 1987, he issued executive order number 12612 containing "fundamental principles" emphasizing dual federalism. The order concludes that "in the absence of clear constitutional or statutory authority, the presumption of sovereignty should rest with the individual states." This order contains criteria that must be followed by department and agencies relative to preemption.

Perhaps the most important initiative of President Reagan was the process of speeding up federal agency delegation of "regulatory primacy" to the states, described in chapter 4, under partial preemption statutes establishing minimum national standards. The statutory requirements are not modified by the delegation, but the states acquired additional discretionary authority in administering the statutes.

The Reagan administration reduced federal government oversight of state regulatory activities under partial preemption statutes and relaxed a number of national regulatory standards. An example of a major administrative decision designed to increase the regulatory authority of the states was an environmental protection agency regulation allowing a state to employ the "bubble" concept in determining whether changes in a stationary source within an industrial plant met the requirements of the *Clean Air Act*. The concept measures air pollution emissions on a plantwide basis instead of an individual source basis.

The Reagan initiated administrative actions were very limited responses to the complaints of state and local government officers. Congressional creation of block grants and the general revenue-sharing program broadened significantly the discretionary authority of subnational governments.

Block Grants

As noted, state and local government officers registered opposition to categorical grants-in-aid with attached conditions because their discretionary authority is reduced. Many officers maintained the grant of greater discretionary authority in the form of block grants, which fold several categorical grants into one grant, would enable them to achieve programmatic goals with fewer dollars.

Although the first Hoover Commission on the organization of the executive branch of the national government in 1949 recommended "a system of grants be established based upon broad categories . . . as contrasted with the present system of extreme fragmentation," the first block grant program was not established by Congress until 1966 when the *Partnership for Health Act* was enacted.[57]

The *Omnibus Crime Control and Safe Streets Act of 1968* was the second block grant program enacted by Congress. Critics, however, argued that Congress shortly thereafter commenced to add categories to the program, which resulted in it becoming "a closely related set of categorical grants masquerading under a block grant guise."[58]

President Nixon in 1972 proposed four modified block grant programs that he labeled "special revenue sharing" and Congress enacted one of the programs—community development—into law in 1974.[59] Referred to popularly as the community development block grant program (CDBG), it differs from a conventional block grant program because (1) the eligible government is required only to submit a simple application, (2) the department of housing and community development cannot reject the application, (3) the recipient local government is not subject to administrative audits by the department, and (4) matching and maintenance-of-effort requirements do not apply to the program.

A total of thirty-two categorical grants-in-aid programs were consolidated into block grants or a special revenue-sharing program between 1966 and 1974, and new block grant programs—insular areas, elderly, and forestry—were authorized by Congress in 1977 and 1978. Although Congress terminated the law enforcement block grant program in 1980, President Reagan in 1981 was successful in persuading Congress in the *Omnibus Budget Reconciliation Act* to establish nine new or modified block grant programs by merging fifty-seven categorical grant-in-aid programs.[60]

Enactment of the block grants terminated the rules and regulations promulgated by implementing departments and agencies for categorical programs. The implementing regulations for the block grant programs are short and not complex. President Reagan in 1984 reported the paperwork burden of state and local governments had been reduced by 90 percent following establishment of the new block grants in 1981 and the rules and regulations covered only thirty-two pages in the *Code of Federal Regulations*.

Analytical reports reveal the block grants achieved the objectives of allowing states additional flexibility in administering the programs. These programs are administered by the states, and a number of mayors of large cities expressed their displeasure with the block grants since their relations with their respective state government are not always friendly and most mayors would prefer to have the grants come directly to the cities. Other critics maintain block grants result in less aid being directed to help poor citizens since states have greater discretion in determining how the funds will be spent. In 1991, the U.S. General Accounting Office (now U.S. Government Accountability Office) issued a report revealing weaknesses in oversight of block grant monitoring by the department of housing and urban development and concluding it cannot ensure that it detects grantee's management problems.[61]

General Revenue Sharing

Not surprisingly, the national financial assistance program most popular with state and local government officers was the general revenue sharing program since it permitted recipient units the most discretionary authority in spending the funds. In enacting the *State and Local Fiscal Assistance Act of 1972* at the urging of President Nixon, Congress appropriated $30.2 billion to be given to the fifty states and approximately 38,000 general-purpose local governments over a five-year period with few attached conditions.[62] The funds could be spent for any legal purpose, but could not be used for discriminatory purposes.

In contrast to national grant-in-aid programs promoting intergovernmental functional contacts and strengthening the position of bureaucrats on all planes of government administering the program, the general revenue sharing program strengthens the ability of subnational elected officer to control bureaucrats since general revenue-sharing funds cannot be spent without an appropriation by the state legislature or local governing body.

The U.S. House of Representatives and the U.S. Senate could not agree on a common formula for distribution of general revenue sharing funds and decided to include two formulas in the law. Each state received the higher amount resulting from calculations utilizing the two formulas. The house formula was based on population, urban population, per capita income, state income tax collections, and tax effort. The senate formula was based on population, relative income, and tax effort. Until 1980, states received one-third of the funds and local governments received two-thirds.

The program was an entitlement one and eligible units were not required to apply for the funds, meet a maintenance-of-effort requirement, appropriate matching funds, or be subject to federal administrative audits. Congress reauthorized the program in 1976, but in its 1980 renewal Congress dropped states as eligible recipients of funds. Although there was agreement the general-purpose local governments still needed general revenue-sharing funds, Congress in 1986 did not reauthorize the program because of the sharply escalating national budgetary deficit.

A U.S. bureau of the census report revealed the program provided a significant proportion of the funds expended by several cities—Baton Rouge, Louisiana (10.8%); Miami, Florida (9.7%); New Orleans, Louisiana (7.8%); Pittsburgh, Pennsylvania (6.4%); and El Paso, Texas (6.2%).[63]

Four major arguments were directed against the program. First, opponents contended the political accountability maxim is violated since the units spending the funds are not responsible for raising the funds. In particular, critics asked to whom are local government officers responsible for spending the funds received from the national government?

Second, a U.S. general accounting office report revealed that "there was no observed tendency to target more aid to governments with high fiscal pressures."[64] Numerous wealthy local governments received general revenue sharing funds on the same basis as poor municipalities.

Third, the program was decried on the ground it "shored up" small local governments that otherwise would have been merged with other local governments, thereby simplifying the fragmented local governmental system and making it more cost effective. This criticism was directed in particular at Midwest townships, many of which are little more than bridge and highway districts, and New England counties with limited court-related, law enforcement, and welfare functions. Approximately one-third of the eligible local governments were "limited-purpose" rather than "general-purpose units."

Fourth, opponents of the program maintained it did not benefit poor citizens whose interests would have been more effectively served by categorical grants-in-aid targeted to assist citizens.

Post-Reagan Responses

Presidents George H. W. Bush, William J. Clinton, and George W. Bush failed to respond to complaints of subnational officers by launching major new initiatives. The increasing national budgetary deficit and the long-lasting recession that commenced in 1989 limited the intergovernmental financial role of the first President Bush. He approved thirty-four preemption bills, but only the *Clean Air Act Amendments of 1990* had a major impact on subnational governments.[65]

President William J. Clinton, a former governor of Arkansas, also was constrained by the budgetary deficit and recession during his early years in office. He issued executive order 12866 directing regulatory departments and agency to initiate planning for regulatory relief and executive order 12875 establishing a national-state-local governmental consultation process relating to promulgation of rules and regulations impacting subnational governments. Clinton approved sixty-four preemption bills, but only the *Riegle-Neal Interstate Banking and Branching Efficiency Act of 1994, Telecommunications Act of 1996*, and *Gramm-Leach-Bliley Financial Modernization Act of 1999* had a major impact on subnational governments.[66]

President George W. Bush, a former governor of Texas, on February 26, 2001, issued a memorandum establishing an interagency working group on federalism, but no record indicates it met.[67] The September 11, 2001, terrorists' attacks and the wars in Afghanistan and Iraq diverted his attention away from a number of domestic issues. He approved ninety-six preemption bills in the period 2001–2007, but only the two *Internet Tax Freedom Acts* had an impact on states levying a sales tax.[68] The other preemption acts involved the periphery of state-exercised powers in comparison with 16 preemption statutes enacted between 1965 and 1999 including the *Water Quality Act of 1965* and the *Gramm-Leach-Bliley Financial Modernization Act of 1999*.[69]

Other Federal Financial Assistance

The national government provides financial assistance to state and local governments, directly and indirectly, by allowing national taxpayers, not subject to the alternative minimum tax, to deduct from their gross income for tax purposes certain taxes paid to subnational governments, exempting the interest received on state and local government bonds (collectively referred to as municipal bonds) from the national income tax, and providing insurance, technical assistance, and services to subnational governments.

TAX DEDUCTIONS

For many years, Congress allowed most subnational taxes to be deducted from a taxpayer's gross income. Such deductions are beneficial to state and local governments as they can increase their taxes without the entire burden of the increase falling on taxpayers.

In 1943, Congress repealed the authorization for the deduction of several state and local government excise taxes and ended in 1964 deductions for state and local excise taxes on alcohol and tobacco products, and operator and motor vehicle registration fees. In 1979, Congress eliminated state motor fuel taxes as a deduction.

With the national budgetary deficits increasing sharply during the 1980s, Congress in 1986 decided to phase out the deductibility of state and local government sales and use taxes. Sales taxes originally were 100 percent deductible, but the percentage was reduced each year with only a 10 percent deduction allowed in 1990, the last year in which a deduction was permitted. Subnational income and property taxes remain fully deductible.

President Reagan in 1985 recommended that Congress repeal authorization for deductibility of state and local taxes. Subnational government officers expressed alarm at the proposal and predicted it would result in sharp reductions in state and local government services, higher subnational governmental taxes, or both. The President's proposal would benefit states with low taxes and expenditures, such as New Hampshire and Wyoming, and low-income taxpayers who do not itemize deductions on their income tax returns.

States with high taxes and expenditures, with New York leading the list, and high-income taxpayers would be the losers under the Reagan proposal. It was estimated in 1985 that repeal of deductibility would result in a national income tax increase per itemizing taxpayers, ranging from $322.81 in Wyoming to $1,646.16 in New York. Taxpayers in fifteen states, according to estimates, would pay more than one-half the money raised by eliminating deductibility.

The President's recommendation would reduce the size of the huge national deficit by removing an indirect subsidy, referred to as tax expenditures, and force state and local governments to curtail spending or risk the wrath of citizens by increasing taxes. In states with the direct initiative allowing voters to place proposed laws and constitutional amendments by petition, a sharp tax increase resulting from elimination of deductibility undoubtedly would stimulate tax revolts.[70] Congress in the *Omnibus Budget Reconciliation Act for Fiscal Year 1990* limited the amount of state and local income and property taxes that may be deducted by individuals with incomes exceeding $100,000 per year.[71]

TAX-EXEMPT MUNICIPAL BONDS

A taxpayer does not have to pay the national income tax on interest received from bonds issued for public purposes by state and local governments. As noted in the section on governmental tax immunity, the U.S. Supreme Court in 1829 ruled states may not tax obligations of the U.S.

government and in 1895 extended the ruling by declaring that Congress could not tax interest received by holders of municipal bonds.

The dollar volume of such bonds has been escalating for decades. The exemption of interest on these bonds from national taxation is a valuable indirect subsidy to state and local governments enabling them to borrow funds at a rate of interest significantly lower than the market rate of interest on taxable private bonds, thereby benefiting subnational governmental taxpayers. Critics of the tax exemption charge high-income citizens, who hold most of the bonds, are the principal beneficiaries of the exemption.

Concern about loss of revenue resulting from the exemption induced Congress to enact the *Revenue and Expenditure Control Act of 1968* removing the exemption from bonds utilized primarily to finance projects benefiting private persons or organizations; that is, industrial development bonds.[72]

The use of tax-exempt bonds to finance single-family home mortgages was restricted by the *Mortgage Subsidy Bond Tax Act of 1980* that placed limits on the prices of homes and restricted purchasers to first-time buyers of a home.[73] The *Social Security Act Amendments of 1983* indirectly made tax-exempt interest received by retirees subject to income taxation by including the interest in the calculations of a social security recipient's income and taxing a portion of the social security payments under a formulated related to that income.[74]

The *Deficit Reduction Act of 1984* placed additional restrictions upon the use of tax-exempt municipal bonds to financial industrial development, including volume limitation on certain types of industrial development bonds and student loan bonds within each state.[75] Two years later, Congress Enacted the *Tax Reform Act* imposing comprehensive restrictions on use of tax-exempt municipal bonds.[76] These securities no longer can be used to finance convention centers, industrial parks, sports facilities, air and water pollution control facilities, and privately owned transportation facilities. In 1987 and 1988, Congress imposed additional restrictions on the use of tax-exempt bond proceeds.

Until 1986, state and local governments issuing municipal bonds often earned an arbitrage profit by reinvesting the borrowed funds for a period of time in private securities paying a rate of interest higher than the interest paid on the municipal bonds. Congress in the *Tax Reform Act of 1986* decided to recoup the profits by requiring these governments to remit such profits to the U.S. Treasury.[77]

This act was challenged in court by South Carolina as violating the rights of states under the Tenth Amendment to the U.S. Constitution. In 1988, the U.S. Supreme Court declared in *South Carolina v. Baker* "that subsequent case law has overruled the holding in *Pollock* that state bond interest is immune from a nondiscriminatory federal tax" and added the

1895 *Pollock* ruling had not been overruled explicitly simply because Congress had exempted municipal bond interest from taxation since 1913.[78] Congress has continued the tax exemption to this day.

TAX CREDITS

Congress authorized the first national tax credit program in the *Revenue Act of 1926* that provided eligible taxpayers with an 80 percent credit against the national inheritance and estate tax for a similar tax paid to a state.[79] The purpose of credit was to encourage each state legislature to enact a uniform inheritance and estate tax based on the national tax. If a state failed to adopt a tax linked to the national tax, taxpayers in the state would be required to pay the total national tax as well as the state tax.

In enacting the *Social Security Act of 1935*, Congress decided that a system of unemployment compensation should be operated by each state. To encourage each state to operate such a system, the act provides a 90 percent tax credit for employers who pay unemployment taxes to a state.[80] In other words, employers are required to pay only 10 percent of the national tax if the concerned states have an unemployment compensation system and taxes levied at the same rate as the national tax.

Under the short-lived *Economic Tax Recovery Act of 1981*, urban public transit authorities were authorized to utilize sale-lease-backs as a device for selling their investment tax credits and depreciation allowances.[81] For example, the act authorized a private corporation to purchases buses from a public transportation authority for $10 million by using $2 million of its own funds and $8 million of the authority's funds. Since the corporation holds title to the buses, it may depreciate the total cost of the buses under the national corporate income tax as a deduction and lease the buses for a fee to the authority responsible for maintenance and operating costs. The authority gained $2 million, and the corporation took advantage of tax-deductible payments and accelerated depreciation allowances over a five-year period under the national corporation income tax.

OTHER ASSISTANCE

Congress authorized loans of funds to subnational governments for construction of publicly owned college and university facilities, transportation systems, and reconstruction after natural disasters, such as floods and hurricanes, and the terrorists attacks on the World Trade Center in New York City on September 11, 2001. In addition, Congress authorized a national guarantee of loans enabling state and local governments to borrow money at a lower rate of interest. When the City of New York verged on the edge of municipal bankruptcy and the credit markets were closed to the city,

Congress in the mid-1970s guaranteed approximately $1.65 billion of the bonds issued by the city.

Seven national governmental agencies—emergency management agency, environmental protection agency, national fire academy, coast guard, department of transportation, department of energy, and department of health and human services—provide funding for or conduct training programs for state and local government emergency response personnel without charge.

In addition, many national agencies provide technical assistance to a wide range of governmental functions to subnational governments free of charge. Furthermore, the federal bureau of investigation operates a national fingerprint service. Without it, criminal investigations by state and locals governments would be more costly and less effective.

Federal Government Coercion

Congress until 1965 relied on conditional grants-in-aid to persuade state and local governments to adopt and implement national policies. Since 1965, Congress increasingly employed its powers of partial and complete preemption to mandate subnational governments to implement a specific policy or to prohibit the exercise of a reserved power by states and their political subdivisions. Furthermore, Congress has employed cross-cutting sanctions, cross-over sanctions, and tax sanctions to coerce these governments to implement national regulatory policies.

FEDERAL MANDATES AND RESTRAINTS

As described in chapter 4, Congress enacted preemption statutes containing mandates that are legal requirements that states and/or local governments must undertake specified activities or provide services meeting minimum national standards. A statutory mandate must be distinguished from a condition-of-aid avoidable by a subnational government that does not apply for or accept a national grant-in-aid. It also must be noted there are judicial mandates contained in court orders requiring a state or a local government to initiate a new policy or program to remedy a past wrong. Busing of schoolchildren to promote racial desegregation of government-operated schools is an example of a judicial remedial mandate.

The federal mandate is the principal irritant in national-subnational relations today. Many mandates, such as removal of asbestos from school buildings and filtering of drinking water, are expensive to implement. The cumulative effect of a large number of national mandates created a particularly difficult problem for a state or local government subject to a state constitutional requirement of operating with a balanced budget or within a constitutional debt limit. Environmental mandates have high compliance costs for small local governments often lacking the tax resources to comply and may result in dissolution of many of these units. Subnational government officers resent federally mandated costs and lobby Congress for reimbursement of such costs.

The *New York Times* editorially identified one of the undesirable results of increased federal mandates on local governments: "Mandates often have perverse effect. They require local officials to spend local money on some worthy services at the expense of others, but take away the discretion as to which needs the money more. . . . Uncle Sam is in no position to balance these claims. Nor can he simply say, raise taxes. He does not know when local taxes become so onerous that taxpayers are driven out. Both tasks call for balancing that must be left to local politics."[82]

Responding to complaints of state and local government officers, Congress enacted the *Unfunded Mandates Reform Act of 1995* that is prospective in nature and does not apply to preexisting mandates.[83] The act established new procedures for any bill imposing a mandate, including preparation by the congressional budget office of estimates of the cost of any mandate exceeding $50 million during its first year, and allowing a member of either house to raise a point of order if a committee report fails to contain required information. John C. Eastman in 2002 concluded that the act has been "very effective in imposing some much-needed discipline on Congress, but the exemptions . . . hamper its ability to achieve the kind of far-reaching reform that was its motivating purpose."[84]

In contrast to a mandate, a restraint forbids a state or a local government to exercise a specific power. Preemption statutes have stripped subnational governments of authority to engage in economic regulation of airlines, bus, and motor carrier firms as noted in chapter 4. The *Bus Regulatory Reform Act of 1982*, for example, prohibits state issuance of a franchise to operate buses between two major cities conditional on an agreement by the carrier to provide service to small communities.[85] To ensure bus service to these communities, many states subsidize the carriers.

CROSS-CUTTING AND CROSS-OVER SANCTIONS
Congress increased its policy influence by using these two types of sanctions. A cross-cutting sanction is a condition, such as affirmative action, attached to all grant-in-aid programs. This type of sanction dates to a 1921 amendment to the *Federal Road Aid Act of 1916* stipulating a state highway department receiving federal funds was subject to an evaluation of their competence by the secretary of agriculture.[86]

A cross-over sanction threatens a state failing to comply with a congressional statute with loss of federal grant-in-aid funds authorized by an earlier statute. The Arab oil embargo induced Congress in 1974 to promote energy conservation by employing a cross-over sanction to persuade each state to lower the maximum speed limit to fifty-five miles per hour by threatening to withhold 10 percent of its federal highway aid.[87] A second congressional response was enactment of a 1975 statute providing for withholding of highway grant funds from a state failing to allow motorists stopped at a red traffic light to make a right turn if no motor vehicle is approaching the intersection from the left.[88]

A 1984 act seeks to curb drunk driving by means of a cross-over sanction threatening states with loss of highway funds if they do not increase their minimum alcoholic beverage purchase age to twenty-one.[89] South Dakota challenged the constitutionality of the act as violating the Twenty-first Amendment to the U.S. Constitution devolving regulatory control of alcoholic beverages to states. The U.S. Supreme Court in 1988 upheld the constitutionality of the act.[90]

The *State Comprehensive Mental Health Services Plan Act of 1986* requires states, with the assistance of national grants, to develop a state comprehensive mental health services plan. States failing to develop such a plan by September 30, 1989, had their alcohol, drug abuse, and mental health block grant reduced the following year.[91]

Two similar cross-over sanctions are included in the *Transportation and Related Agencies Appropriations Act for Fiscal Year 1991*.[92] The first sanction is the withholding of 5 percent of a state's federal highway funds if a state fails to impose a six-month suspension of the driver's license of any person convicted of a drug offence, effective October 1, 1993, with the sanction increasing to 10 percent effective October 1, 1995. This sanction is a contingent one since it does not apply to a state if the governor submits to the secretary of transportation written certification that he or she is opposed to the enactment or enforcement of a mandatory suspension law and the state legislature has approved a resolution expressing its opposition to such a law.

The second sanction is a 25 percent reduction in the funds that may be obligated for federal-aid highways and highway safety construction programs for fiscal year 1991 if a state has a public authority responsible for public transportation in an urbanized area with a 1980 population of three million or more and by October 1, 1990, should the laws of the state not authorize a tax dedicated to paying the nonfederal share of public transportation projects or establishment of a regional or local tax for the same purpose.

Another section of the statute continues the sanction for fiscal year 1992, but authorizes the waiver of the sanction if the governor certifies to the secretary of transportation that he or she is opposed to the levying of such a tax and it would not improve public transportation safety, and submits a written certification that the state legislature had approved a resolution opposing the levying of such a tax. Amazingly, Congress included in the *Department of Transportation and Related Agencies Appropriation Act for Fiscal Year 1992* a stipulation that the crossover sanction in the 1991 act should "be treated as having not been enacted into law."[93] Congress changed its mind again and reinserted the sanction in the *Transportation Equity Act for the 21st Century of 1998.*[94]

Tax Sanctions

The first tax sanction was contained in the *Tax Equity and Fiscal Responsibility Act of 1982* and stipulated subnational governments must issue only registered, instead of traditional bearer, long-term municipal bonds or the interest received by bondholders will be subject to the national income tax.[95] This tax sanction increases the cost of borrowing funds by subnational governments, but the cost increase is minor. The U.S. Supreme Court in *South Carolina v. Baker* upheld the constitutionality of the sanction.[96]

The *Tax Reform Act of 1986* contains a similar tax sanction mandating that subnational governmental issuers of long-term bonds whose interest is exempt from the national income tax must rebate to the U.S. Treasury any arbitrage profit.[97] Depending on the spread between the interest cost of borrowing and the interest earned on borrowed funds invested in other securities until needed, the loss of revenue can be significant.

SUMMARY

The U.S. Constitution grants Congress power to levy any type of tax subject to the restriction all duties and excise taxes must be uniform throughout the nation. States have reserved powers to levy taxes subject to the prohibition in Section 10 of Article I of the U.S. Constitution of the levying of a duty on tonnage or exports or imports without the consent of Congress. The U.S. Supreme Court, however, invalidated state and local taxes held to place an undue burden on interstate commerce.

Although the court interpreted the U.S. Constitution in the nineteenth century as prohibiting states from taxing the national government and its instrumentalities or Congress taxing instrumentalities of states, the court in 1939 overruled earlier decisions granting immunity from income taxation of the salaries of employees of the national government or state governments and their instrumentalities.

State taxation of the income of nonresidents is subject to the equal protection of the laws clause of the Fourteenth Amendment. A particularly difficult problem is the development of an equitable state system of taxing the income of multistate and multinational corporations.

The national government provides states and their political subdivisions with an extensive range of direct and indirect financial assistance based until 1974 exclusively on the theory of cooperative federalism. Although subnational governmental officers often object to conditional grants-in-aid, their governments can avoid objectionable conditions by not applying for the grant.

The explosion in the number and dollar amounts of categorical grants-in-aid in the 1960s generated a major controversy and pressure for converting many of these grants into block grants. In 1966, Congress enacted the first block grant program and subsequently created other block grant programs. In general, these programs have achieved their goal of allowing states greater discretion in the spending of the grant funds.

Today, federal mandates, restraints, cross-cutting sanctions, cross-over sanctions, and tax sanctions are the principal irritants in national-subnational governmental relations. Continuing enactment of expensive national mandates has produced extensive lobbying by state and local government officers for national government reimbursement of mandated costs and defeat of mandate bills in Congress.

This chapter has highlighted the increasing complexity of intergovernmental fiscal relations in the United States. Chapter 7 examines another complex aspect of a federal system—interstate relations.

CHAPTER 7

Interstate Relations

The drafters of the U.S. Constitution were convinced experience with a confederation necessitated incorporation into the proposed fundamental law of provisions governing aspects of relations between sister states. The U.S. Constitution places an obligation on states to cooperate with the national government on specified matters and with each other regardless of substantial differences in their population, geographical area, resources, and other characteristics.

The Constitution contains two types of interstate relations provisions. The first type governs relations between states as legal entities and includes a procedure for settling disputes and a mechanism for joint programs. The second type governs relationships of states with each other involving their respective citizens and includes the application of the laws of one state to persons residing in another state, the return of fugitives from justice, and the requirement that each state treat visiting citizens of other states in the same manner that it treats its own citizens.

Original (trial) jurisdiction over legal disputes between states is vested in the U.S. Supreme Court and political compacts between states are subject to the approval of Congress. Article IV of the Constitution, known as the interstate article, contains provisions relating to full faith and credit, interstate citizenship, and interstate rendition of fugitives from justice. The Fourteenth Amendment also affects interstate citizenship.

Development of national systems of communications and transportation has had an important impact on interstate relations and led Congress to use its delegated powers to assume complete or partial responsibility for regulatory functions previously handled by states as described in chapter 4. In addition, the complexity of the economy and society produced a number of extraconstitutional contacts between states seeking to improve the performance of their mutual obligations.

INTERSTATE CONTROVERSIES

Anticipating disputes would arise between states, the founding fathers included in Section 2 of Article III of the Constitution a grant of original jurisdiction to the U.S. Supreme Court over suits between states. This grant of original jurisdiction is one of only two such grants. The other grant involves cases affecting "ambassadors, other public ministers, and consuls." By statute, Congress in 1789 made the grant of original jurisdiction over interstate controversies to the Court exclusive.[1]

The court exercises its original jurisdiction on a discretionary basis after determining whether the complainant state is a genuine or a nominal party, the controversy is justiciable, and the dispute is appropriate for the court to adjudicate.[2] If the court decides to exercise such jurisdiction, the court appoints a special master to collect data and information, and to prepare a report. The special master operates in a manner similar to a U.S. District Court judge and his or her findings and recommendations may be appealed to the court by a disputing state.

Relations between states today generally are good, but conflicts have occurred primarily over boundaries, water pollution and supply, and debts. The large population growth since 1945 in the relatively arid southwest of the nation has generated disputes over the interstate diversion of river waters.

Boundary Disputes

The seriousness of interstate boundary disputes is reflected in a 1964 page 1 headline in *The New York Times* entitled "Iowa Is Called Aggressor State: Nebraska Fears a Shooting War."[3] The controversy, involving the Missouri River that shifts its course periodically, was settled peaceably.

Commencing with *New York v. Connecticut* in 1799, the U.S. Supreme Court adjudicated a number of boundary disputes between states on the basis of international law. Ambiguous boundaries in land grants, survey errors, and natural changes in the courses of rivers serving as boundaries have been responsible for several boundary controversies. As noted in chapter 2, New Hampshire maintained the Mason Grant of 1629 gave the state land west of the Connecticut River and New York claimed the same territory. In this instance, the court did not settle the suit. Congress resolved the interstate controversy by admitting the disputed territory into the Union as the State of Vermont in 1791.

Relative to recent boundary disputes, the U.S. Supreme Court in *Ohio v. Kentucky* in 1980 held the boundary line was the low-water mark on the northerly side of the Ohio River as it existed in 1792 when Kentucky was admitted to the Union and not the current low-water mark on the northerly side of the river.[4] After suing Nebraska, South Dakota in 1982 agreed with Nebraska that avoidance of litigation was in the best interests of the two states and future boundary disputes involving Rush Island would be submitted to a joint state boundary commission. In 1982, the U.S. Supreme Court in *South Dakota v. Nebraska* issued an order confirming the agreement.[5]

In 1990, the court in *Georgia v. South Carolina* defined the boundary between the two states along the Savannah River downstream from the City of Savannah.[6] The states agreed in the *Treaty of Beaufort of 1787* that the boundary along the river was the "most northern branch or stream" and to the reservation of "all islands [in the river] to Georgia." The court opined islands emerging in the river since 1787 did not affect the boundary line between the states, and the boundary lines around islands on the South Carolina side of the river is the midpoint between the islands and the South Carolina shore. In 1991, the court ruled in *Illinois v. Kentucky* the boundary line between the two states is the low-water mark on the north shore of the Ohio River as it existed in 1792.[7]

The U.S. Supreme Court in 1999 interpreted an 1834 interstate compact entered into by New Jersey and New York, and settled a boundary dispute between involving the filled-in area of Ellis Island in New York harbor by ruling the disputed area was part of New Jersey.[8]

Water Disputes

The development of cities with large populations generated the problem of disposing of sewage. Municipalities historically released untreated sewage into waterways and a serious public health problem was caused if the sewage was released into water used for drinking purposes in a downstream municipality. Missouri sued Illinois because a Chicago sanitary district drainage canal emptied sewage into a tributary of the Mississippi River, causing pollution of one of Missouri's water sources. The U.S Supreme Court in *Missouri v. Illinois* in 1906 held use of the canal could not be enjoined in the absence of proof of the deleterious effects of the canal water.[9]

Since water basins and state boundaries do not coincide, it is not surprising conflicting claims would be made relative to the diversion of river water. Such claims to river water led to U.S. Supreme Court decisions in suits between Kansas and Colorado in 1902, 1907, and 1943.[10] The disputes involved diversion of water from the Arkansas River by Colorado to the detriment of farmers in Kansas, and were resolved in Colorado's favor because the issue was an interpretation of common law riparian rights. The court found Kansas's claims had merit, but the damages were not outweighed by the benefits derived by Colorado in reclamation of arid lands by irrigation. To avoid future disputes, the two states accepted the court's 1943 advice and entered into the *Arkansas River Compact of 1949*.[11] Kansas concluded increased well-pumping in Colorado post 1949 violated the compact and brought an original action against Colorado in the U.S. Supreme Court in 1986. The court in 1995 approved the special master's finding that Kansas had not proven well-pumping was responsible for water depletion in violation of the compact.[12]

The most major water dispute involves the Colorado River that originates in the Rocky Mountains north and west of Denver, Colorado, and flows through Utah to form the Arizona boundary line with Nevada and California. Diversion of Colorado River water made possible the rapid growth of southern California.

In 1952, Arizona sued California for diverting too much water from the river, the fifth interstate suit involving the river. At the time, the Los Angeles and San Diego metropolitan areas were using more Colorado River water than the six other states with access to the river water combined. In 1963, the U.S. Supreme Court in *Arizona v. California* settled the dispute by accepting the general claims of Arizona when there is normal water flow, but ruling the U.S. secretary of the interior has complete authority to allocate the water whenever the flow drops below normal.[13] The court retains jurisdiction over the controversy. It should be noted there are disputes between the upper- and lower-basin states over the waters of the river.

Debt Conflict

The most famous debt controversy is the suit initiated by Virginia against West Virginia in 1906 and finally adjudicated in 1918. The dispute originated in the loyalty of the northwestern counties of Virginia to the Union during the Civil War and the conditions imposed by Congress when these counties were admitted to the Union as a state in 1863. The new state agreed to "take upon itself a just proportion of the public debt of the Commonwealth of Virginia, prior to January 1, 1861."[14]

Virginia for years attempted to secure from West Virginia a settlement of the amount due, but West Virginia disputed the amount. Consequently, Virginia in 1906 filed suit against West Virginia in the U.S. Supreme Court for a determination of the amount due. West Virginia contended the court lacked jurisdiction and therefore could not enforce a judgment should it render one.

The court opined it had jurisdiction over the dispute and permitted West Virginia to answer the complaint in the court's next term. Following numerous technical pleas by West Virginia and the filing of additional suits by Virginia, the court in 1918 ordered West Virginia to pay the bondholders $12,393,929.50, the sum determined by the court in an earlier decision.[15] In 1918, the court postponed a final decision by scheduling for arguments at the next term of the court on the question of the specific methods to be used to enforce the judgment against West Virginia.

This decision is of particular interest since the court suggested several means that might be utilized to enforce its judgment against West Virginia. Among others, the court noted as a possible remedy a writ of mandamus commanding the levy by the West Virginia State Legislature of a tax to raise funds to pay the judgment. In 1919, the legislature met in a special session and enacted a law providing for payment of the amount determined by the court.

Escheats and Taxation

Escheats refer to tangible and intangible unclaimed property that reverts to the state after a stipulated period of time. Two or more states may claim the same property. The Supreme Court has resolved three such controversies.

Taxation disputes are common and involve the question of the right to tax an estate or income of an individual or a corporation.

ESCHEATS
The court in 1965 explicated rules governing the right of a state to assume title of unclaimed property in *Texas v. New Jersey*. The primary rule stipulates that "fairness among the state requires that the right and power to escheat the debt should be accorded to the state of the creditor's last known address as shown by the debtor's books and records."[16] The court recognized its primary rule will not resolve each controversy, and developed a secondary rule awarding in effect the right to escheat abandoned property to the debtor's state of corporate domicile, subject to a claim by a state with a superior right to escheat under the primary rule.

The court resolved a similar controversy involving unclaimed proceeds of the Western Union Company in 1972 between Pennsylvania and New York by utilizing its primary rule to allow the state where the money orders were purchased to escheat.[17]

The third suit involved the right of Delaware or New York to escheat $300 million in unclaimed dividends, interest, and securities. The court utilized its primary rule, but remanded the case to the special master and noted that "if New York can establish by reference to debtors' records that the creditors who were owned particular securities distributions had last known addresses in New York," its right to escheat under the primary rule supersedes Delaware's right under the secondary rule.[18]

ESTATE TAX

The court issued rulings in three estate tax disputes. We limit our focus to the interstate dispute over the $44 million estate of Edward H. R. Green. Florida, New York, Massachusetts, and Texas each claimed the decedent was one of its residents. The court accepted the findings of the special master that Green was domiciled in Massachusetts at the time of his death, spent part of each summer since 1917 in Massachusetts where he constructed a $6,699,000 estate, had never registered to vote in New York, spent winters commencing in 1923 in Florida on the advice of his doctor, and did not have a place of residence in Texas after 1911.[19]

OTHER TAXATION SUITS

These suits involve determination of the jurisdiction of a state to tax, an electrical energy tax, a commuter income tax, a first use tax levied on natural gas, and a negative interstate commerce case.

In 1893, the U.S. Supreme court in *Iowa v. Illinois* was faced with the problem of determining the precise boundary between the two states in view of the enabling statute admitting the Territory of Illinois to the Union describing the boundary as the "middle of the Mississippi River," and the enabling statute admitting Iowa to the Union specified the "middle of the main channel of the Mississippi River." The court traced the history of the disputed area to the *Treaty of 1763* between Great Britain, France, and Spain, the *Treaty of 1783* between Great Britain and the United States, and the *Treaty of 1803* between France and the United States. Employing international law, the court set the midchannel as the boundary line.[20]

Arizona challenged the constitutionality of a New Mexico tax levied on the generation of electrical energy sold at retail and authorizing a tax credit against the gross receipts due the state. Three Arizona public utilities firms sold electricity at retail in New Mexico, but were not eligible for the tax credit. Emphasizing its reluctance to invoke its original jurisdiction, the U.S. Supreme Court in 1976 opined: "If on appeal the New Mexico Supreme Court should hold the . . . tax unconstitutional, Arizona will have been vindicated. If, . . . the tax is held to be constitutional, the issues raised now may be brought to this court by way of direct appeal."[21]

The Supreme Court in 1976 combined a suit filed by Pennsylvania against New Jersey, and a suit by Maine, Massachusetts, and Vermont against

New Hampshire. The suits involved a commuter income tax and the privileges and immunities clause of the U.S. Constitution. At the time, New Hampshire and New Jersey did not tax the domestic income of its residents but did tax the income of nonresidents earned in the state. The states bringing the suits granted their respective citizens a 100 percent tax credit for income taxes paid to sister states. The court opined: "The injuries to the plaintiff's fiscs were self-inflicted, resulting from decisions by their respective state legislature. Nothing required Maine, Massachusetts, and Vermont to extend a tax credit to their residents for income taxes paid to New Hampshire, and nothing prevents Pennsylvania from withdrawing that credit for taxes paid to New Jersey."[22]

Eight states challenged the constitutionality of a Louisiana first-use tax levied on natural gas brought into the state and not previously taxed by a state or the United States. The Supreme Court in 1981 invalidated the tax as violating the interstate commerce clause and added that the state had no right to tax natural gas from the outer continental shelf owned by the United States.[23]

Wyoming challenged an Oklahoma statute requiring electric power plants to burn a mixture of coal containing a minimum of 10 percent mined in the state. This type of suit is known as a negative commerce clause suit because of the adverse effect of the law on Wyoming's tax revenues. The court accepted the special master's findings regarding the impact of the statute on Wyoming and invalidated the statute.[24]

INTERSTATE COMPACTS

Section 10 of Article I of the U.S. Constitution expressly forbids states to enter into any treaty, alliance, or confederation without the consent of Congress.[25] This provision is almost identical to Article VI of the Articles of Confederation and Perpetual union, which stipulates that "no two or more States shall enter into any treaty, confederation, or alliance without the consent of the United States in Congress assembled specifying accurately the purposes for which the state is to be entered into, and how long it shall continue." Several compacts were concluded under the articles, including a 1785 Maryland-Virginia compact relative to use of the Potomac River and the Chesapeake Bay.

The prohibition of compacts without congressional consent was included in the U.S. Constitution to prevent states from splitting the Union by forming alliances among themselves directed against the Union or other states. The constitution, however, recognizes there is a need for cooperative state action to solve common problems extending across state boundary lines, and authorizes Congress to grant its consent to such compacts. Another advantage of compacts is their ability to solve disputes as an alternative to a state bringing a suit in the U.S. Supreme Court. Furthermore, a compact allows states to pool and/or coordinate employment of their resources and to gain economies of scale in provision of certain services.

There is almost no limitation to the subject matter of compacts and a compact with congressional consent may authorize two or more states to take an action that taken by an individual state would violate the U.S. Constitution. The northeast dairy compact, a milk price fixing compact, is an example.

An interstate compact can be bilateral, multilateral, national, or international in scope. Several compacts include the District of Columbia or all or some of the Canadian provinces. Currently, there are twenty-six types of interstate compacts ranging alphabetically in subject matter from agricultural to water. A new type, the federal-interstate compact, emerged in 1961 when four states and Congress each enacted the Delaware River Basin Compact, the first federal-interstate compact. Subsequently, such compacts have been created for the Susquehanna River basin and the Appalachian region.

An imaginative proposed interstate compact to ensure the popular winner of the Presidential election is progressing in state legislatures. The compact becomes effective when states, including possibly the District of Columbia, with a total of 270 Electoral College votes enact the compact providing each party state will award all its electoral votes to the presidential–vice-presidential slate receiving the largest number of popular votes in the nation.[26]

Felix Frankfurter and James M. Landis in 1925 explained that "the combined legislative powers of Congress and of the several states permit a wide range of permutations and combinations for governmental action. Until very recently these potentialities have been left large unexplored. . . . Creativeness is called for to devise a great variety of legal alternatives to cope with the diverse forms of interests."[27] Frederick L. Zimmermann and Mitchell Wendell in 1951 pointed out the compact "bridges jurisdictional gaps and at the same time provides flexibility in the integration of the pattern into the laws of the acting governments."[28]

An interstate compact is a contract protected by Section 10 of Article I of the U.S. Constitution against impairment by states. Because of its contractual nature, a compact takes precedence over any statute subsequently enacted by a participating state legislature.

Joint compact commissions, created by the concerned states, drafted the early compacts and focused primarily on boundary and water controversies. In more recent years, extralegal committees of state officers and interest groups have drafted compacts for submission to state legislatures for enactment into law. A joint compact commission drafted the Port of New York Compact, the first one providing for a commission, whereas a committee of attorneys general and other state officers developed the interstate compact on parolees and probationers.

Political and Nonpolitical Compacts

A literal reading of the interstate compact clause of the U.S. Constitution would lead to the conclusion all compacts become effective only with the consent of Congress. In 1893, however, the U.S. Supreme Court in *Virginia v. Tennessee* drew a distinction between the types of compacts by opining that the required consent only applies to agreements that tend to increase "the political power or influence" of the party states "and thus encroach . . . upon the full and free exercise of federal authority."[29] Although the compact to determine the boundary line between these two states had been signed early in the nineteenth century, the compact had not received the formal consent of Congress. The Supreme Court ruled Congress by its reliance on the terms of the compact for "judicial and revenue purposes" had consented to the compact by implication.

In the final analysis, Congress is the body that usually determines whether a compact is political in nature and its decision is final. Congress, however, has not defined the elements of a compact that would make it political. Whereas New Hampshire and Vermont submitted an interstate school district compact to Congress for its consent, a similarly interstate library compact entered into by other states went into force without being submitted to Congress. In 2006, Congress granted its consent to the revised interstate compact for the placement of children, a nonpolitical compact.[30]

Determining whether an interstate compact has the potential for encroaching on the authority of the national government can be a difficult task. The United States Steel Corporation and other multistate taxpayers challenged the constitutionality of the Multistate Tax Commission, created by an interstate compact, which facilitates the determination of the individual state tax liability of multistate taxpayers. Member states retain jurisdiction over tax rate and tax bases, and may withdraw from the compact at any time.

In 1978, the U.S. Supreme Court held the compact did not violate the U.S. Constitution since the compact did not authorize member states to exercise powers they could not exercise without a compact and hence there is no state encroachment on national powers.[31]

If the boundary line between two states is in dispute, for example, the concerned states could agree to have the boundary line surveyed without the consent of Congress. However, a change in the boundary line would require approval of the national legislature if as a result of the change the number of U.S. representatives from one or both states would be altered. Similarly, if New York owned land in Vermont and the latter state offered to purchase the land, the two states could sign an agreement for the sale of the land and no congressional consent would be needed.

The U.S. Constitution does not indicate at what stage in the compacting process congressional consent must be given to effectuate the compact or whether consent must be expressed or implied. Congress occasionally has granted consent prior to completion of negotiations by the concerned states by granting consent-in-advance: forest-fire fighting compacts in 1911, a compact for supervisions of paroles and probationers in 1934, and flood control compacts in 1936. On rare occasions, Congress granted consent-in-advance with the proviso the national government would participate in the compact formation negotiations.

The most recent court decision on the subject of congressional consent and political compacts was the 1962 decision of the U.S. Court of Appeals for the District of Columbia Circuit in *Tobin v. United States* holding interstate compacts of a political nature are not effective without the consent of Congress, which may place conditions on its consent.[32]

Effects of Consent

The U.S. Supreme Court in 1938 opined that congressional consent does not make a compact the equivalent to a United States treaty or statute, but in 1981 reversed itself by holding that such consent makes a compact federal law in addition to state law.[33]

The Supreme Court in 1874 issued an opinion requiring all U.S. courts to apply the interpretation of a concerned state law by the highest court in the state.[34] The 1981 decision permitted the Supreme Court to interpret the concerned Pennsylvania law and disregard the law's interpretation by the Pennsylvania Supreme Court.

Obstacles to Establishment

The process of establishing an interstate compact typically entails three basic steps. First, representatives of the concerned states must negotiate and reach tentative agreement on the terms of the compact. Second, the compact does not become effective until enacted into law in identical form by the state legislature in each participating state. Third, the consent of Congress is required if the compact is a political one.

The most fundamental obstacle has been the inability of the negotiators to reach agreement quickly on the terms of the compact. They must resolve various financial, substantive, and technical issues posed by the problems to which the compact is to be addressed. The negotiators are constrained by a variety of factors, including their responsibility to the public, limitations on the states' ability to commit funds for future years, and procedural requirements calling for voter approval, legislative approval, or both. As a result, negotiations generally are prolonged and frequently unsuccessful.

Agreement often has been difficult to reach. For example, negotiations between California and Nevada concerning a bilateral compact for the allocation of certain water rights took twelve years, even though only two states were involved and there was only one issue to be resolved.

Political concerns can delay and complicate establishment of a compact in other ways. Obtaining approval by the state legislature can be a lengthy process, and even the need for gubernatorial approval can prolong the period prior to establishment of a compact. Although the New York State Legislature approved the interstate compact for the supervision of parolees and probationers in 1936, the state did not become a compact member until 1944 because of the refusal of Governor Herbert H. Lehman to execute the compact with the other states. On one occasion, a compact was not established because the President vetoed the congressional resolution approving the compact. In 1942, President Franklin D. Roosevelt vetoed the resolution consenting to the *Republican River Compact*.[35]

State legislatures enacted statutes authorizing department heads and others to enter into administrative agreements with their counterparts in sister states. Innumerable formal and informal agreements exist today. These agreements are not subject to the constitutional consent of Congress clause and can involve most of the subjects of interstate compacts. The Connecticut River basin Atlantic salmon restoration compact and the Merrimack River anadromous fish restoration administrative agreement contain nearly identical language.

FULL FAITH AND CREDIT

Section 1 of Article IV of the U.S. Constitution stipulates that "full faith and credit shall be given in each State to the public acts, records, and judicial proceedings of every other State. And the Congress may by general laws prescribe the manner in which such acts, records, and proceedings shall be proved, and the effect thereof." The Second Continental Congress in 1777 adopted a resolution containing similar language subsequently incorporated into the Articles of Confederation and Perpetual Union.

The framers of the U.S. Constitution attempted, by inclusion of the full faith and credit clause, to establish a national legal system by an overriding principle of reciprocal recognition of public acts, records, and final judicial proceedings of each state. In particular, the clause protects the Union against individual state jurisprudence based on provincialism without expanding the power of the national government.

Public acts are the civil statutes enacted by state legislatures. Records are documents such as deeds, mortgages, and wills. Judicial proceedings are final civil court judgments. The constitutional guarantee is designed to facilitate intercourse among the states, particularly in the conduct of legal affairs. With the exceptions of two very general laws enacted in 1790 and 1804 prescribing the method of authenticating public acts and records, Congress failed to clarify the full faith and credit obligations of states until 1994 when it established standards that must be followed by state courts in determining their jurisdiction to issue child support orders and the effect that must be given by courts of sister states to each order.[36] The failure of Congress to clarify further the obligations of states under the clause until 1996 (see below) resulted in the U.S. Supreme Court "legislating" with respect to the guarantee.

Divorce actions raise particularly difficult jurisdictional problems since one of the parties may move to a sister state. Court jurisdiction depends on domicile and the period of required residence within a state to establish domicile varies among the states. In 1975, the U.S. Supreme Court upheld the constitutionality of Iowa's one-year residence requirement prior to the filing of a petition for divorce.[37] The court opined that the requirement was justified on the ground that the state had an interest in requiring persons seeking a divorce in a state court to be genuinely attached to the state.

On occasions, the courts of one state refuse to recognize as valid a divorce decree of a court in a sister state on the ground the court granting the divorce did not have jurisdiction over the parties because they had not fulfilled properly the residence requirement.

Because of the differences in the strictness of the divorce laws between states, a person seeking a divorce may attempt to circumvent the home state's strict laws by obtaining a divorce from another state and resuming residence subsequently in the home state. Although domicile is based upon the intent of an individual to establish a bona fide residence, it is not always easy to determine whether residence was established for the sole purpose of obtaining a divorce.

In *Williams v. North Carolina*, the U.S. Supreme Court in 1945 upheld the decision of the Supreme Court of North Carolina that the state did not have to recognize a Nevada divorce because the parties had not established residence in Nevada.[38]

In 1994, the Hawaiian Supreme Court interpreted the state constitution as permitting the marriage of two persons of the same sex, thereby setting off a national debate on the subject. Congress responded by enacting the *Defense of Marriage Act of 1996* defining a marriage as "a legal union between one man and one woman as husband and wife," declaring that the term "spouse" designates "a person of the opposite sex who is husband or a wife," and authorizing a state to deny full faith and credit to a marriage certificate of two persons of the same sex.[39] It should be noted the Hawaiian State Legislature proposed a constitutional amendment reversing the decision of the court and voters in 1999 ratified the amendment. Currently, thirty-nine states have enacted defense of marriage acts and four states—Maryland, New Hampshire, Wisconsin, and Wyoming—have statutes or court decisions banning same sex marriage. In addition, thirteen states have amended their constitutions to forbid same sex marriage, including four states precluding civil unions.

The controversy over same sex marriage was reopened by a 5 to 4 decision of the Massachusetts Supreme Judicial Court on November 18, 2003, holding unconstitutional a statute denying "the protections, benefits, and obligations conferred by civil marriage to two individuals of the same sex who wish to marry."[40] The decision raised an important legal question: Are same sex nonresidents eligible to marry in the Commonwealth? The answer is no for some nonresidents since a 1913 Massachusetts statute disqualifies individuals from marrying if they are ineligible to marry in their home state.[41] The state senate requested an advisory opinion from the court as to whether a civil union law would comply with the court's decision. The same 4 to 3 majority on February 4, 2004, responded with a negative answer.[42]

Vermont's civil union statute, enacted in 2000, has caused complex legal problems as illustrated by two Virginia women who decided to move to Vermont in order to enter a union. Frederick County Circuit Judge John R. Prosser in Virginia on August 24, 2004, voided the visitation rights order issued by a Vermont judge for Janet Miller-Jenkins, a current resident of Vermont, who entered into a civil union with Lisa Miller-Jenkins and Janet later became pregnant through in-vitro fertilization. Lisa filed a petition in a Vermont court to dissolve the civil union and establish parental rights. The Virginia ruling was based on the ground that Virginia law supersedes Vermont law because Lisa and her daughter reside in Virginia. The Vermont Supreme Court, however, unanimously opined that Vermont courts have exclusive jurisdiction over the case.[43] Only the U.S. Supreme Court can resolve this interstate dispute over court jurisdiction.

Privileges and Immunities

Kindred to the full faith and credit clause are the interstate citizenship provisions guaranteeing the privileges and immunities of sojourners; that is, citizens of one state visiting another state.

Section 2 of Article IV of the national constitution provides that "the citizens of each state shall be entitled to all privileges and immunities of citizens in the several states." Section 1 of the Fourteenth Amendment contains a similar provision: "No State shall make or enforce any law which shall abridge the privileges or immunities of citizens of the United States."

One purpose of the first section is to establish a national economic union in which citizens of one state may do business in another state on terms substantially equal to the terms enjoyed by residents. Making noncitizenship a ground for discrimination violates the privileges and immunities clause since a nonresident is entitled to nondiscriminatory treatment.

The U.S. Constitution does not define "privileges and immunities," but the U.S. Supreme Court in *Paul v. Virginia* in 1868 ruled the clause relieves citizens "from the disabilities of alienage in other States. It inhibits discriminatory legislation against them by other States; it gives them the right of free ingress into other States and egress from them; it insures to them in other States the same freedom possessed by the citizens of those States in the acquisition and enjoyment of property and in the pursuit of happiness, and it secures to them in other States the equal protection of the laws."[44]

Numerous U.S. Supreme Court cases have arisen under the clause because states attempted to favor their own citizens over citizens of other states. Nevertheless, the court has not defined the privileges and immunities and makes its decisions on a case-by-case basis. In 1870, the court in *Ward v. Maryland* struck down a statute requiring nonresidents to pay a $300 annual license fee to trade in goods not manufactured in Maryland while Maryland traders were required to pay only a fee ranging from $12 to $150.[45] In 1948, the court in *Toomer v. Witsell* invalidated a law requiring nonresident fishermen to pay a license fee of $2,500 for each shrimp boat while residents were required to pay only a $25 fee.[46] The court in *Austin v. New Hampshire* in 1975 invalidated a New Hampshire commuter income tax because state residents were not taxed on their domestic or foreign income.[47]

EXCLUSION FROM BENEFICIAL SERVICES

There are, however, exceptions to the privileges and immunities clause. The U.S. Supreme Court has held that this clause does not apply to beneficial services—those resources and institutions in which the state has property rights.

Thus, a state may require out-of-state students to pay a higher tuition rate at state-operated colleges and universities.[48] Similarly, a state in its *parens patriae* (father of its people) capacity also may limit the use of state property by nonresidents or exclude them entirely.[49] Nonresident hunting and fishing license fees typically are substantially higher than fees for residents. The nonresident fees, however, must be uniform for residents of all of the other states. Similarly, a state may not exclude residents of one state from hunting big game unless the state excludes residents of all states.

EXCLUSION FROM POLITICAL AND OTHER PRIVILEGES

Political privileges are also an exception to the privileges and immunities guarantee. A state may require a new resident to dwell in the state for a specified period of time before he or she will be allowed to vote or to hold public office. Prior to universal women suffrage guaranteed by the Nineteenth Amendment to the U.S. Constitution, women allowed to vote in one state could not vote automatically in another state on establishment of residence if the state did not grant the suffrage to women.

An individual may not compel a state to recognize special privileges granted to him or her by his or her home state, such as the right to practice law. Through comity, however, privileges (*e.g.*, recognition of expert witnesses from other states in court) may be granted.

States utilized the police power to regulate various professions and set standards that practitioners must meet, including passing a written examination. Regulation of the law profession had been left to the states until 1985. A Vermont lawyer, who passed the required bar examination and was admitted to the New Hampshire bar in 1980, was prevented from practicing law in the state because a rule of the New Hampshire Supreme Court restricted the practice of law to residents. In 1985, the U.S. Supreme Court invalidated the residence requirement as violative of the privileges and immunities clause.[50] The court noted that a state may discriminate against nonresidents only where there are substantial reasons and the difference in treatment is related closely to the state's objective. Insulating resident practitioners against out-of-state competition was not a substantial reason in the court's opinion.

SPECIAL POSITION OF CORPORATIONS

The U.S. Supreme Court in *Bank of Augusta v. Earle* in 1839 opined that a corporation "must dwell in the place of its creation, and can not migrate to another sovereignty."[51]

Although corporations are legal entities possessing many characteristics of natural persons, they are not considered citizens. Consequently, a state generally may discriminate against foreign corporations (chartered in other states) or alien corporations (chartered in foreign nations) by imposing higher license fees and by levying heavier taxes on them than on domestic corporations, or by prohibiting alien and foreign corporations from conducting business in the state. Hence, many foreign and alien corporations establish domestic subsidiary corporations in the larger states.

The U.S. Supreme Court in *Metropolitan Life Insurance Company v. Ward* in 1985, however, struck down as violative of the equal protection of the law clause an Alabama statute imposing a substantially lower gross premium tax on domestic insurance companies compared to foreign insurance companies even though the *McCarran-Ferguson Act of 1945* devolved to states the power to regulate the business of insurance.[52]

INTERSTATE RENDITION

Nation states govern the process of extraditing fugitives from justice from one nation to another nation by means of international treaties. A need exists for a similar mechanism in a confederation or a federation.

In the United States, a person accused of a state crime can be tried and, if found guilty, punished by the state in which the crime was committed. With the invention of modern modes of transportation, it has become very easy for a fugitive from justice to flee to another state.

To address this problem, Section 2 of Article IV of the U.S. Constitution provides for interstate rendition: "A person charged in any State with treason, felony, or other crime found in another State shall on the demand of the executive authority of the State from which he fled, be delivered up to the State having jurisdiction of the crime." The term "executive authority" was employed because New Hampshire had a president, rather than a governor, as chief executive until 1964.

A nearly identical provision was included in the Articles of Confederation and Perpetual Union.

Procedure in Rendition

A 1793 act of Congress regulates the manner of interstate rendition. The first step in the procedure is the indictment—a formal written accusation charging an individual with having committed a crime—and/or an official record indicating the person was found guilty of a crime.[53] Police officers in the state from which a fugitive has fled often make an informal request that the police in the asylum state hold the fugitive until the necessary formal-ities for rendition have been completed. The governor of the requesting state submits to the governor of the asylum state a formal request for rendition together with a certified copy of the indictment against the fugitive or a copy of the record of the trial if the fugitive has been convicted of a crime. The governor of the requesting state is required by the congressional statute to send an officer to the asylum state to bring back the fugitive.

The asylum state governor examines all documents concerning the accused and may call on the attorney general of the state for advice. The governor frequently holds a hearing before making a decision on the rendition request.

A fugitive can appeal to the state's courts against the governor's order for his or her return. In 1980, the U.S. Supreme Court ruled invalid a writ of habeas corpus, issued by the California Supreme Court, directing the superior court to conduct hearings to determine if the penitentiary in which Arkansas planned to confine the fugitive was operated in conformance with the Eighth Amendment to the U.S. Constitution.[54]

One of the most interesting rendition cases dates to the 1890s. William Hall, standing in North Carolina, shot dead a Mr. Bryson who was standing in Tennessee. All parties agreed a murder had been committee, but there was disagreement relative to which state had jurisdiction; that is, the state where the trigger was pulled or the state where the bullet entered Bryson's body. Although Hall was convicted in a North Carolina trial, the state supreme court reversed the conviction on the ground the crime occurred where the bullet entered the body. The Tennessee governor requested the North Carolina governor to render Hall to Tennessee to stand trial for murder. The North Carolina governor ordered Hall to be transported to Tennessee and Hall appealed to the judiciary. In 1894, the North Carolina Supreme Court in State v. Hall ruled Hall was not a fugitive from justice as he never had been in Tennessee. As a result, Hall escaped punishment for a murder.[55]

By act of Congress, all expenses incurred in the arrest, including transportation of the fugitive, must be paid by the requesting state. Once the fugitive is returned to the requesting state, he or she is subject to the normal legal procedures in criminal cases and may be tried for any offenses that he or she committed.

Role of the Asylum State Governor

The congressional statute regulating interstate rendition, by declaring "it shall be the duty" of the governor of the asylum state, appears to make it mandatory that the governor must return the fugitive to the requesting state. However, Chief Justice Roger B. Taney, writing for the U.S. Supreme Court in 1861 in *Kentucky v. Dennison* opined that the court "is of the opinion, the words—'it shall be the duty'—were not used as mandatory and compulsory, but as declaratory of the moral duty which this compact created, when Congress provided the mode of carrying it into execution."[56] The court specifically ruled it has no power under the congressional statute to force the governor of the asylum state to return a fugitive from justice since no penalty is imposed for his failure to act.

Governors refused rendition requests when they believed fugitives to be innocent or would not be given fair trials in the state from which they fled. A governor occasionally refused to return a fugitive from justice because the requesting state in the past failed to honor a rendition request from his state. In 1977, Governor Edmund S. Brown Jr. of California refused to return American Indian activist Dennis Banks to South Dakota because the governor feared for the safety of Banks in South Dakota. Governor William Clinton of Arkansas in 1985 rejected a New York rendition request on the ground the the nineteen-year-old woman would be subject to a severe penalty—a minimum of fifteen years to life sentence—under a law designed to punish career drug dealers.

The *Kentucky v. Dennison* decision was not challenged in the U.S. Supreme Court for more than 120 years. In 1987, the court in *Puerto Rico v. Branstad* reversed its earlier ruling by explaining it was issued after the southern states had seceded from the Union and a civil war was threatened, and adding that there was no justification for treating the governor's duty to return a fugitive differently than any other constitutional duty enforceable in federal courts.[57]

In 1990, Governor Mario M. Cuomo of New York denied a rendition request from Governor Guy Hunt of Alabama that four executives of a New York company be rendered to Alabama to be tried on charges of transmitting pornographic films by satellite on the ground that they never had been in Alabama. The constitutional provision clearly refers to a person fleeing from a state in which he had been charged. Governor Cuomo, however, signed approximately 400 rendition warrants annually for the return of fugitives to other states.

Other Considerations in Rendition

If a fugitive commits a crime in the asylum state, he or she will be tried and, if convicted, must serve the sentence before being surrendered to the requesting state. Certain states allow police officers from adjoining states in hot pursuit of fugitives to pursue them across their borders, thus obviating the necessity for a rendition hearing.

Congress enacted a statute making it a national criminal offense for an individual to travel to another state or to a foreign nation in order to avoid prosecution or imprisonment by a state for specified felonies. Violators of this statute are returned to the United States judicial district where the felony was alleged to have been committed and may be turned over to state officers.

INTERSTATE TRADE BARRIERS

Many states utilize their police power to discriminate against persons and goods from sister states. At one time, several dairy states had statutes prohibiting the sale of yellow oleomargarine in order to protect butter makers and dairy farmers. In some states, the sale of milk produced in other states was prohibited for the ostensible purpose of protecting the health of consumers by ensuring the milk is fresh. Similarly, the state legislature in Arizona, Florida, and Georgia at one time enacted statutes allowing only eggs produced within their respective state to be labeled "fresh" eggs. In 1973, the Kansas governor vetoed a bill requiring all out-of-state beef and other red meat sold in the state to be labeled as imported.

Numerous state inspection laws have been concerned legitimately with protection of public health, safety, and morals, but other laws have not been. For example, California's quarantine and motor vehicles laws in the Depression of the 1930s were simply subterfuges to prevent the immigration of impoverished persons from other states, particularly ones in the Midwest.

The New York State Legislature in 1984, citing its authority under the Twenty-first Amendment to the U.S. Constitution, enacted a statute allowing grocery stores to offer for sale a diluted wine provided it is made in part from grapes grown in the states. The U.S. District Court invalidated the law because it "is plain and simple economic protectionism of the New York–grown grapes, at the expense of out-of-state grapes, and a violation of the interstate commerce clause of the most simple kind."[58]

License, Tax, and Proprietary Powers Barriers

Licensing and taxing powers are used extensively by states to erected interstate trade barriers. Many state legislatures enacted laws requiring itinerant vendors to obtain licenses, imposing discriminatory license fees and taxes on foreign corporations, and subjecting chain stores to special taxes, frequently based on the total number of stores in the national or regional chain.

States purchase huge quantifies of materials and hire millions of employees. A state in its proprietary capacity often discriminates against other states by purchasing only supplies produced or sold within its own borders and by limiting public employment to its own citizens. Adjacent states may retaliate with similar measures against the selfish state. Preference is given in some states in purchasing to in-state bidders, products, and printing firms. Many states have reciprocal preference laws waiving the restrictions for firms in states waiving restrictions.

A Wyoming ready-mix concrete distributor sued the South Dakota Cement Commission because it restricted sale of cement produced at a state-owned plant to state residents during a period of cement shortage. The U.S. Supreme Court in 1980 upheld the power of the commission and noted a distinction must be made between a state as a market regulator and a state as a market participant.[59]

In 1990, the Florida State Legislature imposed a $295 "impact fee" on each motor vehicle purchased or titled in another state and subsequently registered in Florida allegedly to recover part of the cost of highway construction and maintenance. The Florida Supreme Court struck down the fee by opining that it violated the interstate commerce clause of the U.S. Constitution.[60]

Employing ingenuity, the City of Virginia Beach, Virginia, imposed a personal property tax on satellite transponders located on communications satellites circling the Earth. Judge Thomas S. Shadrick of the Virginia Beach Circuit Court invalidated the tax on the ground that the city lacked authority to levy the tax and the Virginia Supreme Court upheld his decision in 2002.[61]

In theory, Congress's regulatory jurisdiction is limited to interstate commerce and states may regulate intrastate commerce. It is apparent state regulation of intrastate commerce may affect interstate commerce as the U.S. Supreme Court determined in the famous case *Gibbons v. Ogden* in 1824.[62]

Removal of Barriers

Congressional statutes, judicial decisions, and reciprocal state legislation may remove interstate trade barriers. Congress has the authority to enact a national law uniform throughout the United States to replace nonharmonious state regulation of matters, such as interstate commercial vehicles. For example, Congress enacted the *Surface Transportation Assistance Act of 1982* preempting completely state size and weight limits on commercial vehicles operating on interstate highways and on portions of the national-aid highway system as determined by the secretary of transportation. State size and weight limits remain in effect on other highways.[63]

The U.S. Supreme Court in 1984 struck down as violative of the interstate commerce clause a 20 percent excise tax imposed by Hawaii on the sale of liquor at wholesale with the exceptions of locally produced alcoholic beverages.[64] In 1987, the U.S. District Court for the Eastern District of New York overturned the decision of the New York State commissioner of agriculture not to allow a New Jersey dairy to sell milk in New York City.[65]

The U.S. Supreme Court in 1994 examined a challenged pricing order issued by the Massachusetts commissioner of food and agriculture imposing an assessment on all fluid milk sold by dealers to Massachusetts retailers with the funds collected distributed only to dairy farmers in the commonwealth in spite of the fact approximately two-thirds of the milk is imported from other states. The court opined that the order discriminates against interstate commerce and therefore was unconstitutional.[66]

Cases alleging a tax levied by a state violates the interstate commerce clause of the U.S. Constitution typically are brought in the U.S. District Court, but can be brought in the courts of a state levying the tax. In 1986, for example, the Maine Supreme Court declared unconstitutional as violative of the interstate commerce clause a state highway use tax on out-of-state truckers.[67]

Through reciprocal arrangements, states have extended privileges and relaxed restraints to citizens and business firms in other states in return for the same treatment by other states. For instance, a number of states incorporated reciprocal provisions in their tax laws in order to protect citizens against double income taxation by other states. A familiar result of interstate comity is the general recognition of state motor vehicle registrations and drivers' licenses throughout the United States. The ten Canadian provinces also recognize state registrations and operators' licenses. States, except New York, similarly recognize a professional license issued by another state provided it recognizes a similar license issued by the other states

The Differential Tax Rate Problem

With each state free to determine the amount of a general sales tax and excise taxes on alcohol, motor fuel, tobacco products, and other items, the differential in tax rates deprives some states of tax revenue and creates special problems for merchants located near state boundary lines in a state with the higher tax rates as citizens often make purchases in states where the tax rates are lower.

To combat this problem, states enacted use taxes at the same rate as the excise taxes or sales tax on items purchased in other states and used in the use tax state. This tax is effective relative to the purchase of motor vehicles because the state motor vehicle department in a state with a sales tax will register a motor vehicle only if a sales or use tax receipt is provided. Collecting the use tax on other items is difficult.

Tax evasion may be the result of casual smuggling, organized smuggling, or purchase through tax-free outlets. Relative to the latter, many national government treaties with Indian tribes preclude state taxation of sales on Indian reservations. In addition, state taxes are not collected on sales on military bases.

Congress sought to assist states in curtailing cigarette smuggling or buttlegging by enacting the *Jenkins Act of 1940* stipulating it is a federal crime for a person or firm to utilize the postal service to evade payment of state and local government excise taxes.[68] This act is avoided by a persons or firm simply utilizing another mode of transportation. Congress also enacted the *Contraband Cigarette Act of 1978* making it a federal crime to distribute, possess, purchase, receive, ship, or transport more than 60,000 cigarettes lacking the tax indicia of the state where they were found.[69] The act also encouraged states to enter into interstate compacts to combat cigarette smuggling, but no such compact has been entered into. The *USA Patriot Improvement and Reauthorization Act of 2005* reduced the number of cigarettes to 10,000.[70]

State excise taxes on cigarettes varied widely in 2007 with the lowest tax rate, 7 cents per package in South Carolina, and the highest tax rate in New York City where the combined state and city excise taxes totaled $7.00 a package.

A similar problem, bootlegging, is attributable to casual and organized smuggling of alcoholic beverages to avoid high state excise taxes. Eighteen states control directly the retail and wholesale sale of alcoholic beverages and thirty-two states have licensing systems to control sales. New Hampshire uses the former system and has located many of its state-operated liquor stores near the boundaries of the neighboring states of Maine, Massachusetts, and Vermont, and its state liquor commission spends approximately 80 percent of its advertising appropriations in sister states. The state has no sales tax and beverage bottle tax, and when Massachusetts imposed a bottle deposit the price of a case of beer increased by nearly three dollars and encouraged its residents to make their purchases in New Hampshire where the lack of a sales tax encourages out-of-state visitors to purchase products taxed in their respective home state.

EXTRACONSTITUTIONAL RELATIONS

With the passage of time, states established a number of extraconstitutional relationships, including development of common judicial decisions, enactment of uniform state laws, and conferences of administrative officer and legislators. These relationships have been promoted by the organization of national and regional associations of state officers and have become particularly influencial since 1950.

Judicial Decisions

There has developed over the decades what has been labeled a "Common Law" of the states. Although the consolidated statutes of each state fill many volumes, statutory law does not always contain a specific section relating to a matter in controversy. A search of the decisions of the courts of the fifty states typically will produce several cases where similar facts have been presented to a court which made a determination. The courts in one state often are guided by the rulings of sister state courts. While many courts follow in general the rulings of courts in other states, there often are significant differences in their decisions.

To facilitate the development of a common law of the states, the American Law Institute, established in 1923, prepared a volume—*The Restatement in the Courts*—highlighting the major points of agreement in the decisions of courts in various states on the same subject.[71]

Uniform State Laws

Since each state may legislate for itself by employing its reserved or residual powers, diversity rather than uniformity has been characteristic of statutes on the same subject in the different states.

In addition to borrowing sections from constitutions of other states, state legislatures commonly borrow statutes from one another.[72] Initially, the borrowing was on an informal basis and a state legislature might not borrow the exact wording or all provisions of a statute enacted by a sister state legislature.

In an effort to eliminate, or at least reduce, conflict among laws of the states, the national conference of commissioners on uniform laws was founded in 1892. A conference, sponsored by the organization, is held annually for approximately one week and is attended by three commissioners, all attorneys, appointed by the governor of each state. Currently, commissioners represent all states, the District of Columbia, Puerto Rico, and the U.S. Virgin Islands.

The conference drafted and recommended enactment of numerous model acts. The first model act—negotiable instruments and warehouse receipts act—has been enacted by all state legislatures as has the uniform commercial code. Reflecting technological changes, the conference drafted the uniform electronic transactions act in 1999 validating electronic signatures.

Conferences of Administrative Officers

National and regional groups of administrative officers meet on a regular basis in order to solve common problems. The national governors' association has held annual meetings since 1908 to promote closer relations between states and its work is supplemented by regional governors' associations. The association and the national conference of state legislators lobby Congress and national administrative departments and agencies.

Another organization promoting interstate cooperation is the council of state governments, organized in 1935, whose primary function is the researching and dispensing of information on state, interstate, and national problems. The council annually publishes *The Book of the States*, an authoritative source of information on important state problems, facts and figures on state finance, and changes in state constitutions and laws affecting state politics and administration. In contrast to the other two major associations, the council does not lobby.

Many groups of more specialized administrative officers—including attorneys general, budget officers, purchasing agencies, secretaries of state—organized national associations to promote interstate cooperation. The state heads of departments and agencies have entered into numerous formal and informal administrative agreements with their counterparts in sister states as noted above.

SUMMARY

It is essential to include in a constitution establishing a federal system provisions relating to interstate relations. Among other provisions, the U.S. Constitution authorizes states to enter into interstate compacts with the consent of Congress to solve common problems, construct interstate facilities, provide mutual assistance in emergencies, regulate, and lower service providing costs. Congressional consent was made a requirement for the effectuation of a compact because of fear compacts might produce alliances directed against the Union. The U.S. Supreme Court, however, ruled the requirement does not apply to nonpolitical compacts; that is, compacts that do not encroach on the powers of Congress.

In practice, compacts have proven to be extremely flexible mechanisms for addressing a variety of interstate and national problems. Not all compacts have been successful in achieving their respective goals and critics maintain agencies established by compacts are responsible to no one. Compacts may centralize certain political powers on the regional level, but this type of power centralization differs significantly from the power centralization produced by congressional preemption since the compacts are entered into voluntarily by the party states.

The process of establishing a compact is time-consuming and frequently is nonproductive. Formation of regulatory compacts peaked in the 1950s and early 1960s, and declined subsequently with the dramatic increase in the number of congressional preemption statutes removing regulatory authority from the states and the growing complexity of many interstate problems.

To prevent the serious legal problems that would result from a state refusing to recognize the civil acts, records, and judicial proceedings of other states, the drafters of the U.S. Constitution included a full faith and credit provision. Congress and the U.S. Supreme Court have not clarified fully the clause and suits often are filed in courts as a result.

The U.S. Constitution contains a privileges and immunities clause designed to promote interstate citizenship. Interpreted literally, the clause prevents a state from discriminating against visitors from sister states. In practice, courts have allowed exceptions relative to state beneficial services and political privileges such as voting and office holding.

To prevent criminals and individuals accused of crimes in a state from escaping justice, the U.S. Constitution authorizes a system of interstate rendition governed in part by a congressional statute. Although the statute mandates that a governor return a fugitive at the request of the governor of the demanding state, the U.S. Supreme Court in 1861 opined the duty of the asylum state governor was discretionary. The court reversed this decision in 1987 when the duty was made mandatory.

Trade barriers erected by individual states can be a serious problem in a confederation or a federation. The U.S. Constitution seeks to prohibit the erection of barriers by authorizing Congress to regulate commerce between the states. Nevertheless, state legislatures have employed their reserved powers—police, proprietary, tax—to create barriers that have been challenged in court on many occasions on the ground they violate the interstate commerce clause. The barriers can be removed by congressional preemption, judicial decisions, and reciprocity.

A serious problem for many states is the differential in their general sales and excise tax rates. The high tax rate states lose revenues and their merchants lose sales to merchants in the low tax rate states. Disputes between neighboring high and low tax rate states unfortunately reduce their willingness to cooperate on certain other matters.

Establishment of national and regional associations of state officers has facilitated cooperation among states and solution of many common problems. The increasing use of preemption powers by Congress since 1965 induced the national governors' association and the national conference of state legislatures to lobby Congress to prevent enactment of most preemption bills or to promote enactment of bills providing relief from earlier preemption statutes and preemption decisions of courts reversible by Congress. These associations also lobby Congress to reimburse states for costs incurred in complying with national mandates described in chapter 4.

Whereas this chapter has focused on the complex horizontal relationships between states, chapter 8 examines the vertical relationships between a state government and its political subdivisions, and notes the increase in the discretionary authority of certain types of local governments in many states since 1900.

CHAPTER 8

State-Local Relations

Local governments, in terms of services provided, are the units that have the most direct impact on the daily lives of citizens. There is no common system of local governments in the United States since the powers and organizational structure of the 87,525 substate governments have been adapted to the customs and peculiar needs of the people in each state.

Substate governments may be classified in two broad categories—municipal corporations and quasi-municipal corporations. The former generally have individual charters establishing each municipality as an artificial legal person and outlining its organizational structure and powers. Unless the state constitution provides to the contrary, a municipal corporation is subject to the control of the state legislature through ordinary legislation or charter amendment. Quasi-municipal corporations are nonchartered units—chiefly many counties, Midwest townships, and all special districts—that nevertheless are legal entities.

There are four major differences between the two types of units. First, a municipality is formed by the state legislature at the request of a majority of the voters who reside in the area whereas a quasi-municipal corporation is created by the legislature usually without consent of the residents.

Second, a municipal corporation engages in a wide range of proprietary, or business, functions in addition to performing governmental functions as an agent of the state. A quasi-municipal corporation exercises few or no proprietary functions and is almost entirely an agent of the state.

Third, a municipal corporation historically was liable to suit when performing proprietary functions, but was immune from suit without its consent when performing governmental functions that are the older traditional functions such as public health and public safety. A quasi-municipal corporation generally has the same immunity from suit as the state. Many states, however, have waived state and municipality immunity from suit and as a result a municipality may be sued relative to a governmental or proprietary function without its consent in these states. Similarly, quasi-municipal corporations in these states may be sued without their consent.

Fourth, a municipal corporation possesses relatively broad sublegislative powers to enact ordinances and local laws in contrast to a quasi-municipal corporation that possesses little or no ordinance-making power.

Initially, only cities and villages (termed boroughs in a few states) were municipal corporations. Counties, special districts, towns, and townships were quasi-municipal corporations. Today, some or all counties in a state are municipal corporations as are towns in the New England States and New York, and townships in New Jersey and Pennsylvania. Midwest townships, on the other hand, are quasi-municipal corporations with relatively few functional responsibilities.

All local governments are subject to varying degrees of control by their respective state governments. Originally, all local governments were considered in law to be "creatures" of their respective state government possessing no inherent powers of self-government. In the twenty-first century, many municipalities possess relatively broad discretionary powers while other units, as in Vermont, are subject to tight control by the state government and may initiate no new action without state permission. The trend has been toward granting additional discretionary powers to general-purpose local governments, but state legislatures with a few exceptions continue to possess authority to dominate local governments completely.

State-local relations bear several similarities with national-state relations depending on the system for distributing authority in a given state. A federal system involves a constitutional division of powers between two planes of government and constitutional provisions in several states establish a state-local governmental division of powers. Intergovernmental lobbying is common on both planes with states pressuring Congress to grant additional funds to the states and to reject most preemption bills, and local government officers lobbying the state legislature to increase local government financial assistance and to defeat bills mandating actions by political subdivisions. In contrast to the national plane where states generally do not seek authorization of Congress to exercise a power, local government officers often request their state legislature to enact laws authorizing all general-purpose local governments or a particular unit to exercise a specific power.

The complexity of state-local relations varies considerably among the states, depending in part upon the numbers and types of local governments and the systems employed to distribute powers between a state and its political subdivisions. To understand the local government systems in the various states, the reader must become familiar with the constitutional and statutory provisions granting discretionary authority to the different types of local governments, and the revenues of these units. Without adequate revenues, local governments are unable to exercise fully their discretionary powers.

As the superior government, the state possesses the legal authority and financial resources enabling it to play a key role in solving local government problems. In general, the state initiates three types of actions to assist local governments—grants in-aid and revenue sharing, authorization of actions facilitating local solutions of problems, and direct state action to solve local problems.

LOCAL DISCRETIONARY AUTHORITY

The U.S. Constitution contains no provisions relative to local governments, but the U.S. Supreme Court has interpreted the constitutional prohibitions of specified types of state actions, described in chapter 3, to include similar actions initiated by local governments.

The original state constitutions delegated no powers to local governments and placed few restrictions, other than protection of civil liberties, upon the powers of the state legislatures. Hence, the legislature was omnipotent relative to determining the powers exercisable by substate governmental units. With the passage of time, constitutions initially were amended in many states to restrict the powers of the legislature relative to local governments and subsequently to grant powers to certain types of local governments in several states.[1] Three systems distributing political power between a state and its local government are employed.

The Ultra Vires Rule

This rule limits the powers of local governments to those conferred expressly by a charter or law and any action exceeding these powers is *ultra vires*; that is, invalid. This English common law rule commonly is referred to as Dillon's rule in the United States because Judge John F. Dillon authored a commentary on the powers of municipalities.[2] In 1868, Judge Dillon of the Iowa Supreme Court issued two decisions based on the *ultra vires* rule providing for a strict construction of municipal powers. In *City of Clinton v. Cedar Rapids and Missouri Railroad Company* he wrote: "Municipal corporations owe their origin to, and derive their powers and rights wholly from the Legislature. . . . As it creates, so may it destroy."[3] In *Merriam v. Moody's Executors*, he opined a municipality could exercise only the following powers: "First, those granted in express words; second, those necessarily implied or necessarily incident to the powers expressly granted; third, those absolutely essential to the declared objects and purposes of the corporation—not simply convenient, but indispensable; fourth, any fair doubt as to the existence of a power is resolved by the courts against the corporation."[4]

In 1903, the U.S. Supreme Court in *Atkins v. Kansas* held the rule did not violate the U.S. Constitution because "what they lawfully do of a public character is done under the sanction of the state . . ." and "their powers may be restricted or enlarged, or altogether withdrawn at the will of the Legislature."[5] Twenty years later, the court issued a similar decision in *Trenton v. New Jersey* opining a municipality possesses no inherent right of local self-government.[6]

Dillon's Rule in the nineteenth century enabled the state legislature, if it so desires, to control all aspects of municipal governance. Employing its powers on a partisan basis, a legislature frequently would authorize one city to exercise a specific power and deny the request of a second city for permission to exercise the same power. Furthermore, the legislature often interfered arbitrarily with the internal operations of a municipality by enacting what were labeled "ripper laws."

Abuses associated with special laws applying to individual municipalities in the nineteenth century triggered a public reaction in several states in the form of constitutional amendments prohibiting enactment of such laws. Initially, these prohibitions, dating to an 1850 Michigan constitutional amendment, related to specific topics such as laying out or discontinuing roads, changing county seats, and incorporating villages.[7] Today, the constitutions of forty-one states forbid enactment of a special law without a request from the concerned local government. The Massachusetts constitution allows enactment of a special law on the receipt of a recommendation from the governor for approval of the law and a two-thirds affirmative vote of each house of the General Court (state legislature).[8]

The prohibition of special legislation, however, has been evaded in a number of states by enactment of classified laws ostensibly recognizing different conditions in the various local governments. Courts have upheld most classified laws based upon population, but struck down classified laws employing geographical criteria. The New York Court of Appeals in *Farrington v. Pinckney* in 1956 validated as a general law a statute applying to cities with a population exceeding one million; only New York City had a population meeting the criterion.[9] To prevent abuse of classified legislation, the constitution in several states established a maximum number of classes and/or a minimum number of local governments in a class such as two.

Constitutions and constitutional amendments ratified in the second half of the nineteenth century often contain procedural requirements for enactment of special laws. Section 2 of Article XII of the New York constitution of 1894 stipulated all special city acts were subject to a suspensive veto by the concerned cities. On approval by the state legislature, the special act was transmitted to the mayor and/or city council of the concerned city for review. If the city disapproved of the act, it was returned to the state legislature, which could override the suspensive veto and send the act to the governor for his or her approval or veto.

Recognizing the fact the special law process was time-consuming and cumbersome when subject to procedural requirements, state legislatures in the latter part of the nineteenth century commenced to enact acceptance statutes; that is, the statutes become effective within a municipality only if accepted by the governing body or by the voters in a referendum. There are two types of acceptance statutes. The first type is a general law containing several municipal charters and a municipality's voters may adopt any one of the charters or substitute one charter for another. The second type empowers a municipality accepting the statute to exercise the powers authorized by it.

An *Imperium in Imperio*

Constitutional restrictions placed on the powers of the state legislature to control local governments prevented legislative interference in local affairs with the exception of abusive classified laws, but were inadequate in an age of rapid economic and social changes necessitating prompt local government reactions. Political subdivisions governed by the *ultra vires* rule were delayed in initiating a new regulatory action or service delivery program by the necessity of obtaining permission from the state legislature, a body meeting biennially for a short session in the nineteenth century. Acceptance statutes, while helpful, were not tailored to meet specific local problems and often were not accepted by municipalities because of the difficulty under state law of amending or repealing the acceptance.

Critics of the governance system maintained citizens of local governments possessing knowledge of their municipality's problems were prevented from making important decisions. Proponents of a constitutional grant of powers directly to municipal corporations also argued such a grant will result in more economical and efficient administration as municipalities engage in experimentation to solve problems and provide services. In addition, proponents maintained such a grant would free the state legislature of the need to consider special bills, thereby allowing more time to be devoted to bills addressing the solution of statewide problems.

The national municipal league (now national civic league) in 1921 developed a model constitutional provision establishing within a state what may be labeled a type of dual federalism or an *Imperium in Imperio* under which municipal corporations would be granted certain autonomous powers protected against interference by the state legislature. In 1923, New York voters ratified a constitutional amendment (now Article IX) establishing an *Imperium in Imperio* for cities and New York's lead was followed soon thereafter by several other states including Illinois. By subsequent constitutional amendments, New York extended the system to counties, towns, and villages.

This separate entity approach to distributing political power between the state and its general-purpose local governments failed to achieve most of its goals because state courts interpreted narrowly the scope of powers granted to the local units. The New York constitutional amendment, for example, forbids the state legislature to enact a law relating to the "property, affairs, or government" of a municipality if the law is "special or local in terms of its effect." The 1929 New York State Legislature enacted a multiple-dwelling law applicable to cities with a population exceeding 800,000, which applied only to New York City in spite of the constitutional prohibition of special laws to control local affairs. The New York Court of Appeals, the highest state court, in 1929 upheld the constitutionality of the law by developing in *Adler v. Deegan* a "state concern" doctrine holding the state legislature has authority to enact a law involving the concerns of a municipality if there is a substantial "state concern" with the problem addressed by the law.[10] Courts in other *Imperium in Imperio* states adopted the "state concern" doctrine in their decisions. It must be pointed out the courts do not always rule against municipalities in cases involving a dispute between the state and one of its municipal corporations.

Courts generally interpreted narrowly the constitutional provisions designed to create an *Imperium in Imperio*. Terrance P. Hass in 2006 reviewed Rhode Island's experience under its 1952 home rule constitutional amendment, concluded the state supreme court initially tended to give a narrow reading to the amendment but more recently included a broader interpretation in its opinions, and added "this slow progression of home rule is probably just a reluctant recognition of a persistent fact of Rhode Island's history, that towns came first."[11]

Devolution of Powers

Somewhat surprisingly, the development and spread of the "state concern" doctrine did not lead immediately to major efforts by local government associations to change the system of power distribution. It was not until 1952 that the American municipal association (now national league of cities) engaged Dean Jefferson B. Fordham of the University of Pennsylvania law school to study the distribution of powers and to develop recommendations for a new system.

Fordham in 1953 prepared a report containing model constitutional provisions for a new system of granting authority to general-purpose local governments avoiding the problem of narrow judicial interpretation of municipal powers.[12] Under the proposal, the state constitution would devolve to each municipal corporation adopting a charter all powers capable of devolution subject to preemption by general law with two exceptions. Such a municipality would not be empowered to enact "civil law governing civil relations" or "define and provide for the punishment of a felony." This devolution of powers approach is designed to exclude the judiciary from determining the dividing line between state powers and municipal powers. General-purpose local governments would derive their powers directly from the state constitution in common with the derivation of the powers of the state legislature. Recognizing it might be undesirable to allow municipalities to exercise all delegated powers with two exceptions, Fordham proposed the state legislature should be granted authority to remove a power(s) from all municipalities or all municipalities of a given class by means of a preemption statute. The legislature, however, would be forbidden to remove a power from a single municipality. No constitutional devolution of powers provision, with the exceptions of the ones in Alaska and Pennsylvania, grant broad financial powers to local governments.

There is in most states a dual or tripartite system of distributing powers between the state and its general-purpose local governments because not all states adopted the devolution of powers approach and where it has been adopted the approach applies typically only to certain types of general-purpose local governments and not all Fordham recommended powers have been devolved. New York is unique in that it employs the *Ultra Vires* rule, *Imperium in Imperio*, and devolution of powers systems to allocate powers. The result is considerable confusion as to the powers of local governments and their attorneys requesting advisory opinions from the attorney general, commissioner of education, and/or state comptroller.

TYPES OF MUNICIPAL CHARTERS

Counties, towns, townships, and other rural units of government usually were created by special acts of colonial or state legislatures. As a town became urbanized, it petitioned the state legislature for issuance of a charter conferring municipal status on the town, there by allowing it to exercise a wider array of powers. Today, five types of municipal charters are in use in the various states.

Special Charters

The oldest type is a charter granted to a city by a special act of the state legislature. In theory, a special charter is custom-tailored to the needs of the city, granting it exactly the organizational structure and the powers the city needs. In practice, the special charter system suffers from two major disadvantages. First, the legislature often acts capriciously, forcing on cities unwieldy or burdensome governmental structures and imposing limitations on city action. Second, the excessive time expended by state legislatures on local problems leads to the neglect of state problems. For these reasons, many state constitutions have been amended to prohibit the granting of special charters.

General Charters

Under the general charter system, each city—large or small—is granted exactly the same charter by the state legislature. In theory, the system provides for equal corporate privileges for all cities. In practice, the system is grossly unequal for it burdens small cities with administrative paraphernalia they do not want and deprives large cities or urgently needed powers and facilities. The system also fails to take into account local political conditions, geographical considerations, and economic differences. Although the system is useful in facilitating incorporation of smaller cities, it is impractical in general use and is not used exclusively in any state.

Classified Charters

In order to avoid the defects of both special and general charters, the classified charter system has been adopted by several state legislatures for some or all types of general-purpose local governments. Cities, for example, are classified according to population and a uniform charter is provided for all cities within the same population class.

Unfortunately, classification often has been employed by the state legislature to evade constitutional prohibitions against issuance of special charters. If the law stipulates "the following charter shall apply to all cities with populations between 70,001 and 75,000," it is reasonable to assume that the charter will apply to only one city. In several states, each large city is in a different population class and has a different charter.

Even with reasonable classification, the system has the following defects: (1) It fails to take account of different environmental characteristics of cities with approximately the same populations, and (2) it requires a change of charter—no matter how satisfactory the existing one is—if a city's population increases or declines beyond the limits of the city's class.

Optional Charters

In 1913, the Ohio State Legislature enacted an optional charter plan that has been copied by fourteen other states. Under this plan, the legislature drafts a number of charters and the voters of a city, by means of a referendum, are authorized to adopt the particular charter best fitted for the city's needs. For example, all cities except Boston in Massachusetts may choose between six different charters—three mayor-council charters, two council-manager charters, and one commission charter. A few states have adopted the optional charter plan for counties.

This system has the advantages of securing a degree of uniformity and at the same time permitting some local self-determination. Nevertheless, the system is objected to by critics who argue each city should possess the authority to draft and adopt a charter containing provisions city voters believe are most desirable to meet their needs.

Home Rule Charters

Home rule in the United States refers loosely to general-purpose local governments being authorized to conduct their affairs without interference by the state government. More specifically, home rule is the privilege granted by the state constitution or state legislature to municipal corporations to draft, adopt, and amend their charters. Constitutional home rule grants local governments greater protection than legislative home rule since the state constitution is more difficult to amend than a statute. The Illinois constitutional home rule provision is unique in containing an opt-out provision stipulating that a home rule government by referendum may elect not to be a home rule unit.[13]

The Missouri Constitution of 1875 was the first one to contain a municipal home rule provision, but home rule was limited to cities with a population in excess of 100,000 and only St. Louis met this criterion.[14] Constitutions commonly specify the matters subject to local control, but a major problem in these states involves distinguishing between local and state or general affairs. It must be pointed out the interests of the state are paramount and are not subordinated in most instances to those of the city or county under home rule. As noted, Fordham proposed the devolution of powers approach granting all governmental powers with two exceptions to general-purpose local governments, but reserving the power of preemption to the state legislature.

Home rule proponents cite four main advantages: (1) It eliminates or greatly reduces legislative interference in city affairs. (2) It permits citizens to determine the form and administrative organization of their local government. (3) The state legislature is relieved of the time-consuming burden of special legislation and can devote its exclusive attention to state and interstate problems. (4) Home rule permits citizens to have a greater voice in the determination of local governmental policies and thus encourages more citizens to become interested in and involved in local affairs.

Opponents cite four major disadvantages. (1) Frequent changes in the charter may cause instability in a local government. (2) Owing to proposals to amend the charter, the ballot may become excessive in length at each election and discourage citizens from casting a vote on each referred issue. (3) Home rule allows local political machines increased freedom from state supervision and interference. (4) The system makes more difficult the solution of areawide problems since solutions to these problems may be blocked if a strategically located municipality refuses to cooperate with its neighbors. In practice, these concerns have proven to be minor because charters are not amended often, local political machines have become extinct or weak, and the state legislature possesses plenary authority to solve areawide problems.

The amount of discretionary authority possessed by general-purpose local governments varies by type of local government, function, and state. In general, states tend to grant cities more authority to change the structure of their governments than authority relative to finance, functional areas, and personnel.[15] At one extreme, Arkansas, Georgia, Indiana, and Vermont grant no authority to cities relative to their structure. At the other extreme, nineteen states grant blanket governmental structure powers to their cities.

LOCAL GOVERNMENT FINANCE

The importance of local governments in the United States is indicated by their expenditures—$1,257,580,779,000 in 2004. These governments historically relied upon the property tax for the bulk of their revenues, but it has declined in importance in recent decades as the amount of intergovernmental financial assistance has increased sharply, and certain cities and counties levy a sales tax and a use tax. It is important to note local government finance is subject to prohibitions, restrictions, and procedural requirements contained in the state constitution, statutes, or both.

Constitutional and Statutory Provisions

The state legislature historically possessed unlimited power to regulate the system of local government finance. Abuses in the early decades of the nineteenth century led to amendment of state constitutions to incorporate restrictions upon the powers of local governments to incur debt and to tax. In particular, debt and tax levy limits were established based on the assessed value of real property. These limits often vary by type of local government and exceptions are made for certain cities. In several states, including Massachusetts, the constitutional debt limit may be exceeded by a specified percentage with the approval of a state board.

In addition to these restrictions, the constitution or statutes of twenty-seven states require real property to be assessed at full value for purposes of property taxation. In general, this requirement has been ignored and under-assessment has been common.

The constitution and/or statutes of states require all property or all property of a given class be taxed at a uniform rate. This requirement is contained in the constitution and statutes of West Virginia.[16] Nevertheless, the West Virginia Supreme Court in 1987 allowed a nonuniform tax rate.[17] On appeal, the U.S. Supreme court opined in 1989 the West Virginia State Legislature possesses the power to classify property and to establish a different tax rate for each class provided the "divisions and burdens are reasonable."[18] The court added that in the absence of reasonable divisions and burdens, taxing properties at different tax rates violates the equal protection of the laws clause of the Fourteenth Amendment to the U.S. Constitution.

Constitutions and statutes also exclude from taxation real property owned by eleemosynary, religious, and private educational organizations along with property owned by the national and state governments. Constitutional provisions in several states provide for a homestead exemption under which a homeowner does not have to pay a tax unless the property is assessed at more than a stated value.

Currently, Article VIII of the New York Constitution forbids local governments to "give or loan money or property to or in aid of any individual, or private corporation or association, or private undertaking . . ." In New Jersey, New Mexico, and North Carolina, local governments are required to submit their budgets for approval to a state division or commission for approval. And many state constitutions and statutes require all local governments to operate with balanced budgets.

Escalating property taxes and financial stress in recent years resulted in local governments placing more reliance on user charges to finance specific services, such as solid waste removal. A major development is the levying of impact fees on real estate developments to pay for road improvements, sewer lines, and schools. Several state legislatures granted authority to some or all general-purpose local governments to levy the fees.

The Town of Guilderland, New York, in 1987, enacted a local law requiring applicants for a building permit that will generate additional highway traffic to pay an impact fee with the proceeds dedicated to a fund for improving and expanding the town's road system. The town board enacted the law on the basis of the constitutional grant of power to towns to control their own property, structure of government, and local affairs. In 1988, the Appellate Division of the State Supreme Court invalidated the local law because it will inhibit new construction in the town and shift new development to neighboring municipalities.[19] The court specifically noted development is a "state concern" and impact fees do not relate solely to the constitutional grant of powers to municipalities to control their own "property, affairs, or government."[20]

State Financial Aid

State financial aid to local governments must be viewed in relation to the proportion of public services delivered by state governments. States provide approximately one-half of the noneducation public services, but the percentage ranges from 38.0 percent in Nevada to 78.6 percent in Vermont.[21] If the state provides the bulk of the services to citizens, there obviously is less need for state financial aid for local governments.

One advantage of the state providing a high proportion of the public services is the reduction in the severity of fiscal disparities between local governments since reliance on unevenly distributed local property tax bases is reduced. Conditional grants-in-aid also help to establish more and better quality local government services throughout the state. Furthermore, state aid also is a more equitable method of financing services whose benefits overflow local government boundary lines. A municipality's highways, parks, and several other facilities are utilized by citizens of neighboring municipalities who cannot be taxed for the use of the facilities although municipality could levy user charges. On the negative side, the centralized provision of services in a state may result in higher costs and in services less responsive to the preferences of citizens within a local government. A study by the U.S. Advisory Commission on Intergovernmental Relations concluded the size of a city in the population range of 25,000 to 250,000 has no significant relationship to economies of scale, but the law of diminishing returns applies as size exceeds 250,000, resulting in significant diseconomies of scale.[22] Although this study focused only on cities, its findings suggest state provision of traditional municipal services suffers from diseconomies of scale.

State financial assistance to local governments increased from $5,679,000,000 in 1954 to $149,009,000,000 in 1988 to $379,125,561,000 in 2004. The largest amount of assistance is dedicated to public education followed by public welfare, general support, and highways. The reader must be aware that responsibility for a number of functions or functional components has been transferred from local governments to the state government in several states. In consequence, state financial assistance to local governments for these functions was terminated upon the transfers. A decrease in state aid, for example, occurred in Delaware, Massachusetts, and Vermont as responsibility for local government expensive welfare programs was shifted to the state government.

State financial assistance to local school districts is designed to produce a greater equalization of educational opportunities throughout a state. A complex formula is utilized to distribute the aid and representatives of districts with wide differences in real property values supporting each student seek to have the state legislature change the formula to benefit their interest. The problem of distributing aid to school districts is avoided in Hawaii where there is a single state-administered school district.

While the aid formulas appear to be scientifically based on factors, such as the number of pupils in a school district and the taxable property in the district, the formulas generally were designed by the state legislature with political goals in mind to ensure the aid is distributed to favor specific geographical areas of the state. In 1988, the New York State Legislature made one change in the school aid formula because New York City otherwise would receive more of the proposed statewide increase in aid under the current formula than the legislature desired to give to the city. Hence, the formula was changed to provide each student in the city's schools would count as 94 percent of a student, thereby resulting in a reduction of $90 million in aid the city otherwise would have received.[23]

Courts in several states in the 1970s forced the state legislature to change the system of financial aid to school districts. In 1971, the California Supreme Court in *Serrano v. Priest* ruled that the heavy reliance on the general property tax to finance public schools resulted in major disparities between school districts relative to revenue raised per student and thereby violated the state constitution and the equal protection of the laws clause of the Fourteenth Amendment to the U.S. Constitution.[24] The Connecticut Superior Court in 1974 rendered a similar decision.[25]

Although the U.S. Supreme Court in *San Antonio Independent School District v. Rodriguez* in 1973 rejected a challenge to the Texas system of financing public schools, the Texas Supreme Court in *Edgewood Independent School District v. Kirby* in 1989 overruled the decision of the Texas Court of Appeals and held the system of financing public schools violated the state constitution.[26] The Texas Supreme Court pointed out the wealthiest district had over $14 million of property wealth per student compared to the poorest district with $20,000 per student, a ratio of 700 to 1.

As noted, state financial aid programs are justified in part on the ground they help to eliminate fiscal disparities between local governments. The 1972 Minnesota State Legislature enacted an innovative law to reduce such disparities within the seven-county Twin Cities metropolitan area of Minneapolis and St. Paul.[27] The law provides for a partial sharing of the revenue produced by the growth in the commercial-industrial property tax base in the area. Revenue produced by 40 percent of the growth in this tax base is deposited in the state treasury and distributed to municipalities in accordance with a formula based on need and population. No other state legislature has adopted this tax base sharing system.

In 2006, Minnetonka Beach had the highest property tax base per capita ($3,990) and Landfall had the lowest base per capita ($152).[28] The disparity between these two governments decreased to 6 to 1 when the tax-base sharing formula was applied.

A number of local governments are financially distressed because of loss of tax base and employment associated with the closing of factories, exodus of many middle-class citizens to suburban municipalities, an influx of low-income persons heavily dependent on governmental services, an aging population with a high proportion of retired citizens, termination of the national revenue sharing program, and reductions in several national grants-in-aid. Several states in the 1980s launched special programs to assist these municipalities.

During the Great Depression of the 1930s, state governments were forced to place a number of local governments in financial receivership. In 1975, New York City was facing bankruptcy and the state legislature enacted laws to assist the city. Among other actions, the state-controlled emergency financial control board and the municipal assistance corporation were created to solve the city's fiscal problems.[29] The City of Yonkers, New York, experienced exceptionally serious problems and the 1975 state legislature created an emergency financial control board for the city.[30] More recently, the state legislature created a similar control board for the City of Troy in 1995, Nassau County in 2000, and Erie County in 2005.[31] A control board was established in 2006 for Springfield, Massachusetts.

THE STATE MANDATE PROBLEM

Local government officers object strongly to the state legislature mandating that their governments initiate a specific activity or provide a service meeting minimum state standards. Based upon the assumption state legislators

were unaware of the financial burden placed on local governments by mandates, associations of local governments pressured twenty-two state legislatures to adopt a rule requiring a fiscal note to be attached to all bills with
spending implications for local governments. Experience with the notes
revealed they had little impact in curtailing the number of new mandates.
In consequence, local governments decided to seek state reimbursement of
mandated costs.

State mandates can be directed at a single local government, all local
governments, or a class of local governments. In addition, mandates can
assume the form of transfers of functional responsibilities. The state legislature in Florida in 1970 transferred responsibility for property tax administration to counties and the state legislature in New York in 1972 transferred
responsibility for public welfare from cities and towns to counties.[32]

A Mandate Typology

Examination of state statutes reveal mandates may be placed in fifteen
classes:

Due process mandates require notices of proposed local government decisions and public hearings.

Entitlement mandates provide automatic eligibility for receipt of a
   benefit to persons such as senior citizens who receive real property tax exemptions.

Environmental mandates require local governments to initiate
   expensive program such as water pollution abatement.

Equal Treatment mandates seek to ensure all citizens and employees are treated equitably.

Ethical mandates direct local governing bodies to adopt a code of
   ethics.

Good neighbor mandates seek to eliminate or reduce problems overspilling local government boundary lines.

Informational mandates are designed to inform citizens about local
   government activities by the holding of open meetings of governing bodies, ensuring government information is readily available, and requiring advance public notices of meetings of public
   bodies.

Infrastructure mandates require modernization or replacement of
   bridges, local government building, sewage and other facilities.

Membership mandates specify local governments must be members of a given association such as officials and code administrators international and to pay a membership fee.

Personnel mandates pertain to hours of work, fringe benefits, compulsory binding arbitration of impasses with local government employee unions, and retirement benefits.

Record keeping mandates specify accounting standards and systems for maintenance of financial and other records.

Structural mandates require the use of a given organizational structure for the local government.

Service level mandates require local governments to provide services meeting or exceeding state minimum standards.

Tax base mandates provide exemptions from the real property tax to specified classes of citizens and/or business firms.

Training mandates require specified newly appointed and/or elected officers to complete a training course on a periodic basis.

It is apparent that several classes of mandates, such as entitlement and tax base mandates, overlap each other.

State Mandate Reimbursement

Public dissatisfaction with state mandates resulted in the amendment of fifteen state constitutions to restrict the power of the legislature and administrative agencies to mandate costs on political subdivisions. The major argument advanced in favor of a constitutional guarantee of freedom from mandated costs is based on the proposition the unit mandating a public expenditure should be responsible for financing it. Proponents of reimbursement also argue local governments lose control over a significant portion of their budgets and are deprived of funds needed to implement programs under their discretionary powers.

Opponents of such a constitutional guarantee stress the dangers associated with introducing rigid constitutional provisions relating to state-local relations and local government finance in an era when swift and decisive action is essential if the needs of citizens are to be met. They also explain the financial problems associated with mandates can be solved through reform of the state's tax structure, revision of state aid programs, and restructuring of the local government system.

The constitutional provisions either restrict the authority of the state government to issue mandates, or authorize local governments to ignore unfunded mandates, or require full or partial reimbursement by the state of costs associated with mandates. Section 1 of Article II of the Constitution of Alaska stipulates special acts necessitating appropriations by a local government do not become effective unless approved by the concerned voters. Initiative proposition 4 of 1979 amended the Constitution of California by directing the state to reimburse local governments for all costs attributable to state mandates.

Section 5 of Article 8 of the Constitution of Hawaii requires the state to "share in the cost" of all new state mandates. Section 14 of Article VI of the Louisiana Constitution stipulates a special law requiring increased expenditures for wages and employee fringe benefits does not become effective until approved by the concerned local governing body or the state legislature appropriates funds to cover implementation costs. Section 23 of part 3 of Article IV of the Maine Constitution directs the state legislature to reimburse cities and towns for at least one-half of the revenue loss resulting from property tax exemptions. Section 18 of Article VII of the Florida Constitution stipulates that local governments do not have to implement state mandates if they are unfunded by the state unless the mandates have been approved by a two-thirds vote of each house of the state legislature or deal with specified policy areas including criminal law. Constitutional provisions in the other nine states are similar to the ones listed above.

In addition, sixteen state legislatures enacted one or more statutes providing local governments with mandate relief. The 1999 Minnesota State Legislature, for example, responded to complaints directed at administrative rules and regulations by enacting a law allowing cities and counties to challenge rules and regulations by demonstrating they no longer are needed, no longer are reasonable, or there is a less costly or less intrusive method of achieving the rules' goals.[33] The 2003 New Hampshire General Court enacted a statute exempting towns with a population of 5,000 or less from the mandate to clean up an inactive municipally owned unlined landfill provided it is monitored in accordance with state rules.[34]

DIRECT STATE ACTION

State governments facilitate the solution of local government problems by conducting studies, granting funds, providing technical assistance, and creating special districts on a local and/or regional basis. State legislatures also authorize intergovernmental service agreements, transfers of functional responsibilities between counties and other local governments, state-operated municipal bond banks lowering local government borrowing costs, state-operated investment pools allowing substate units to earn higher interest on their daily balances, and state-operated insurance pools lowering premiums costs for local government. Not all states have taken each of the above facilitating actions.

While helpful, facilitating state actions are incapable of solving all local government problems, particularly metropolitan problems. In the nineteenth century, the Massachusetts General Court decided to solve problems associated with urbanization overspilling the boundaries of Boston by merging several towns with the city. In 1898, the New York State Legislature abolished all local governments within a five county area and replaced them with the newly created City of New York. Such mergers without voter referenda are unusual today.

State Controlled Public Authorities

Convinced that only the state government possesses the authority and financial resources to solve the sewage problem in the greater Boston area, the Massachusetts General Court created the state-controlled metropolitan sewage commission, metropolitan parks commission, and metropolitan water commission in 1889, 1893, and 1895, respectively.[35] Each was unifunctional, but the sewage and water commissions were merged in 1901 into a new board that in 1919 was amalgamated with the parks commission to form the metropolitan district commission.[36] In 2003, the General Court decided to merge the commission with the department of environmental management to form the department of conservation and recreation.[37]

New York has been the leader in creating unifunctional state-controlled public authorities to solve metropolitan and other problems. The fifty-seven regional and statewide authorities include the environmental facilities corporation, job development authority, urban development authority, and five regional transportation authorities. Interstate compacts, described in chapter 7, were employed to create the port authority of New York and New Jersey and the Lake Champlain bridge authority. An international treaty between Canada and the United States established the Buffalo and Fort Erie public bridge authority. The popularity of many authorities is attributable to the fact they are financed by user charges rather than by the general taxpayers.

In New York State, the early authorities were established to finance, construct, and operate bridges, roads, and tunnels on a self-sustaining basis. In 1960, the state commenced to utilize public authorities to evade the constitutional requirement of voter approval of the issuance of bonds pledging the "full faith and credit" of the state to support bonds. The New York State housing finance agency was established and authorized to borrow funds supported by what has been labeled a "moral obligation" clause in the bond indenture (contract).[38] The clause suggests that the state legislature will appropriate funds to replenish the agency's reserve fund, required by the indenture, if the fund falls below a stipulated level. Most New York state authorities created since 1960 have been authorized to issue "moral obligation" bonds.

Examples of public authorities in other states include the Maryland environmental service and the New Jersey water supply authority created in 1970 and 1981, respectively. The former operates more than 100 water supply, waste water treatment, and solid waste facilities for local governments and state agencies. The latter was established during a period of serious water shortage and is authorized to issue bonds to obtain funds to construct and operate water systems throughout New Jersey.

The Twin Cities Metropolitan Council

One of the major criticisms directed against unifunctional public authorities in metropolitan areas is the lack of coordination of their activities. Each authority tends to develop a politically strong constituency, thereby making their amalgamation a political impossibility. The last amalgamation of state authorities in New York State occurred in the New York City metropolitan area in 1967.[39]

Several state-controlled unifunctional authorities were established in the Twin Cities metropolitan area of Minnesota and each tended to operate independently of the others. To solve this and other problems, the 1967 Minnesota State Legislature established the metropolitan council with members appointed by the governor with the advice and consent of the Senate.[40]

The governance system in the metropolitan area is a federated one with powers divided between the council, public authorities, counties, and municipalities. The council lacks responsibility for providing services and may not direct the other units to initiate a specific action. The council is basically a policy formation body and can review and suspend indefinitely the development plan of each metropolitan authority. Furthermore, each local government in the area is required to prepare a comprehensive plan consistent with the regional airports, parks, sewers, and transportation plans developed by the council which can suspend proposed projects of local governments for up to one year.

The position of the council was strengthened by the 1974 Minnesota State Legislature enactment of a statute authorizing the council to appoint members other than the chairperson of each metropolitan commission with the exception of the airport commission.[41] The governor with the advice and consent of the Senate appoints the chairpersons of the commissions.

The Twin Cities model of metropolitan governance is characterized by the separation of policy execution from policymaking with the council's policies executed by the other metropolitan bodies. Hence, the council is not burdened by operating responsibilities and can devote its total energy to the development of policies for the area.

Although the council improved coordination of policy implementation, the most important areawide problems continue to be attacked on a piecemeal basis with the state legislature playing a major referee role between competing commissions and interests.

State Assumption of Responsibilities

In addition to creating state-controlled public authorities to assume responsibility for certain functions, state legislatures have transferred responsibility for several traditional municipal responsibilities to state departments and agencies.

The 1966 Rhode Island State Legislature abolished city and town health departments and transferred their functions to the state health department. In Vermont, the state health department is responsible for nearly all public health programs, social welfare was transferred from cities and towns to the state in 1967, and all town-operated airports were shifted to the state in 1968.

Massachusetts and Delaware in 1968 and 1970, respectively, shifted responsibility for social welfare to the state. In 1972, Massachusetts made forest fire patrols a state rather than a county responsibility and a Florida constitutional amendment was ratified providing for abolition of municipal courts and transfer of their responsibilities to the state court system. The 1990 New Jersey State Legislature transferred responsibility for many social welfare programs, including general assistance, to the state.

Although Maryland law does not make the state responsible for sewage and solid waste disposal, the state secretary of health and mental hygiene may direct the Maryland environmental service to install and operate necessary facilities if a municipality fails to comply with an order of the secretary.

Because of the sewage problems within the Winnipesaukee River basin, the 1972 New Hampshire General Court directed the state water supply and pollution control commission to acquire, construct, and operate all sewage and waste disposal facilities within the basin, thereby relieving municipalities of responsibility for sewage treatment. In 1987, the Minnesota State

Legislature enacted a statute preempting local government regulation of pesticides except for application warning ordinances.

Maryland assumed complete responsibility for assessing real property for tax purposes in 1975. Although Hawaii is the only other state to have transferred to the state complete responsibility for property tax assessment, the 1973 Wisconsin State Legislature made the state responsible for assessing manufacturing property.

A number of state legislatures enacted laws completely or partially preempting city and town responsibility for land use regulation. A 1970 Vermont law requires a developer to obtain a permit from one of seven district environmental commissions for a proposed development exceeding ten acres in a city or town with zoning regulations and one acre in a city or town without zoning regulations. A 1974 Tennessee law directs the state community development board to adopt minimum standards for development of new communities. The 1973 New York State Legislature created the Adirondack Park Agency to regulate land use in the large Adirondack park reserve. And a 1975 Texas law placed regulation of strip mining of coal, lignite, and uranium under the jurisdiction of the Texas railroad commission. Florida and North Dakota also assumed complete responsibility for regulating mining.

The 1975 Florida State Legislature adopted an interesting default system mandating each local government to adopt a comprehensive development plan by 1979 or responsibility for preparation of the plan would be shifted to the state land planning agency. In the same year, the New York State Legislature directed each local government to adopt a freshwater wetland protection plan. Failure of a city, town, or village to adopt a plan meeting state standards results in the county becoming responsible for the function. If the county fails to develop a local law within ninety days, the county is deemed to have defaulted its responsibility to the state Department of Environmental Conservation.

SUMMARY

The legal relationship existing between a state government and its political subdivisions varies by type of local government and from state to state. All local governments in several states are subject to Dillon's Rule and may not initiate a new action without permission from the state legislature. Although the legislature in such a state possesses complete authority to control all local governments unless restricted by the state constitution, the legislature often grants relatively broad powers to municipalities in several functional fields as in Virginia.

Constitutional provisions providing for an *Imperium in Imperio* system of distribution political power within a state failed to grant general-purpose local governments significant new discretionary powers with the exception of the power to restructure the governments. On the other hand, adoption of constitutional provisions devolving powers has increased significantly the discretionary powers of municipalities.

No state constitution provides for devolution of all powers with two exceptions to municipalities as recommended by Fordham. The state legislature retains complete control over finance and personnel, and by general law may remove devolved powers from local governments. As a result, most states utilize two systems for distributing powers between the state and its political subdivisions—the *ultra vires* rule and *Imperium in Imperio* or devolution of powers. New York is unusual in employing the three systems simultaneously, thereby making it extremely difficult to determine all the powers exercisable by a municipality. Furthermore, sections of municipal statutes in many states contain antiquated and confusing terminology. The New York municipal laws are the most confusing since they contain a number of conflicting provisions.

Most state governments are important providers of financial assistance to their political subdivisions to support certain governmental functions. The bulk of the state aid supports education, but large amounts also are granted for highways and welfare.

Controversies surrounding the system of allocating state financial aid for education led to court suits in a number of states. The U.S. Supreme Court rejected challenges to state school finance systems based on alleged violation of the U.S. Constitution, but courts in a few states, including New York, have ruled the system violates a provision of the state constitution.

The principal irritant in state-local relations is the state mandate. Fifteen state constitutions contain provisions limiting the ability of the state legislature to impose mandates on general-purpose local governments or requiring state reimbursement of mandated costs.

State Legislatures continue to display ambivalence toward granting greater discretionary authority to their political subdivisions. While expressing concern about the impact of state mandates on local units, the legislatures continue to impose new mandates, with the exception of New Hampshire where the constitutional requirement for state reimbursement of mandated costs convinced the state legislature not to impose new mandates. Simultaneously, a number of legislatures in recent years broadened the grant of discretionary powers to some or all of their general-purpose local governments. Available evidence suggests these trends will continue in the foreseeable future.

The concluding chapter integrates the information on the increasing centralization of political power in the national government and present a general theory of federalism in the United States encompassing national-state, interstate, and state-local relations.

CHAPTER 9

Power Centralization
in the Federal System

The United States federal system, the oldest in the world, can be described accurately in the twenty-first century with two words—complex and metamorphic. The system combines centripetal and centrifugal forces to produce constantly changing patterns of national-state-local governmental responsibilities, and retains elements of a confederate system and elements of a unitary system as the drafters of the U.S. Constitution intended. The secular trend since 1937, with occasional minor dips, is in the direction of policy-making centralization in Congress and state and local government administration of many national policies. Although the system has become more centralized, power sharing continues to be an important feature.

The original thirteen states were sovereign polities organized on a unitary basis with respect to their political subdivisions. These states in 1781 joined a confederacy subsequently replaced by a federal system in 1789. The trend toward centralization of political power commenced during the tenure of Chief Justice John Marshall of the U.S. Supreme Court (1801–1835) as the court interpreted broadly the delegated powers of Congress and developed the dormant interstate commerce doctrine, but the trend generally was interrupted after his departure as chief justice until 1937.

Power centralization in the national government was chiefly the product of conditional grants-in-aid and tax credits in the period 1935–1970. Although the preemption revolution dates to 1965 as described in chapter 4, congressional employment of preemption powers has had its greatest impact on subnational governments since the mid-1970s. The loose constructionists of Congress's enumerated powers generally defeated the strict constructionists and the general paramountcy of the delegated regulatory

187

powers of Congress over the concurrent and reserved powers of the states has become well-established. Not surprisingly, philosophical differences over the desirability of a strong national government dating to 1781 continue to this day.

If the drafters of the U.S. Constitution were resurrected and viewed in the twenty-first century the federal system they established in 1789, they would be amazed by the concentration of political power in Congress. Recognizing that they were launching an experiment in national governance and that the economy and society would change in the future, they included provisions for the flexible employment of delegated powers by Congress that would be the architects responsible for redesigning important aspects of the federal system on a continuing basis as needed. They clearly did not desire constitutional provisions establishing procrustean spheres of congressional powers and state powers, and included the supremacy of the law clause and two methods of proposing constitutional amendments to facilitate changes in national-state relations. Nevertheless, the drafters would be surprised by the systemic changes, particularly congressional and national court regulation of states and their political subdivisions.

The revolutionary changes in national-state relations are highlighted by the declared purposes of the *Americans with Disabilities Act of 1990*:

1. to provide a clear and comprehensive national mandate for the elimination of discrimination against individuals with disabilities;
2. to provide clear, strong, consistent, enforceable standards addressing discrimination against individuals with disabilities;
3. to ensure that the Federal Government plays a central role in enforcing the standards established in this Act on behalf of individuals with disabilities; and
4. to invoke the sweep of congressional authority, including the power to enforce the Fourteenth Amendment and to regulate commerce, in order to address the major areas of discrimination faced day-to-day by people with disabilities.[1]

Employment of its powers to enforce the Fourteenth Amendment and to regulate interstate commerce allows Congress to regulate subnational governments and to preempt completely their powers relative to individuals with disabilities. Interestingly, the act defines the term "public entity" to mean "any State or local government," but exempts from the definition of "employer" the U.S. government and corporations "wholly owned by the Government of the United States." Subnational government officers are critical of the exemption of the national government and its instrumentalities from the standards contained in many preemption laws applicable to state and local governments.

ADVANTAGES AND DISADVANTAGES
OF THE FEDERAL SYSTEM

Our review of national-state relations since 1789 facilitates an evaluation of the validity of the alleged advantages and disadvantages of a federal system, listed in chapter 1, pertaining directly to the United States.

Advantages

Experience with federalism in the United States reveals that there is relatively little need for constitutional amendments to provide greater uniformity of regulatory policy and administration since Congress possesses broad authority to establish such uniformity in many functional fields by enacting statutes assuming complete responsibility for a function or partial responsibility with states allowed a degree of discretionary authority in establishing policy. The sharp increase in enactment of preemption statutes since 1965 resulted in states losing all or a degree of control over several of their traditional affairs. Furthermore, Congress employed effectively cross-cutting, cross-over, and tax sanctions, described in chapter 6, to persuade states to enact uniform laws in critical areas such as the maximum highway speed limit and the minimum alcoholic beverage purchase age.

States nevertheless retain a number of important reserved powers, particularly provision of services, which prevent an overconcentration of governmental authority in the national government and thereby make impossible enactment and implementation of national policies that might prove harmful to sections of a geographically large nation with diverse regional needs and policy preferences.

Experience also demonstrates states continue to serve as laboratories for innovative governmental policies subsequently adopted by a number of other states and Congress. The federal system clearly has the advantage of enabling an individual state to develop and implement programs to solve its nonpreempted special problems by exercise of reserved powers instead of waiting for Congress to develop a consensus to enact a statute providing a national solution.

One major advantage of a federal system, in contrast to a unitary system, is the provision of greater opportunities for citizen participation in the governance process. A prominent characteristic of the United States governance system is the active role played by citizens, as part-time government officers and individuals, in developing and implementing solutions to public problems.

Disadvantages

Mixed support for the alleged disadvantages of a federal system outlined in chapter 1 is provided by United States experience. The system has proved to be a flexible one capable of responding to serious challenges, including two world wars and the Great Depression, rather than a rigid one in which power can be redistributed between the national and state planes only by means of formal constitutional amendments. To date, there have been only twenty-seven formal amendments and only four have a great impact on national-state relations.

The first ten amendments, the Bill of Rights, were adopted as the result of promises made by proponents of the proposed constitution to secure its ratification. The Twelfth, Twentieth, and Twenty-fifth Amendments, respectively, made changes in the method of voting for presidential and vice-presidential electors, and the inaugural dates for the president and the vice president; and established a procedure for determining whether the President "is unable to discharge the powers and duties of his office . . ." These amendments and the Thirteenth Amendment, which abolish slavery, did not affect national-state relations.

The Twenty-first Amendment repealed the Eighteenth Amendment and its national prohibition of the manufacture, sale, and consumption of alcoholic beverages, thereby returning control of alcoholic beverages, with exceptions noted in a subsequent section, to the states. The Twenty-second amendment did not affect national-state relations since it only established a two-term limit for the President. Similarly, such relations are unaffected by the Twenty-third Amendment authorizing the District of Columbia to appoint presidential and vice-presidential electors.

The Twenty-fourth Amendment forbids states to require payment of a poll or other tax as a condition for voting in any election for presidential and vice-presidential electors, or U.S. representatives and senators. This amendment was directed against southern states with poll taxes designed to discourage black citizens from registering and voting, and has had a minor impact on national-state relations.

The Twenty-sixth Amendment lowered the voting age in all elections to eighteen years without affecting the balance of power between Congress and the states. And the Twenty-seventh Amendment forbids Congress to vary the compensation for senators and representatives until "an election of Representatives shall have intervened."

In sum, only the Fourteenth, Fifteenth, Sixteenth, and Seventeenth Amendments affect significantly the nature of the federal system. The Fourteenth Amendment has had a great impact on the powers of states only since the U.S. Supreme Court, commencing in the mid-1920s, incorporated most of the guarantees of the Bill of Rights into the Amendment, thereby protecting them from abridgment by state and local governments. The Fifteenth Amendment serves as the basis for the contingent *Voting Rights Act of 1965* as amended and forbids any state or local government covered by the act from making any change in its electoral system, no matter how minor, without the permission of the U.S. Attorney General or the District Court for the District of Columbia.

The Sixteenth Amendment's authorization of a graduated income tax made it possible for Congress to raise large sums of money and to authorize conditional-grants-in-aid to subnational governments, thereby allowing Congress to influence the exercise of reserved powers of the states.

By removing the power of state legislatures to appoint U.S. senators, the Seventeenth Amendment facilitated enactment of preemption statutes by Congress. In the absence of the amendment, it is reasonable to assume the U.S. Senate would not approve most bills providing for nullification of important powers of the states if they were opposed to the bills.

As alleged, the existence of concurrent powers has resulted in conflicts between the national and state planes of government, but has not been responsible for significant uneconomical, overlapping of functional responsibilities. In times of an emergency, Congress may not be able to mobilize the total resources of the country as rapidly as the government of a unitary system, yet this inability has not proven to be a major problem in the United States.

There is no denying the serious problems caused by lack of national regulatory uniformity in several important functional areas, particularly as communications, financial, manufacturing, and transportation systems have become national and international in scope. The lack of a central banking system until 1913 hindered the development of the economy and the lack of uniformity in highway laws continues to be a problem. With respect to the latter, however, Congress employed its preemption and cross-over sanction powers, explained in chapters 4 and 6, to establish more uniformity in this critical functional area. A number of other nonuniformity problems have been solved by states voluntarily enacting uniform state laws and entering into interstate compact and interstate administrative agreements, a subject explored in chapter 7.

Evidence does not support Harold J. Laski's 1939 charge that federalism in the United States is obsolete or his 1948 contention the states never have had real sovereignty.[2] The federal system continues to be one whose nature has become more dynamic in response to the great increase in the scope and complexity of governmental challenges in the Twenty-first Century.

METAMORPHIC NATIONAL-STATE RELATIONS

Our review of intergovernmental relations reveals Congress today plays three principal intergovernmental roles—facilitator, inhibitor, and initiator. As a facilitator, Congress provides financial assistance—grants-in-aid, loans, guarantees of loan, and tax credits—and technical assistance to promote effective subnational governmental regulation and provision of quality services. As an inhibitor, Congress employs its complete preemption powers to nullify state and local government regulatory laws and rules, and to prohibit future enactment of such laws and regulations. As an initiator, Congress enacts minimum standards partial preemption statutes to provide the framework for new regulatory programs involving the national and state governments.

Congress's dominant role in the period 1935–1970 was a facilitating one. The period 1970–1980 was a transitional one during which the facilitating role declined in importance as the inhibiting and initiating roles assumed central stage. Although the pace of enactment of preemption statutes decreased slightly after 1980, Congress continued to enact such statutes in important areas in the 1990s, including banking, communications, and finance. The bulk of the preemption statues enacted post-2000, while important, affect the periphery of the powers of the states.

By March 1, 2008, Congress had enacted 589 preemption statutes since 1789. Note should be made of the fact congressional economic deregulation of the banking, communications, and transportation industries since 1978 occurred simultaneously with increasing congressional regulation of states and their political subdivisions as polities.

In general, the growth of national powers has been gradual and based chiefly on congressional exercise of latent powers and the U.S. Supreme Court decisions during the chief justiceship of John Marshall in the early decades of the nineteenth century. As described in chapter 6, Congress commenced in 1893 to add conditions to new grant-in-aid programs, thereby enabling it to increase its influence over the policies of states and their political subdivisions. Tax credits first were employed in 1926 and 1935 to persuade states to enact an inheritance tax based on the federal one and to establish a state unemployment compensation system based on federal law, respectively. The proliferation of conditional grant-in-aid programs in the late 1950s and 1960s facilitated broad congressional supervision of many state regulatory and service programs based upon the reserved powers of the states.

In 1965, a consensus developed in Congress that a national problem—water pollution—could not be solve by conditional grants-in-aid, interstate cooperation, or both. To eliminate this problem, Congress devised an innovative approach to restructuring national-state relations. As explained in detail in chapter 4, minimum standards preemption involves Congress enacting minimum national regulatory standards. A state can retain responsibility for regulating a given field provided it submits to the concerned federal department or agency a plan with standards as rigorous as the national ones and demonstrates it has the necessary qualified personnel and equipment. If the federal department or agency approves the plan, regulatory primacy is delegated to the state. A state may adopt more stringent standards and a number of states have done so in various regulatory fields. Congress also has enacted a series of other statutes authorizing a state to establish standards stricter than the national standards without seeking regulatory primacy.[3]

Fluid economic and societal changes, including nationalization and internationalization of the economy, generate pressures by interest groups and others, of varying intensity for readjustment of the respective competences of the three planes of government. The American political system since 1965 has become more metamorphic as interplane relationships change continually with congressional enactment of conditional grants-in-aid, cross-cutting sanctions, cross-over sanctions, tax sanctions, and preemption statutes; issuance by U.S. departments and agencies of new implementing rules and regulations; and states' refusal, or acceptance, or return of "regulatory primacy" under minimum standard preemption statutes. It also is important to note individual states have launched new regulatory programs subsequently adopted by sister states and by Congress in some instances.

These developments ensure the system is in a perpetual state of locomotion describable as kaleidoscopic rather than linear in nature, and often generate confusion relative to whether national government agencies or states are responsible for solving a given problem. The intergovernmental maze produced by congressional enactment of preemption statutes, however, cannot be eliminated by a "rational" reassignment of functional responsibilities because of the great interdependence of the three planes of government with actions by one plane affecting the other planes.

To understand the major reason for the sharp increase in the number and importance of preemption statutes, one must study the influence of major interest groups and their political action committees channeling election campaign funds to candidates for seats in Congress. Groups regulated by the national and state governments are major sources of campaign finance. Historically most interest groups were economic ones although there were a few public interest groups such as the league of women voters. Coinciding with the post-1965 increased pace of enactment of preemption statutes has been the establishment of numerous public interest groups seeking enactment of preemption statutes to protect the environment. Television news programs in particular generated broad public support for environmental preemption statutes by highlighting environmental disasters such as the Exxon Valdez oil spill in Alaska. The proliferation of federal mandates and restraints, described in chapter 4, induced associations of state and local governments to become more active in lobbying Congress to prevent enactment of preemption bills and to seek congressional relief from existing preemption statutes and preemptive court decisions.

The national judiciary will play a greater role in interpreting preemption statutes in the future because of their lack of precision. In general, Congress enacts a preemption statute containing only a skeleton of policy for two reasons. First, attempts by sponsors of a bill to include more specific provisions will result in the loss of congressional support for the bill as more specific provisions affect adversely important interest groups not alarmed by a bill containing general provisions. Second, many preemption bills relate to technical subjects, such as contaminants in drinking water. Congress, a generalist body, lacks the expertise to develop specific standards and must rely upon experts in the bureaucracy to develop the standards. Experience reveals technical standards incorporated in administrative rules and regulations affecting negatively a major interest group are challenged in court upon issuance. The courts are called on to decide whether the rules and regulations are in accordance with congressional intent, *ultra vires*, or both. In addition, courts are the agencies for determining implied preemption in the absence of a congressional declaration of intent to displace completely or partially a state law or the English Common Law followed by all states except Louisiana.

The wide-ranging use of preemption powers since 1965 suggests Congress is a nearly omnipotent regulatory policy-maker. Separation of facts from rhetoric charging national power aggrandizement reveals such a conclusion is unwarranted. The U.S. Supreme Court, as the referee of national-state relations, occasionally strikes down as unconstitutional a preemption statute on the ground it exceeds the delegated powers of Congress. Furthermore, Congress is a government of enumerated and implied powers, and lacks authority to provide most services directly to the citizenry within states. Because Congress lacks this authority, it employs conditional grants grants-in-aid, cross-cutting sanctions, cross-over sanctions, minimum standards preemption, and tax credits to induce states and local governments to implement national policies relative to governmental services.

In 1953, Herbert Wechsler wrote:

> National action has thus always been regarded as exceptional in our polity, an intrusion to be justified by some necessity, the special rather than the ordinary case. . . . Even when Congress acts, its tendency has been to frame enactments on an *ad hoc* basis to accomplish limited objectives, supplanting state-created norms only so far as may be necessary for the purpose. Indeed, with all the centralizing growth throughout the years, federal law is still a largely interstitial product, rarely occupying any field completely, building normally upon legal relationships established by the States.[4]

This statement remains generally valid in the first decade of the Twenty-first Century although Congress has assumed exclusive responsibility for a small number of additional regulatory functions.

Writing in 1970, Richard H. Leach concluded "that the old federalism of disparate programs, policies, and administrative procedures has given way to a new federalism which stresses intergovernmentalism and administrative devolution."[5] Although this conclusion was based on the important roles the federal conditional grants-in-aid were playing in 1970, the assessment is broad enough to encompass the current federal system and its heavy reliance on congressional leadership in establishing policies to be implemented, through conditional grants-in-aid and minimum standards regulatory preemption, by states and their political subdivisions. Leach's conclusion that "federalism functions only when the parties to it accept compromise as a working principle" remains an accurate one.[6]

Devolution of substantial discretionary authority to states to administer national policies relieves overburdening at the federal agency level, but increases the need for national monitoring of the performance of states in implementing congressional statutes and the extent to which their programs are integrated into coherent national policies. Unfortunately, federal agencies do not possess adequate information and capacity to monitor and appraise effectively the performance of states in executing national policies.

The Powers of the States

The greatly expanded use of preemption powers by Congress suggests that there has been an equivalent loss of political power by states. Surprisingly, expansive use of preemption powers paradoxically has increased and not reduced the exercise of political powers by states. In the national-state context, political power in the United States is not a "zero sum" system with an increase in the exercise of partial preemption powers by Congress automatically resulting in a corresponding decrease in the exercisable reserved powers of the states. With the exception of complete preemption statutes with no provisions for a turnback of regulatory authority to states, the exercise of preemption powers generally encourages the utilization of latent powers by all or most states and has revitalized the regulatory state activities to a degree. To prevent the complete exercise of regulatory powers by the national government, states with a few exceptions seek the delegations to them of "regulatory primacy" by the concerned national department or agency under minimum standards preemption as explained in chapter 4.

Fortunately, Congress is aware complete preemption without a provision for state administrative involvement, with a few exceptions, cannot be successful throughout the United States because of the wide diversity of local and regional conditions, and the national government's lack of complementary powers.

Recognition also must be accorded the fact partial preemption statutes have been enacted in an innovative manner to increase the discretionary authority of states. Examples of such laws include (1) the *Marine Sanctuaries Act Amendments of 1984* authorizing the drafting of regulations by regional fisheries management councils whose members are selected in part by state government officers, (2) the *Coast Guard Authorization Act of 1984* whose implementing regulations provide a state blood alcohol content (BAC) standard for operating a marine recreational vessel is the national BAC standard within the state, (3) the *Abandoned Shipwreck Act of 1987* asserting a federal title to an abandoned historic shipwreck and immediately transferring the title to the concerned state, and (4) the *Riegle-Neal Interstate Banking and Branching Efficiency Act of 1994* containing an "opt-in" provision allowing a state legislature to enact a law permitting interstate branching through *de novo* branches and to "opt-out" of the act by allowing a state legislature to prohibit interstate branching within the state.[7]

Furthermore, Congress enacted seven statutes devolving regulatory authority to states. Congress in 1789 devolved to states authority to regulate marine port pilots and reaffirmed the devolution in 1983.[8] The *McCarran-Ferguson Act of 1945* declares regulation of the business of insurance is a state responsibility although the industry is involved in interstate commerce.[9] The *Submerged Lands Act of 1953* devolves to states jurisdiction over submerged lands up to three miles from the shoreline.[10] The *Interstate Horseracing Act of 1978* permits interstate simulcasts of horse races if the concerned state regulatory body and the concerned horsemen's association do not object.[11] Congress in 1946 completely preempted regulation of ionizing radiation, but enacted the *Low-level Radioactive Waste Policy Act of 1980* devolving responsibility for disposal of such wastes to states.[12] The *Vessel Safety Standards Act of 1983* devolves to states authority to regulate navigation on navigable waters of the United States.[13] And the *Liability Risk Retention Act of 1986* devolves authority to states to regulate risk retention groups.[14]

Congress also enhanced the regulatory powers of states by enacting the *Financial Institutions, Reform, Recovery, and Enforcement Act of 1989* stipulating all appraisals of properties involving federal government transactions—including transactions of the federal deposit insurance corporation, federal national mortgage association, federal home loan mortgage corporation, and federally chartered banks—must be made by state-licensed or state-certified appraisers.[15]

Minimum standards preemption and delegation of regulatory primacy are compromises between the Scylla of complete centralization and the Charybdis of complete decentralization of political power. This type of preemption in a functional area preserves a degree of political decentralization in policy making since states detail policy within the framework of national statutes, administrative regulations, or both and also fosters nearly complete decentralization of program administration. In addition, minimum standards preemption statutes relieves states of responsibility for solving difficult problems if states so choose and also affords a state the opportunity to challenge another state for its failure to act in compliance with a preemption statute designed to prevent a problem, such as water pollution, overspilling its boundaries. The challenge initially can assume the form of a protest to the federal department or agency responsible for overseeing implementation of the minimum standards preemption statute and/or a suit in the U.S. District Court seeking a writ of injunction or a writ of mandamus.

Surprisingly, the great expansion in the exercise of preemption powers by Congress had not produced a sharp increase in national administration of regulatory programs. The federal government directly administers few programs today that it was not responsible for administering prior to 1965.

Minimum standards preemption accelerates implementation national policies in various functional areas and in effect multiplies federal resources by incorporating resources of states in a number of national programs. Although this statement suggest Congress "commandeers" the resources of reluctant states to achieve national policy goals, this suggestion is not entirely accurate as a state in the absence of minimum standards preemption may desire to initiate more stringent regulatory programs but does not do so for fear that industrial firms will be discouraged from expanding their facilities within the state, which also will acquire an antibusiness image hindering industrial recruitment efforts.

In general, this type of preemption has produced a degree of national uniformity in regulatory policies combined with diversity resulting from individual states adapting their regulatory policies to special conditions and their preferences in decision-making and implementation systems. Nevertheless, it must be admitted national-state relations have become more coercive as the result of expanded use of cross-cutting and cross-over sanctions, tax sanctions, mandates, and restraints. The large national budgetary deficit deprives to a great extent the ability of Congress to employ new financial incentives to induce desired subnational governmental actions, thereby increasing the pressures for congressional employment of coercive powers.

One complete preemption statutory provision is a clear abuse of congressional powers. The law mandating the location of toll collection booths for the Verrazano Narrows bridge in New York City is a misuse of Congress's power to regulate commerce among the states and has resulted in increased traffic congestion at the entrance to the Lincoln tunnel connecting the city to New Jersey, additional air pollution, and loss of significant toll revenues as noted in chapter 4.

Although state officers complain about cross-over sanctions, they implement the national policies contained in the sanction statutes to avoid loss of national grant-in-aid funds in another functional area. State officers most dislike expensive federal mandates.

In 1982, as described in chapter 4, Congress commenced to become more responsive to complaints of subnational government officers and enacted ten statutes granting a degree of relief to states and/or their local governments from certain provisions of earlier preemption laws and two U.S. Supreme Court decisions viewed as burdensome, unwise, or both by the officers.

Today, the preemption policy-making process may be viewed as an innovation-response model. A preemption power is employed by Congress to initiate a new policy that in its implementation phase often generates more opposition and complaints than were encountered during the bill enactment process. If states are united in their opposition to specific provisions of a preemption statute, Congress often responds within a year or two by enacting into law one or more preemption relief bills addressing the objections of the states.

States historically served as experimental laboratories developing innovative programs subsequently adopted by other states and Congress. The expansive employment of congressional powers of partial preemption might lead to the conclusion the inventiveness of states has been reduced significantly. Evidence, however, reveals states continue to be innovative in policy development.

Interestingly, Congress took an innovative approach to solving a problem by enacting the *Hotel and Motel Fire Safety Act of 1990* that does not preempt laws of state and local governments or impose mandates on them.[16] The act seeks to encourage employees of the national government who travel on official business to stay in hotels and motels meeting the guidelines contained in the *Federal Fire Prevention and Control Act of 1974*.[17] The 1990 act also stipulates that federal funds, including grants to state and local governments, may not be used to sponsor or pay for a meeting, convention, conference, or training seminar in a facility failing to meet federal fire safety guidelines.

A THEORY OF UNITED STATES FEDERALISM

The two widely publicized theories of federalism in the United States—dual and cooperative—are confined to national-state relations and inadequately explain such relations. National-state relations involve only part, although the most important part, of intergovernmental relations. Cooperative and friendly interstate relations are essential in a federal system where states possess broad and important reserved powers. Furthermore, a federal system exists within a number of states, such as New York and Illinois, where the state constitution devolves important powers upon general-purpose local governments. What is needed is a general theory of United States federalism incorporating a synthesis of elements of dual and cooperative federalism and new elements including an explanation of the employment of the political process by subnational governments to obtain preemption relief, and the coordination and accountability problems resulting from continuous changes in national-state-local relations.

The insufficiencies of dual and cooperative federalism theories are apparent in their neglect of the use of preemption and other coercive powers by Congress to induce subnational governments to comply with national policies or to prohibit the exercise of subnational regulatory powers.

Dual federalism is valid in postulating that Congress possesses a number of autonomous powers, but as a static model is inaccurate in suggesting that states possess many important regulatory powers free of potential formal and informal congressional encroachment. While the Twenty-first Amendment to the U.S. Constitution devolves to states complete authority over the importation, sale, and consumption of alcoholic beverages within their respective borders, Congress can control importation of alcoholic beverages into the United States, regulate interstate beverage shipments, and tax such beverages. In 1984, the U.S. Supreme Court in *Bacchus Imports, Limited v. Dias* opined that the amendment did not remove entirely from the ambit of the commerce clause state regulation of alcoholic beverages.[18] As explained in chapter 6, Congress employed a cross-over sanction to intrude into an area reserved to the states—minimum alcoholic beverage purchase age. Furthermore, states have nearly complete control over the structure and powers of their political subdivisions subject to provisions of their respective state constitutions, the U.S. Constitution, and congressional mandates.

The theory of cooperative federalism explains accurately that many types of national-state relations, including ones structured by preemption statutes, are cooperative in nature. It should be noted the theory implies the existence of autonomous and concurrent state powers (dual federalism) employable in cooperation with the national government to solve public problems.

Minimum standards partial preemption is premised on active state cooperation with the national government. Lacking adequate staff and other resources, the national government would be unable to implement its standards in the absence of state cooperation. With relatively few exceptions, states have applied for and accepted federal delegation of "regulatory primacy" and have not returned primacy to the concerned national agency.

In enacting complete preemption statutes, Congress assumes states will be cooperative and will not encroach upon the federal sphere of responsibility. In addition, several statutes have provisions for a limited turnback of regulatory authority and thereby are inherently cooperative in nature; a majority of the states have accepted such turnback of authority.

While retaining a degree of explanatory value, the theory of cooperative federalism fails to note the structuring of national-state relations by coercive use of formal statutory preemption, cross-cutting sanctions, cross-over sanctions, and tax sanctions. In historical perspective, the theory accurately explains a transitional phase between essentially a dual system and today's more coercive, although primarily cooperative, system. The current federal system should be viewed as a continuum in terms of national-state relations, ranging from nil to cooperative to coercive with the precise location of a given relationship on the continuum determined by the concerned functional component.

Central to a general theory of United States federalism is the premise there is no necessary optimal degree of centralization of decentralization of political powers within the nation. The theory also must be based in part on the premise vertical coordination problems are inherent in a system with functional assignments frequently shifting between planes of government. In addition, achievement of coordinated interplane implementation of national policies is hindered by congressional piecemeal enactment of partial preemption statutes distributing responsibilities to several federal administrative agencies for a single function.

Similarly, the theory must incorporate as a premise the inherent horizontal coordination problems on the national plane resulting from the unplanned proliferation of preemption statutes. Specifically, the most serious organizational problems are overlapping of responsibilities, lack of coordination by federal agencies, and rivalry among agencies resulting in wasted public resources and impediments to the achievement of congressional goals.

While the precise extent of malcoordination can be determined only by a comprehensive survey, evidence of coordination problems are contained in a number of official government reports, including ones issued by the U.S. government accountability office, and newspaper accounts.

Democratic theory posits the importance of establishing governmental and public officer responsibility to facilitate the ability of voters to hold governments and officers accountable for their actions and inactions. A general theory of federalism must explain the inherent accountability and responsibility problems caused by extensive enactment of congressional coercive statutes producing a constantly changeable intertwining of two or three planes of government relative to many functions and functional components.

As noted, extensive use of coercive powers by Congress paradoxically has increased and not reduced the exercise of political powers by states. The general theory must explain that political power in the national-state context in the United States is not a "zero-sum" system with an increase in the exercise of preemption power by Congress automatically resulting in a corresponding decrease in the exercisable reserved powers of states. With the exception of complete preemption statutes with no provisions for a turnback of regulatory authority, exercise of a preemption power generally has encouraged utilization of latent powers by all or most states.

A general theory of United States federalism must be a nonequilibrium one containing postulates relating to national-state relations, interstate relations, state-local relations in states with constitutions devolving powers on general-purpose local governments, such as Illinois and New York, and the role of the U.S. Supreme Court in adjudicating national-state and interstate disputes.

The nuances of complex national-state relations can be understood by viewing the federal system through a kaleidoscope whose revolving produces a continuous metamorphosis of the national political landscape with each piece of colored glass reflecting (1) the changing numbers and types of preemption statutes removing completely or partially regulatory powers from subnational governments and containing mandates and restraints, opt-in and opt-out provisions; (2) intertwining of national and state powers; (3) conditional grants-in-aid; (4) cross-cutting, cross-over, and tax sanctions; (5) administrative cooperation; (6) occasional preemption relief; and (7) congressional devolution of certain of its legislative powers to state legislatures, limited executive and administrative powers to governors affecting the gubernatorial-legislative balance of powers, and limited enforcement powers to attorneys general.

The kaleidoscopic view reveals congressional dependence upon states for implementation of many national policies. The views in the kaleidoscope are changed by the relative emphasis Congress places on its three roles— initiator, inhibitor, and facilitator—at any one time. The national-state kaleidoscope also can be tailored to an individual state to reflect the asymmetrical relations between the national government and each state.

The national-state kaleidoscope does not reveal the full complexity of the United States federal system. A comprehensive federalism theory also must include competitive, cooperative, and conflicting postulates pertaining to relations between sister states, and similar postulates relating to state-local relations in states with constitutional devolution of powers on general-purpose local governments.

CONCLUSIONS

Present-day concerns that the original constitutional balance of powers between states and Congress has been destroyed are specious to a degree since the framers of the U.S. Constitution were aware they were embarking on a new ship of state without accurate navigational instruments. They understood the importance of a fundamental document permitting mid-course changes in direction as experience was gained and new endogenous and exogenous developments occurred. Tensions between the national and state planes of government naturally arise in a system in which the national legislature today is the chief engineer with nearly complete authority to structure relations between the planes. Nevertheless, Congress is a partial government dependent on states for assistance, as explained in chapter 3.

"State' Righters" continue to protest the increased centralization of political powers in the national government, but their voices today are relatively muted compared to the protests of state and local government officers of the costs imposed on their units by federal mandates. Unreimbursed federal mandates, as noted in chapter 4, create serious problems for fiscally strained units and for subnational governments subject to strict state constitutional tax levy and debt limits. Minor relief has been provided by the *Unfunded Mandates Reform Act of 1995*.[19]

Although Congress in effect employs an "egg-beater" in restructuring intergovernmental relations that necessitates litigation on occasions for a determination of the scope of a preemption statute, congressional exercise of its plenary powers in a functional area generally has preserved a degree of political decentralization in policy making with states detailing policies within the framework of national statutes and administrative regulations, and has fostered nearly total decentralization of program administration. Minimum standards preemption has produced a degree of national uniformity in regulatory policies combined with diversity resulting from individual states adapting their regulatory policies to special conditions and their preferences in decision-making and implementation systems. Nevertheless, the federal system in the United States has become more coercive since 1965.

Congress approaches preempting state and local governmental regulatory authority on an ad hoc basis and has failed to conduct a comprehensive examination of the desirability and effectiveness of the various types of partial and complete preemption statutes. The results of its failure are problems of accountability, coordination, costs, effectiveness, and responsibility.

A strong argument can be made that Congress should rely more heavily on contingent preemption statutes to achieve national goals. A statute, for example, would not apply to a state or a local government unless the concerned government failed to meet national minimum standards. This type of preemption is similar to the current minimum standards preemption, but there is no need for a state to develop a plan for submission to a national department or agency for approval prior to exercising regulatory authority.

In sum intergovernmental relations, vertical and horizontal, have increased greatly in complexity since the mid-1960s; currently exhibit elements of coercion, conflict, and cooperation; and generally are based on a mutuality model with each plane relying on one or both of the other planes for their performance of certain essential functions.

Notes

PREFACE

1. Joseph F. Zimmerman, *Federal Preemption: The Silent Revolution* (Ames: Iowa State University Press, 1991).
2. Joseph F. Zimmerman, *Interstate Relations: The Neglected Dimension of Federalism* (Westport, CT: Praeger Publishers, 1996), and Joseph F. Zimmerman, *State-Local Relations: A Partnership Approach* (New York: Praeger Publishers, 1983).

CHAPTER 1

1. Daniel J. Elazar, *American Federalism: A View from the States*, 3rd ed. (New York: Harper & Row, Publishers, 1984), pp. 110–49.
2. Ibid., p. 115.
3. Ibid., p. 117.
4. Ibid., pp. 118–19.
5. Kenneth C. Wheare, *Federal Government*, 4th ed. (New York: Oxford University Press, 1964), p. 10.
6. Elazar, *American Federalism*, p. 2
7. Carl J. Friedrick, *Trends of Federalism in Theory and Practice* (New York: Frederick A. Praeger, 1968), p. 7.
8. Richard H. Leach, *American Federalism* (New York: W. W. Norton and Company, Incorporated, 1970), p. 2.
9. *The Federalist Papers* (New York: New American Library, 1961), p. 324.
10. Jack L. Walker, "The Diffusion of Innovations Among the American States," *American Political Science Review* 63, September 1969, pp. 880–99.
11. Friedrick, *Trends in Federalism in Theory and Practice*, p. 58.
12. Ibid.
13. Harold J. Laski, "The Obsolescence of Federalism," *The New Republic* 98 (May 1939), pp. 362–69, and Harold J. Laski, *The American Democracy: A Commentary and an Interpretation* (New York: The Viking Press, 1948), p. 139.

14. Edward S. Corwin, "The Passing of Dual Federalism," *Virginia Law Review* 36, February 1950, p. 4.
15. John C. Calhoun, *A Disquisition on Government* (New York: Political Science Classics, 1947).
16. Gaillard Hunt, ed., *The Writings of James Madison* (New York: G. P. Putnam's Sons, 1901), vol. II, pp. 332–33.
17. Daniel J. Elazar, *The American Partnership: Intergovernmental Cooperation in the Nineteenth Century United States* (Chicago: University of Chicago Press, 1962).
18. *South Carolina v. Baker*, U.S. 405 U.S. 505 at 1514, 108 S.Ct. 1355 at 1362 (1988).
19. Arthur N. Holcombe, "The Coercion of States in a Federal System." In MacMahon, Arthur W., ed., *Federalism: Mature and Emergent* (Garden City, NY: Doubleday and Company, 1955), p. 137.
20. *Water Quality Act of 1965*, 79 Stat. 903, 33 U.S.C. §1151.
21. Joseph F. Zimmerman, *Congressional Preemption: Regulatory Federalism* (Albany: State University of New York Press, 2005).

CHAPTER 2

1. Henry S. Commager, ed. *Documents of American History to 1898*, 8th ed. (New York: Appleton-Century-Crofts, 1968), vol. I, p. 120.
2. Ibid., pp. 128–32.
3. Martin Diamond, "What the Framers Meant by Federalism." In Goldwin, Robert A., ed., *A Nation of States: Essays on the American Federal System*, 2nd ed. (Chicago: Rand McNally College Publishing Company, 1974), p. 29.
4. Gaillard Hunt, ed. *The Writings of James Madison* (New York: G. P. Putnam's Sons, 1901), vol. II, p. 362.
5. Ibid., p. 365.
6. Max M. Farrand, ed., *The Records of the Constitutional Convention of 1789* (New Haven: Yale University Press, 1966), vol. II, p. 24.
7. Ibid., p. 27.
8. *Voting Rights Act of 1965*, 79 Stat. 437, 42 U.S.C. §1973.
9. Farrand, *The Records of the Constitutional Convention*, vol. II, p. 240.
10. Ibid., pp. 364–65.
11. Ibid., p. 362.
12. John P. Kaminski, and Gaspare J. Saladino, eds., *The Documentary History of the Ratification of the Constitution* (Madison: State Historical Society of Wisconsin, 1981), vol. XIII, p. 348.
13. *The Federalist Papers* (New York: New American Library, 1961), p. 246.
14. Ibid., p. 292
15. Ibid., p. 296
16. Ibid., p. 204.
17. Ralph Ketcham, ed., *The Antifederalist Papers and the Constitutional Convention* (New York: New American Library, 1986), pp. 270–310.
18. Ibid., p. 272.

19. Charles A. Beard, *An Economic Interpretation of the Constitution of the United States* (New York: The Macmillan Company, 1913).
20. William B. Munro, *The Government of the United States* (New York: The Macmillan Company, 1937), pp. 43–44.
21. Ibid., p. 44.
22. Robert E. Brown, *Charles Beard and the Constitution* (Princeton: Princeton University Press, 1956).
23. William H. Riker, *Federalism: Origin, Operation, Significance* (Boston: Little Brown and Company, 1964), pp. 17–20.
24. Ibid., p. 19.

CHAPTER 3

1. Vine Deloria Jr., and Clifford Little, *The Nations Within: The Past and Future of American Indian Sovereignty* (New York: Pantheon Books, 1984).
2. Gaillard Hunt, ed., *The Writings of James Madison* (New York: G. P. Putnam's Sons, 1901), vol. VI, p. 333.
3. *McCulloch v. Maryland*, 17 U.S. 316 at 421, 4 Wheaton 316 at 421 (1819).
4. *Noble State Bank v. Haskell*, 219 U.S. 104 at 111, 31 S.Ct. 193 at 200 (1911).
5. Joseph F. Zimmerman, *Pragmatic Federalism: The Reassignment of Functional Responsibility* (Washington, DC: U.S. Advisory Commission on Intergovernmental Relations, 1976).
6. *An Act to Establish a Uniform System of Bankruptcy of 1898*, 30 Stat. 544, 11 U.S.C. §1.
7. *McCarran-Ferguson Act of 1945*, 59 Stat. 33, 15 U.S.C. §1011.
8. *Calder v. Bull*, 3 U.S. 386, 3 Dallas 386 (1798).
9. *Dartmouth College v. Woodward*, 17 U.S. 518, 4 Wheaton 518 (1819).
10. *State v. Reese*, 91 U.S. 214, 2 Otto 214 (1875).
11. *Oregon v. Mitchell*, 400 U.S. 112, 91 S.Ct. 260 (1970).
12. Joseph F. Zimmerman, *The Silence of Congress: State Taxation of Interstate Commerce* (Albany: State University of New York Press, 2007).
13. Ibid.
14. *McCulloch v. Maryland*, 17 U.S. 316, 4 Wheaton 316 (1819).
15. 42 Stat. 1499 (1923).
16. 53 Stat. 574 (1939).
17. 5 Stat. 797 (1845).
18. *Pacific States Telephone and Telegraph Company v. Oregon*, 223 U.S. 118, 32 S.Ct. 224 (1912).
19. Joseph F. Zimmerman, *The Initiative: Citizen Law-Making* (Westport, CT: Praeger Publishers, 1999).
20. *Chisholm v. Georgia*, 2 U.S. 419, 2 Dallas 419 (1793).
21. Joseph F. Zimmerman, *The Recall: Tribunal of the People* (Westport, Ct: Praeger Publishers, 1997).
22. *Sterns v. Minnesota*, 179 U.S. 223, 21 S.Ct. 73 (1900).

23. *Coyle v.* Smith, 221 U.S. 559, 31 S.Ct. 688 (1911).
24. Zimmerman, *The Silence of Congress: State Taxation of Interstate Commerce.*
25. *State v. Reese,* 91 U.S. 214, 2 Otto 214(1875).
26. *Voting Rights Act of 1965,* 79 Stat. 437, 42 U.S.C. §1973.
27. *Marbury v. Madison,* 5 U.S. 137, 1 Cranch 137 (1803).
28. *Fletcher v. Peck,* 10 U.S. 87, 6 Cranch 84 (1810).
29. Gaillard Hunt, ed., *The Writings of James Madison* (New York: G.P. Putnam's Sons, 1901), vol. VIII, p. 451.
30. *McCulloch v. Maryland,* 17 U.S. 316 at 421, 4 Wheaton 316 at 421 (1819).
31. Woodrow Wilson, *Congressional Government: A Study in American Politics* (Boston: Houghton Mifflin Company, 1925), pp. 36–37.
32. *Missouri v. Holland,* 252 U.S. 416, 40 S.Ct. 382 (1920).
33. Daniel J. Elazar, *The American Partnership*: A View from the States (Chicago: University of Chicago Press, 1962).
34. *Lacey Act of 1900,* 31 Stat. 187, 16 U.S.C. §701.
35. *Contraband Cigarette Act of 1978,* 92 Stat, 2463, 18 U.S.C. §2341.
36. *Revenue Act of 1951,* 65 Stat. 452, 2 U.S.C. §31b.
37. *States v. Kahriger,* 345 U.S. 22, 73 S.Ct. 510 (1953).

CHAPTER 4

1. *Copyright Act of 1790,* 1 Stat. 124, 7 U.S.C. §301, and *Patent Act of 1790,* 1 Stat. 109, 35 U.S.C. §1.
2. *Consolidated Appropriations Act for Fiscal Year 2005,* 118 Stat. 418, 42 U.S.C. §7547(b-c); and *Satellite Home Viewer Extension and Reauthorization Act of 2004,* 118 Stat. 3393, 17 U.S.C. §101.
3. Joseph F. Zimmerman, *Congressional Preemption: Regulatory Federalism* (Albany: State University of New York Press, 2005).
4. *The Federalist Papers* (New York: New American Library, 1961), p. 292.
5. *Americans with Disabilities Act of 1990,* 104 Stat. 329, 42 U.S.C. §12101.
6. Robert H. Walker, ed., *The Reform Spirit in America: A Documentation* (New York: G. P. Putnam's Sons, 1979), pp. 25–26.
7. *An Act Relating to Lighthouses and Beacons of 1789,* 1 Stat. 1790.
8. W. Brooke Graves, ed., "Intergovernmental Relations in the United States," *The Annals of the American Academy of Political and Social Science* 207, January 1940, pp. 1–218.
9. Richard H. Leach, ed., "Intergovernmental Relations in America Today," *The Annals of the American Academy of Political and Social Science* 416, November 1974, pp. 1–169.
10. John Kincaid, ed., "American Federalism: The Third Century," *The Annals of the American Academy of Political and Social Science* 509, May 1990, pp. 11–152.
11. *Air Quality Act of 1967,* 81 Stat. 485, 42 U.S.C. §1857.
12. Zimmerman, *Congressional Preemption: Regulatory Federalism.* See also *Beyond Preemption: Intergovernmental Partnerships to Enhance the New Economy* (Washington, DC: National Academy of Public Administration, 2006).

13. Felix Morley, *Freedom and Federalism* (Chicago: Henry Regnery Company, 1959), p. 239.
14. Edward I. Koch, "The Mandate Millstone," *The Public Interest* 61, Fall 1980, p. 44.
15. Brevard Crihfield, and H. Clyde Reeves, "Intergovernmental Relations: A View from the States," *Annals of the American Academy of Political and Social Science* 416, November 1974, pp. 99–107.
16. *Policy Positions: 1980–81* (Washington, DC: National Governors' Association, 1980).
17. *Surface Transportation Assistance Act of 1982*, 96 Stat. 2097, 23 U.S.C. §101, and *Motor Vehicle Width Regulations of 1983*, 97 Stat. 59, 49 U.S.C. §2316.
18. *Commercial Motor Vehicle Safety Act of 1986*, 100 Stat. 3207, 49 U.S.C. §2701.
19. *Flammable Fabrics Act of 1967*, 81 Stat. 574, 15 U.S.C. §1191.
20. *Gun Control Act of 1968*, 82 Stat. 1226, 18 U.S.C. §921.
21. *Federal Railroad Safety Act of 1970*, 84 Stat. 972, 45 U.S.C. §431.
22. *Rice v. Santa Fe Elevator Corporation*, 331 U.S.218, 67 S.Ct. 1146 (1947).
23. *Ray v. Atlantic Richfield Company*, 435 U.S. 151, 98 S.Ct. 988 (1978).
24. *Oregon v. Mitchell*, 400 U.S. 112, 91 S.Ct. 260 (1971).
25. *National League of Cities v. Usery*, 426 U.S. 833, 96 S.Ct. 2465 (1976). See also *Fair Labor Standards Amendments of 1974*, 88 Stat. 55, 29 U.S.C. §203(d).
26. *Garcia v. San Antonio Metropolitan Transit Authority*, 469 U.S. 528, 105 S.Ct. 1005 (1985).
27. Joseph F. Zimmerman, "The Federal Voting Rights Act and Alternative Election Systems," *William & Mary Law Review* 19, Summer, 1978, pp. 621–60.
28. *Voting Rights Act Amendments of 1975*, 89 Stat. 438, 42 U.S.C. §1973.
29. *Hazardous Materials Transportation Uniform Safety Act of 1990*, 104 Stat. 3255, 49 App. U.S.C. §1801.
30. Zimmerman, *Congressional Preemption*, pp. 73–87.
31. *Safe Drinking Water Act Amendments of 1986*, 100 Stat. 651, 42 U.S.C. §300.
32. *Equal Employment Opportunity Act of 1972*, 86 Stat. 103, 42 U.S.C. §2000(e)(5); *Fair Labor Standards Amendments of 1974*, 88 Stat. 55, 29 U.S.C. §203(d); *Safe Drinking Water Act Amendments of 1986*, 100 Stat. 651, 42 U.S.C. §300; and *Federal Mine and Health Act of 1977*, 91 Stat. 1290, 30 U.S.C. §801.
33. *Low-Level Radioactive Waste Policy Act of 1980*, 94 Stat. 3347, 42 U.S.C. §2021d.
34. *Atlantic Striped Bass Conservation Act Amendments of 1986*, 100 Stat. 989, 16 U.S.C. §1851.
35. *Gramm-Leach-Bliley Financial Modernization Act of 1999*, 113 Stat. 1338, 12 U.S.C. §1811.
36. *Abandoned Shipwreck Act of 1987*, 102 Stat. 432, 43 U.S.C. §2101.
37. *Nuclear Waste Policy Act of 1982*, 96 Stat. 2217, 42 U.S.C. §10135.
38. *Omnibus Budget Reconciliation Act of 1988*, 98 Stat. 437, 23 U.S.C. §158.
39. *Yucca Mountain High Level Radioactive Waste Site Act of 2002*, 116 Stat.735, 42 U.S.C. §10135.
40. Joseph F. Zimmerman, *Federal Preemption: The Silent Revolution* (Ames: Iowa State University Press, 1991).
41. *Water Quality Act of 1965*, 79 Stat. 903, 33 U.S.C. §1151.

42. *Air Quality Act of* 1967, 81 Stat. 485, 42 U.S.C. §1857; *Safe Drinking Water Act of 1974,* 83 Stat. 1676, 42 U.S.C. §300; and *Surface Mining Control and Reclamation Act of 1977,* 91 Stat. 445, 30 U.S.C. §1201.
43. Letter to author from Chief Annello L. Check of the Division of Permit and Environmental Analysis of the U.S. Department of the Interior dated February 13, 1987, and letter to author from Acting Assistant Director for Program Support Richard G. Bryson of the Office of Surface Mining dated February 13, 2003.
44. Patricia M. Crotty, "The New Federalism Game: Options for the States." A paper presented at the annual meeting of the Northeastern Political Science Association, Philadelphia, November 14–16. 1985.
45. *Port and Tanker Safety Act of 1978,* 92 Stat. 11471, 33 U.S.C. §1221, 46 U.S.C. §214; and *National Gas Policy Act of 1978,* 92 Stat. 3351, 15 U.S.C. §3301, 42 U.S.C. §8201.
46. *Occupational Safety and Health Act of 1970,* 84 Stat. 1590, 5 U.S.C. §5108.
47. *Wholesome Meat Act of 1967,* 81 Stat. 584, 21 U.S.C. §601.
48. *Poultry Products Inspection Act of 1968,* 82 Stat. 791, 21 U.S.C. §451.
49. *Toxic Substances Control Act of 1976,* 90 Stat. 2038, 15 U.S.C. §2617.
50. *Environmental Pesticide Control Act of 1972,* 82 Stat. 973, 33 U.S.C. §1281.
51. *Cable Communications Policy Act of 1984,* 98 Stat. 2792, 47 U.S.C. §546.
52. *Coastal Zone Management Act of 1972,* 86 Stat. 1280, 16 U.S.C. §1451.
53. Joseph F. Zimmerman, "Federal Preemption Under Reagan's New Federalism," *Publius: The Journal of Federalism* 21, Winter 1991, pp. 7–28.
54. *Bus Regulatory Reform Act of 1982,* 96 Stat. 1104, 49 U.S.C. §10521; *Fair Credit and Charge Card Disclosure Act of 1988,* 102 Stat. 2960, 15 U.S.C. §1601; and *Ocean Dumping Ban Act of 1988,* 102 Stat. 4139, 33 U.S.C. §1401A.
55. *Clean Air Act Amendments of 1990,* 104 Stat. 2399, 42, U.S.C. §§7407, 7511c. See also Joseph F. Zimmerman, "Congressional Preemption During the George W. Bush Administration." *Publius: The Journal of Federalism* 37, Summer 2007, pp. 432–54.
56. *Riegle-Neal Interstate Banking and Branching Efficiency Act of 1994,* 108 Stat. 2338, 12 U.S.C. §1811; *Telecommunications Act of 1996,* 110 Stat. 56, 47 U.S.C. scattered sections; and *Gramm-Leach-Bliley Financial Modernization Act of 1999,* 113 Stat. 1338, 12 U.S.C. §1811.
57. *Internet Tax Freedom Act of 1998,* 112 Stat. 2860, 47 U.S.C. §151; *Internet Nondiscrimination Act of 2001,* 115 Stat. 703, 47 U.S.C. §609; and *Internet Tax Freedom Act of 2004,* 118 Stat. 2615, 47 U.S.C. §609.
58. Zimmerman, "Congressional Preemption During the George W. Bush Administration," pp. 1–21.
59. *Gibbons v. Ogden,* 22 U.S. 1 at 197, 4 Wheatton 1 at 197 (1824).
60. Herbert Wechsler, "The Political Safeguards of Federalism: The Role of the States in the Composition and Selection of the National Government," *Columbia Law Review* 54, 1953, pp. 543–60.
61. *Garcia v. San Antonio Metropolitan Transit Authority,* 469 U.S. 528 at 556, 105 S.Ct. 1007 at 1020 (1985).
62. *Surface Transportation Assistance Act of 1982,* 96 Stat. 2097, 23 U.S.C. §101; *Tandem Truck Safety Act of 1984,* 98 Stat. 2829, 42 U.S.C. §2301, and *Motor Carrier Safety Act of 1984,* 98 Stat. 2832, 42 U.S.C. §2501.

63. *Nuclear Waste Policy Act of 1982*, 96 Stat. 2217, 42 U.S.C. §10125; *Tax Reform Act of 1984*, 98 Stat. 494, 26 U.S.C. §1; *Virus, Serum, and Toxin Act Amendments of 1985*, 99 Stat. 1654, 21 U.S.C. §154a; *Competitive Equality Banking Act of 1987*, 101 Stat. 552, 12 U.S.C. §226; *Marine Plastic Pollution Research and Control Act of 1987*, 101 Stat. 1460, 33 U.S.C. §1901; and *Age Discrimination in Employment Amendments of 1986*, 100 Stat. 3342, 29 U.S.C. §623.
64. *Parker v. Brown*, 317 U.S. 341, 63 S.Ct. 307 (1943).
65. *City of Lafayette v. Louisiana Power and Light Company*, 435 U.S. 389 at 416, 98 S.Ct. 1123 at 1138 (1978).
66. *Community Communications Corporation v. City of Boulder*, 455 U.S. 40, 102 S.Ct. 835 (1982).
67. *Local Government Antitrust Act of 1984*, 98 Stat. 2750, 15 U.S.C. §34.
68. *National League of Cities v. Usery*, 426 U.S. 833, 96 S.Ct. 2465 (1975).
69. *Garcia v. San Antonio Metropolitan Transit Authority*, 469 U.S. 528, 105 S.Ct. 1005 (1985).
70. *Fair Labor Standards Amendments of 1985*, 99 Stat. 787, 29 U.S.C. §201.
71. Howard H. Baker, Jr., *Hearing Before the Subcommittee on Air and Water Pollution of the Committee on Public Works, United States Senate on "Problems and Progress Associated with Control of Automobile Exhaust Emissions"* (Washington, D.C: U.S. Government Printing Office, 1967), p. 116.
72. *Voting Rights Act of 1965*, 79 Stat. 437, 42 U.S.C. §1973, and *Hazardous Material Transportation Uniform Safety Act of 1990*, 104 Stat. 3244, 49 App. U.S.C. §1801.
73. *Congressional Record*, May 25, 1983, pp. S 7556–567.
74. *Tandem Truck Safety Act of 1984*, 98 Stat. 2829, 42 U.S.C. §2301; and *Surface Transportation Assistance Act of 1982*, 96 Stat. 2097, 23 U.S.C. §101.
75. *Environmental Pesticide Control Act of 1972*, 82 Stat. 973, 33 U.S.C. §1281.
76. *National Health Planning and Resources Development Act of 1974*, 88 Stat. 2247, 42 U.S.C. §300m-3.
77. *Safe Drinking Water Act of 1974*, 88 Stat.1676, 42 U.S.C. §300.
78. *Metal and Nonmetallic Mine Safety Act of 1966*, 80 Stat. 783, 42 U.S.C. §2011.
79. *Wholesome Meat Act of 1967*, 81 Stat, 595, 21 U.S.C. §71.
80. *Water Pollution Control Act Amendments of 1972*, 86 Stat. 816, 33 U.S.C. §1151.
81. Joseph F. Zimmerman, *Federally Induced Costs Affecting State and Local Governments* (Washington, DC: U.S. Advisory Commission on Intergovernmental Relations, 1990).
82. *Safe Drinking Water Act Amendments of 1986*, 100 Stat. 651, 42 U.S.C. §300.
83. Sector Study Committee, *Municipalities, Small Business, and Agriculture: The Challenge of Meeting Environmental Responsibilities* (Washington, DC: U.S. Environmental Protection Agency, 1988), pp. 2–19.
84. *Safe Drinking Water Act Amendments of 1996*, 110 Stat. 1613, 42 U.S.C. §300f.
85. House Committee on Education and Labor, *Report to Accompany H.R. 3530, 99th Congress, 1st Session* (Washington, DC: U.S. Government Printing Office, 1985), p. 30.
86. *Fair Labor Standards Amendments of 1985*, 99 Stat. 787, 129 U.S.C. §201.
87. *Asbestos Hazard Emergency Response Act of 1986*, 100 Stat. 2970, 15 U.S.C. §2641.
88. *Tax Equity and Fiscal Responsibility Act of 1982*, 96 Stat. 324, 26 U.S.C. §1.

89. *Low-Level Radioactive Policy Act of 1980*, 94 Stat. 3347, 42 U.S.C. §2021d.
90. *Airline Deregulation Act of 1978*, 92 Stat. 1708, 49 U.S.C. §1305.
91. *Bus Regulatory Reform Act of 1982*, 96 Stat. 1104, 49 U.S.C. §10521.
92. *Omnibus Budget Reconciliation Act for Fiscal Year 1986*, 98 Stat. 437, 23 U.S.C. §158.
93. *Social Security Act of 1935*, 49 Stat. 620.
94. *Social Security Amendments of 1983*, 97 Stat. 71, 42 U.S.C. §418.
95. *Age Discrimination in Employment Act of 1967*, 81 Stat. 602, 29 U.S.C. §621, and *Age Discrimination in Employment Act Amendments of 1986*, 100 Stat. 1874, 29 U.S.C. §621.
96. *Age Discrimination in Employment Act Amendments of 1986*, 100 Stat. 3342, 29 U.S.C. §623.
97. *Marine Protection Research and Sanctuaries Act of 1972*, 86 Stat. 1052, 33 U.S.C. §1401.
98. *Ocean Dumping Ban Act of 1988*, 102 Stat. 4139, 33 U.S.C. §1401A.
99. *Atomic Energy Act of 1954*, 68 Stat. 9191, 42 U.S.C §2011.

CHAPTER 5

1. *The Federalist Papers* (New York: New American Library, 1961), p. 476.
2. Ibid., p. 485.
3. *Judiciary Act of 1789*, 1 Stat. 73 at 90–91, 28 U.S.C. §1251(a). See also Joseph F. Zimmerman, *Interstate Disputes: The Supreme Court's Original Jurisdiction* (Albany: State University of New York Press, 2006).
4. *Houston v. Moore*, 18 U.S. 1, 5 Wheaton 1 (1820).
5. *Chisholm v. Georgia*, 2 U.S. 419, 2 Dallas 419 (1793).
6. *The Federalist Papers*, pp. 227 and 229.
7. William B. Munro, *The Government of the United States* (New York: The Macmillan Company, 1937), p. 514.
8. Morris Dees, "Finding the Forum for Victory," *National Law Review* 13, February 11, 1991, pp. S3–4.
9. *Removal of Causes Act of 1920*, 41 Stat. 554, 28 U.S.C. §1441. The removal clause dates to the *Judiciary Act of 1789*, 1 Stat. 73.
10. John W. Winkle, III, "Dimensions of Judicial Federalism," *The Annals of the American Academy of Political and Social Science* 416, November 1974, pp. 67–76.
11. James T. Young, *The New American Government and Its Work* (New York: The Macmillan Company, 1935), p. 182.
12. George B. Braden, "Umpire to the Federal System," *The University of Chicago Law Review* 10, October 1942, p. 45.
13. *Hines v. Davidowitz*, 312 U.S. 52 at 67, 61S.Ct. 399 (1941).
14. *Rice v. Santa Fe Elevator Corporation*, 331 U.S. 218, 67 S.Ct. 1146 (1941).
15. *City of Burbank v. Lockheed Air Terminal Incorporated*, 411 U.S. 624 at 632, 93 S.Ct. 1854 at 1859 (1978).
16. *Hodel v. Virginia Surface Mining and Reclamation Association*, 452 U.S. 264 at 287, 101 S.Ct. 2352 at 2365 (1981). See also *Surface Mining Control and Reclamation Act of 1977*, 91 Stat. 445, 30 U.S.C. §1201.

17. *Older Workers Benefit Protection Act of 1990*, 104 Stat. 978, 19 U.S.C. §621, and *Public Employee Retirement System of Ohio v. Betts*, 492 U.S. 158, 109 S.Ct. 2854 (1989).

18. *The Federalist Papers*, p. 568.

19. Munro, *The Government of the United States*, pp. 53–81.

20. *The Federalist Papers*, pp. 465–66.

21. *Marbury v. Madison*, 5 U.S. 137, 1 Cranch 137 (1803).

22. *Fletcher v. Peck*, 10 U.S. 87, 6 Cranch 87 (1810).

23. *McCulloch v. Maryland*, 17 U.S. 316 at 421, 4 Wheaton 316 at 421 (1819).

24. *Gibbons v. Ogden*, 22 U.S. 1, 9 Wheaton 1 (1824).

25. *Brown v. Maryland*, 25 U.S. 419, 12 Wheaton 419 (1927).

26. Munro, *The Government of the United States*, p. 55.

27. *Cohens v. Virginia*, 19 U.S. 264 at 380, 6 Wheaton 264 at 380 (1821).

28. *Briscoe v. Bank of the Commonwealth of Kentucky*, 36 U.S. 257 at 326, 11 Peters 257 at 326 1837).

29. *Charles River Bridge v. Warren Bridge*, 36 U.S. 420, 11 Peters 420 (1837).

30. *Cooley v. The Board of Wardens of the Port of Philadelphia*, 53 U.S. 299, 12 Howard 299 (1851).

31. 1 Stat. 54 (1789). See also the *Shipping Statute of 1983*, 97 Stat. 553, 46 U.S.C. §8501.

32. *Dred Scott v. Sanford*, 60 U.S. 393 at 405, 19 Howard 393 at 405 (1857).

33. *Civil Rights Act of 1866*, 14 Stat. 27, 42 U.S.C. §1981.

34. *Texas v. White*, 74 U.S. 700, 7 Wallace 700 (1869).

35. *Hammer v. Dagenhart*, 247 U.S. 251, 38 S.Ct. 529 (1918).

36. *Carter v. Carter Coal Company*, 298 U.S. 238 at 308, 56 S.Ct. 855 at 871 (1936).

37. *Plessy v. Ferguson*, 163 U.S. 537, 16 S.Ct. 1138 (1896).

38. *West Cost Hotel Company v. Parrish*, 300 U.S. 379, 47 S.Ct. 578 (1937).

39. *Virginian Railway v. System Federation No. 40*, 300 U.S. 515, 57 S.Ct. 592 (1937). See also the *Railway Labor Act of 1926*, 44 Stat. 557, 45 U.S.C. §151.

40. *National Labor Relations Board v. Jones & Laughlin Steel Corporation*, 301 U.S. 1, 57 S.Ct. 615 (1937).

41. *United States v. Carolene Products Company*, 304 U.S. 144 at 152, 58 S.Ct. 778 at 784 (1938).

42. *Fair Labor Standards Act of 1938*, 52 Stat. 1060, 29 U.S.C. §301.

43. *Brown v. Board of Education*, 347 U.S. 483, 74 S.Ct. 686 (1954).

44. *Katzenbach v. McClung*, 379 U.S. 294, 85 S.Ct. 377 (1964).

45. *South Carolina v. Katzenbach*, 383 U.S. 301, 86 S.Ct. 803 (1966).

46. *Voting Rights Act Amendments of 1975*, 89 Stat. 438, 42 U.S.C. §1973. See also *Voting Rights Language Assistance Act of 1992*, 106 Stat. 921, 42 U.S.C. §1071.

47. *United States v. Reese*, 92 U.S. 214, 2 Otto 214 (1875).

48. *Palko v. Connecticut*, 302 U.S. 319, 58 S.Ct. 149 (1937).

49. *Malloy v. Hogan*, 378 U.S.1, 84 S.Ct. 1489 (1964).

50. Ibid.

51. *Miranda v. Arizona* 384 U.S. 436, 86 S.Ct. 1602 (1966).

52. *Baker v. Carr*, 369 U.S. 186, 82 S.Ct. 691 (1962).

53. *Gray v. Sanders*, 372 U.S. 368, 83 S.Ct. 801 (1963).

54. *Reynolds v. Sims*, 377 U.S. 533, 95 S.Ct. 751 (1964).
55. *Chapman v. Meiers*, 420 U.S. 1, 95 S.Ct. 751 (1975).
56. *Avery v. Midland County*, 390 U.S. 474, 88 S.Ct. 111 (1968).
57. *League of Latin American Citizens v. Perry*, 126 S.Ct. 2594 (2006).
58. *Gordon v. Lance*, 403 U.S.1, 91 S.Ct. 1889 (1971).
59. *Buckley v. Valeo*, 424 U.S. 1 at 143, 96 S.Ct. 612 at 693 (1976). See also the *Federal Election Campaign Act of 1971*, 85 Stat. 3, 2 U.S.C. §§431–41, and *Federal Election Campaign Act Amendments of 1974*, 88 Stat. 1263, 2 U.S.C. §§431–37.
60. *Buckley v. Valeo*, 424 U.S. 1 at 39, 96 S.Ct. 612 at 644.
61. Ibid., 424 U.S. 1 at 52, 96 S.Ct. 612 at 651.
62. Ibid., 424 U.S. 1 at 52–53, 96 S.Ct. 612 at 651.
63. *First National Bank of Boston et al. v. Bellotti*, 435 U.S. 765, 98 S.Ct. 1407 (1978).
64. *Randall v. Sorrell*, 126 S.Ct. 2479, 165 L.Ed. 482 (2006). See also Vermont *Public Act 64 of 1997*, 17 V.S.A. §§2801 *et seq.*
65. Joseph F. Zimmerman, "Election Systems and Representative Democracy: Reflections on the Voting Rights Act of 1965," *National Civic Review* 84, Fall/Winter 1995, pp. 287–309.
66. *Perkins v. Matthew*, 400 U.S. 379, 91 S.Ct. 431 (1971).
67. *City of Richmond v. United States*, 422 U.S. 358, 95 S.Ct. 2296 (1975).
68. *Clark v. Roemer*, 500 U.S. 646, 111 S.Ct. 2096 (1991).
69. *Gitlow v. New York*, 268 U.S. 652 at 666, 45 S.Ct. 625 at 630 (1925).
70. *Palko v. Connecticut*, 302 U.S. 319 at 324–25, 58 S.Ct. 149 at 151 (1937).
71. *Malloy v. Hogan*, 378 U.S.1, 84 S.Ct. 1489 (1964).
72. *Duncan v. Louisiana*, 391 U.S. 145, 88 S.Ct. 1444 (1968).
73. *Brown v. Board of Education*, 349 U.S. 294, 75 S.Ct. 753 (1955).
74. *Memorandum Regarding Final Orders: Civil Action No. 72–911–G* (Boston: U.S. District Court, 1985).
75. Joseph F. Zimmerman, "Federal Judicial Remedial Power: The Yonkers Case," *Publius: The Journal of Federalism* 20, Summer 1990, pp. 45–61.
76. *U.S. Constitution*, Art. I, §6.
77. *Tenney et al. v. Bandhove*, 341 U.S. 367, 71 S.Ct. 783 (1951), and *Lake County Estates, Incorporated v. Tahoe Regional Planning Agency*, 440 U.S. 391, 99 S.Ct. 1171 (1979).
78. *Spallone v. United States*, 493 U.S. 265, 110 S.Ct. 625 (1990).
79. Ibid., 493 U.S. 265 at 280, 110 S.Ct. 625 at 634–35.
80. *Fair Labor Standards Amendments of 1974*, 88 Stat. 55, 29 U.S.C. §203(d), and *National League of Cities v. Usery*, 426 U.S. 833, 96 S.Ct. 2465 (1976).
81. *Washington v. Davis*, 426 U.S. 229, 96 S.Ct. 2040 (1976).
82. *Village of Arlington Heights et al. v. Metropolitan Housing Development Corporation*, 429 U.S. 252, 97 S.Ct. 555 (1977).
83. *Maine v. Thiboutot*, 448 U.S. 1, 100 S.Ct. 2502 (1980), and *Owen v. City of Independence*, 445 U.S. 622, 100 S.Ct. 1389 (1980).
84. *Federal Energy Regulatory Commission v. Mississippi*, 456 U.S. 742, 102 S.Ct. 2126 (1982). See the *Public Utility Regulatory Policies Act of 1978*, 92 Stat. 3117, 16 U.S.C. §2601.
85. *Garcia v. San Antonio Metropolitan Transit Authority*, 469 U.S. 528, 105 S.Ct. 1005 (1985).

86. *Folie v. Connelie*, 435 U.S. 291, 98 S.Ct. 1067 (1978).
87. *Michigan Department of State Police v. Sitz*, 496 U.S. 444 110 S.Ct. 2481 (1990); *Oregon Department of Human Resources v. Smith*, 494 U.S. 872, 110 S.Ct. 1595 (1990); and *North Dakota v. United States*, 495 U.S. 423, 110 S.Ct.1986 (1990).
88. *Gregory v. Ashcroft*, 501 U.S. 452, 111 S.Ct. 1295 (1991); *Barnes v. Glen Theatre*, 501 U.S. 560, 111 S.Ct. 2456 (1991); and *Wisconsin Public Intervenor v. Mortier*, 501 U.S. 597, 111 S.Ct. 2476 (1991). See also the *Insecticide, Fungicide, and Rodenticide Act of 1975*, 89 Stat. 751, 7 U.S.C. §136.
89. *United States v.* Lopez, 540 U.S. 549 at 567, 115 S.Ct. 1624 at 1634 (1995), and the *Gun-Free School Zones Act of 1990*, 104 Stat. 4844, 18 U.S.C. §922(q)(2)(A).
90. *Prinz v. United States*, 521 U.S. 898, 117 S.Ct. 2365 (1997), and *Brady Handgun Violence Prevention Act of 1993*, 107 Stat. 1536, 18 U.S.C. §921.
91. *Seminole Tribe of Florida v. Florida*, 517 U.S. 44 at 76, 116 S.Ct. 1114 at 1133 (1996), and *Indian Gaming Regulatory Act of 1988*, 108 Stat. 2472, 25 U.S.C. §2710(d)(3).
92. *Rhode Island Department of Environmental Management v. United States*, 304 F.3d 31 (1st Cir. 2002).
93. *Federal Maritime Commission v. South Carolina State Ports Authority*, 535 U.S. 743, 122 S.Ct. 1864 (2002).
94. *Lapides v. Board of Regents of the University System of Georgia*, 535 U.S. 613, 122 S.Ct. 1640 (2002). See also the *Removal of Causes Act of 1920*, 41 Stat. 554, 28 U.S.C. §1441.
95. *United States v. Morrison*, 329 U.S. 598 at 618, 120 S.Ct. 1740 at 1753 (2000), and *Civil Rights Remedies for Gender-Motivated Violence Act of 1994*, 108 Stat. 1941, 42 U.S.C. §12981.
96. *Central Virginia Community College v. Katz*, 546 U.S. 356, 126 S.Ct. 990 (2006).
97. *United States v. Georgia*, 546 U.S. 151, 126 S.Ct. 877 (2006).
98. Edwin Meese, III, "The Attorney General's View of the Supreme Court: Toward a Jurisprudence of Original Intention," *Public Administration Review* 45, November 1985, p. 704.
99. William J. Brennan Jr., "The Constitution of the United States: Contemporary Ratification," a paper presented at a text and teaching symposium, Georgetown University, Washington, DC, October 12, 1985.
100. Robert H. Bork, "The Constitution, Original Intent, and Economic Rights," an address presented at the University of San Diego Law School, November 18, 1985, p. 8.
101. Ibid.

CHAPTER 6

1. *State and Local Government Finances by Level of Government and by State: 2003–04* (Washington, DC: U.S. Bureau of the Census, 2004).
2. Joseph F. Zimmerman, *The Silence of Congress: State Taxation of Interstate Commerce* (Albany: State University of New York Press, 2007).

3. Joseph F. Zimmerman. *State-Local Relations: A Partnership Approach*, 2nd ed (Westport, CT: Praeger Publishers, 1995), pp. 53–60.

4. *McCulloch v. Maryland*, 17 U.S. 516, 4 Wheaton 516 (1819).

5. *Weston v. Charleston*, 27 U.S. 449, 2 Peters 449 (1829).

6. *Collector v. Day*, 78 U.S. 113 at 127, 11 Wallace 113 at 127 (1870).

7. *Pollock v. Farmers Loan and Trust Company*, 157 U.S. 429, 15 S.Ct. 673 (1895).

8. *Brushaber v. Union Pacific Rail Road Company*, 240 U.S. 1, 36 S.Ct. 236 (1916).

9. *South Carolina v. United States*, 199 U.S. 437, 26 S.Ct. 110 (1905),

10. *New York v. United States*, 326 U.S. 572, 66 S.Ct. 310 (1946).

11. *Gillespie v. Oklahoma*, 257 U.S. 501, 42 S.Ct. 171 (1922).

12. *Panhandle Oil Company v. Knox*, 277 U.S 218, 48 S.Ct. 451 (1928), and *Indian Motorcycle Company v. United States*, 283 U.S 570, 51 S.Ct 601 (1931).

13. *Metcalf & Eddy v. Mitchell*, 269 U.S. 514, 46 S.Ct. 172 (1926), and *Willicuts v. Bunn*, 282 U.S. 216, 51 S.Ct. 125 (1931).

14. *James v. Dravo Contracting Company*, 302 U.S. 134, 58 S.Ct. 208 (1937).

15. *Helvering v. Gerhardt*, 304 U.S. 405, 58 S.Ct. 969 (1938).

16. *Graves v. New York*, 306 U.S. 466, 59 S.Ct. 595 (1939).

17. *Public Salary Act of 1939*, 53 Stat. 574, 4 U.S.C. §111.

18. *Buck Act of 1940*, 54 Stat. 1059, 4 U.S.C. §§105–10.

19. *Van Allen v. Assessors*, 70 U.S. 573, 3 Wallace 573 (1866), and *First National Bank v. Anderson*, 290 U.S. 341, 46 S.Ct. 135 (1926).

20. *Graves v. New York*, 306 U.S. 466 at 477, 59 S.Ct. 595 at 596–97.

21. *Shaffer v. Carter*, 252 U.S. 37, 40 S.Ct. 221 (1920).

22. *Travis v. Yale & Towne Manufacturing Company*, 252 U.S. 60, 40 S.Ct. 228 (1920).

23. *Austin v. New Hampshire*, 420 U.S. 656, 95 S.Ct. 1191 (1975).

24. *Alcan Aluminum Limited v. Franchise Tax Board of California*, 1987 WL 153861 (N.D. Ill. 1987).

25. *Alcan Aluminum Limited v. Franchise Board of California*, 860 F.2d 688, 47 USWL 2289 (7th Cir., 1988).

26. *Franchise Tax Board of California v. Alcan Aluminum*, 493 U.S. 331, 110 S.Ct. 661 (1990). See the *Tax Injunction Act of 1937*, 50 Stat. 738, 28 U.S.C. §1341.

27. *Allied Signal, Incorporated v. Director, Division of Taxation*, 504 U.S. 768, 112 S.Ct. 2251 (1992).

28. "An Ordinance for Ascertaining the Mode of Disposing of Lands in the Western Territory," *Journal of the American Congress, from 1774 to 1788* (Washington, DC: 1823), pp. 395–400. See in particular, p. 398.

29. 1 Stat. 138 (1790).

30. 2 Stat. 490 (1808).

31. 5 Stat. 201 (1837).

32. 2 Stat. 225 (1803).

33. 3 Stat. 430 (1818).

34. *Morrill Act of 1862*, 12 Stat. 503.

35. *McGee v. Mathias*, 71 U.S. 143, 4 Wallace 143 (1866).

36. *Massachusetts v. Mellon*, 262 U.S. 447, 43 S.Ct. 597 (1923).

37. *Hatch Act of 1887*, 24 Stat. 440, 7 U.S.C. §362.

38. *Carey Act of 1894*, 28 Stat. 422, 43 U.S.C. §641.

39. *Weeks Act of 1911*, 36 Stat. 961, 16 U.S.C. §552.
40. *Federal Road Aid Act of 1916*, 39 Stat. 355.
41. 42 Stat. 212 (1921).
42. *Social Security Act of 1935*, 49 Stat. 620, 42 U.S.C. §301.
43. *Hatch Act of 1939*, 53 Stat. 1147, 5 U.S.C. §118i, and *Hatch Act of 1940*, 54 Stat. 767, 5 U.S.C. §118i.
44. Joseph P. Harris, "The Future of Federal Grants-in-Aid," *The Annals of the American Academy of Political and Social Science* 207, January 1940, p. 14.
45. *Federal Road Aid Act of 1916*, 39 Stat. 355.
46. *United States Housing Act of 1937*, 50 Stat. 888, 12 U.S.C. §1701.
47. *Fiscal Balance in the American Federal System* (Washington, DC: U.S. Advisory Commission on Intergovernmental Relations, 1981). See also Carl W. Stenberg, *State Involvement in Federal-Local Grant Programs: A Case Study of the "Buying In" Approach* (Washington, DC: U.S. Advisory Commission on Intergovernmental Relations, 1970).
48. *National Interstate and Defense Highways Act of 1956*, 70 Stat. 374, 23 U.S.C. §101.
49. Carl W. Stenberg, "Federal-Local Relations in a Cutback Environment: Issues and Future Directions," a paper presented at the annual conference of the American Politics Group of the United Kingdom Political Studies Association, Manchester, England, January 4, 1980.
50. *Indiana Laws of 1947*, chap. 377.
51. *Categorical Grants: Their Role and Design: An Assessment and Proposed Policies* (Washington, DC: U.S. Advisory Commission on Intergovernmental Relations, 1978), p. 42.
52. Ibid., pp. 52–53.
53. Stenberg, "Federal-Local Relations," p. 13.
54. W. Brooke Graves, *American Intergovernmental Relations: Their Origins, Historical Development, and Current Status* (New York: Charles Scribner's Sons, 1964), pp. 808–09.
55. David B. Walker, *Toward a Functioning Federalism* (Cambridge, MA: Winthrop Publishers, 1981), p. 220.
56. Ibid., p. 122.
57. The Commission on the Organization of the Executive Branch of Government, *Oversees Administration, Federal-State Relations, Federal Research* (Washington, DC: U.S. Government Printing Office, 1949), p. 36. See also the *Partnership for Health Act of 1966* contained in the *Comprehensive Health Planning and Public Health Services Amendments of 1966*, 80 Stat. 1180, 42 U.S.C. §§243, 246.
58. Michael D. Reagan and John. G. Sanzone, *The New Federalism*, 2nd ed. (New York: Oxford University Press, 1981), pp. 129–30.
59. *Housing and Community Development Act of 1974*, 88 Stat. 633, 42 U.S.C. §5301.
60. *Omnibus Budget Reconciliation Act of 1981*, 95 Stat. 357.
61. *Community Development: Oversight of Block Grant Monitoring Needs Improvement* (Washington, DC: U.S. General Accounting Office, 1991), p. 9.
62. *State and Local Fiscal Assistance Act of 1972*, 86 Stat. 919, 33 U.S.C. §1221.
63. U.S. Bureau of the Census, *Expenditures of General Revenue Sharing and Antirecession Fiscal Assistance Funds: 1977–78* (Washington, DC: U.S. Government Printing Office, 1980), pp. 97, 99, 102–03, and 105.

64. *How Revenue Sharing Formulas Distribute Aid: Urban-Rural Implications* (Washington, D.C.: U.S. General Accounting Office, 1980).
65. *Clean Air Act Amendments of 1990*, 104 Stat. 2399, 42 U.S.C. §§7407, 7511c.
66. *Riegle-Neal Interstate Banking and Branching Efficiency Act of 1994*, 108 Stat. 2338, 12 U.S.C. §1811; *Telecommunications Act of 1966*, 110 Stat. 56, 47 U.S.C §223; and *Gramm-Leach-Bliley Financial Modernization Act of 1999*, 113 Stat. 1338, 12 U.S.C. §1811.
67. *Weekly Compilation of Presidential Documents* 37, March 5, 2001, p. 344.
68. *Internet Nondiscrimination Act of 2001*, 115 Stat. 703, 47 U.S.C. §609, and *Internet Tax Freedom Act of 2004*, 118 Stat. 2615, 47 U.S.C. §609.
69. *Water Quality Act of 1965*, 79 Stat. 903, 33 U.S.C. §1151.
70. Joseph F. Zimmerman, *The Initiative: Citizen Law-Making* (Westport, CT: Praeger Publishers, 1999).
71. *Omnibus Budget Reconciliation Act of 1990*, 104 Stat. 1388.
72. *Revenue and Expenditure Control Act of 1968*, 82 Stat. 251, 26 U.S.C. §103(c).
73. *Mortgage Subsidy Bond Tax Act of 1983*, 94 Stat. 2599, 26 U.S.C. §103(a).
74. *Social Security Act Amendments of 1983*, 97 Stat. 65, 42 U.S.C. §418.
75. *Deficit Reduction Act of 1984*, 98 Stat. 494, 26 U.S.C. §1.
76. *Tax Reform Act of 1986*, 100 Stat. 2085, 26 U.S.C. §1.
77. Ibid.
78. *South Carolina v. Baker*, 485 U.S. 505 at 521–22, 108 S.Ct. 1355 at 1366–367 (1988).
79. *Revenue Act of 1926*, 44 Stat. 9, 48 U.S.C. §845.
80. *Social Security Act of 1935*, 49 Stat. 620, 42 U.S.C. §301.
81. *Economic Recovery Tax Act of 1981*, 95 Stat. 399, 26 U.S.C. §103.
82. "Fighting Federal Mandates," *New York Times*, August 16, 1980, p. 20.
83. *Unfunded Mandates Reform Act of 1995*, 109 Stat. 48, 2 U.S.C. §1501.
84. John C. Eastman, "Re-entering the Arena: Restoring a Judicial Role for Enforcing Limits on Federal Mandates," *Harvard Journal of Law & Public Policy* 25, Summer 2002, p. 952.
85. *Bus Regulatory Reform Act of 1982*, 96 Stat. 1104, 49 U.S.C. §10521.
86. *Federal Road Aid Act of 1921*, 42 Stat. 212, and *Federal Road Aid Act of 1916*, 39 Stat. 355.
87. *Emergency Highway Energy Conservation Act of 1974*, 87 Stat. 1046, 23 U.S.C. §154.
88. *Energy Policy and Conservation Act of 1975*, 89 Stat. 933, 42 U.S.C. §6201.
89. *National Minimum Drinking Age Amendments of 1984*, 98 Stat. 437, 23 U.S.C. §158.
90. *South Dakota v. Dole*, 483 U.S. 203, 107 S.Ct. 1793 (1988).
91. *State Comprehensive Mental Health Services Plan Act of 1986*, 100 Stat. 3494, 42 U.S.C. §201.
92. *Department of Transportation and Related Agencies Appropriations Act for Fiscal Year 1991*, 104 Stat. 2184, 23 U.S.C. §104.
93. *Department of Transportation and Related Agencies Appropriations Act for Fiscal Year 1992*, 105 Stat. 944, 23 U.S.C. §159.
94. *Transportation Equity Act for the 21st Century of 1998*, 112 Stat. 126, 23 U.S.C. §159.
95. *Tax Equity and Fiscal Responsibility Act of 1982*, 96 Stat. 324, 26 U.S.C. §1.
96. *South Carolina v. Baker*, 485 U.S. 505, 108 S.Ct. 1355 (1988).
97. *Tax Reform Act of 1986*, 100 Stat. 2085, 26 U.S.C. §1.

CHAPTER 7

1. *Judiciary Act of 1789*, 1 Stat. 80–81.

2. Joseph F. Zimmerman, *Interstate Disputes: The Supreme Court's Original Jurisdiction* (Albany: State University of New York Press, 2006), pp. 30–34.

3. Donald Janson, "Iowa Is Called Aggressor State: Nebraska Fears Shooting War," *New York Times*, July 26, 1964, pp. 1, 24.

4. *Ohio v. Kentucky*, 444 U.S. 335, 100 S.Ct. 599 (1980).

5. *South Dakota v. Nebraska*, 458 U.S. 276, 102 S.Ct. 3477 (1982).

6. *Georgia v. South Carolina*, 497 U.S. 376, 110 S.Ct. 2903 (1990).

7. *Illinois v. Kentucky*, 500 U.S. 380, 222 S.Ct. 1877 (1991).

8. *New Jersey Laws of 1833–34*, pp. 118–21; *New York Laws of 1834*, chap. 8; and *New Jersey v. New York*, 526 U.S. 589, 119 S.Ct. 1743 (1999).

9. *Missouri v. Illinois*, 200 U.S. 496 at 521–22, 26 S.Ct. 268 at 270 (1906).

10. *Kansas v. Colorado*, 185 U.S. 125, 22 S.Ct. 552 (1902); 206 U.S. 46 at 114–17, 27 S.Ct. 46 (1907); and 320 U.S. 383, 64 S.Ct. 176 at 184 (1943).

11. *Arkansas River Compact of 1949*, 63 Stat. 145.

12. *Kansas v. Colorado*, 514 U.S. 673 at 685, 115 S.Ct. 1733 at 1743 (1995).

13. *Arizona v. California*, 373 U.S.546 at 594, 83 S.Ct.1468 at 1494–495 (1963).

14. 13 Stat. 731 (1863).

15. *Virginia v. West Virginia*, 246 U.S. 565 at 594–95, 38 S.Ct. 400 at 403 (1918).

16. *Texas v. New Jersey*, 379 U.S. 674 at 680–81, 85 S.Ct. 626 at 630 (1965).

17. *Pennsylvania v. New York*, 407 U.S. 206 at 215–16, 92 S.Ct. 2075 at 2080 (1972).

18. *Delaware v. New York*, 507 U.S. 490 at 509, 113 S.Ct. 1550 at 1561 (1993).

19. *Texas v. Florida et al.*, 306 U.S. 398, 59 S.Ct. 563 (1939).

20. *Iowa v. Illinois*, 147 U.S. 1 at 10, 13 S.Ct.239 at 242 (1893).

21. *Arizona v. New Mexico*, 425 U.S. 794 at 798, 96 S.Ct. 1845 at 1847 (1976).

22. *Pennsylvania v. New Jersey*, 426 U.S. 660 at 664, 96 S.Ct. 2333 at 2335 (1976).

23. *Maryland v. Louisiana*, 451 U.S. 725 at 757, 759, 101 S.Ct. 2114 at 2134–135 (1981).

24. *Wyoming v. Oklahoma*, 502 U.S. 437 at 453–54, 112 S.Ct. 789 at 799–800 (1992).

25. Joseph F. Zimmerman, *Interstate Cooperation: Compacts and Administrative Agreements* (Westport, CT: Praeger Publishers, 2002).

26. For details, consult John R. Koza, Barry Fadem, Mark Grueskin, Michael S. Mandell, Robert Ritchie, and Joseph F. Zimmerman, *Every Vote Equal: A State-Based Plan for Electing the President by National Popular Vote* (Los Altos, CA: National Popular Vote Press, 2006). The compact appears on pages 248–49.

27. Felix Frankfurter and James M. Landis, "The Compact Clause of the Constitution— A Study of Interstate Adjustments," *Yale Law Journal* 34, May 1925, p. 688.

28. Frederick L. Zimmermann and Mitchell Wendell, *The Interstate Compact Since 1925* (Chicago: The Council of State Governments, 1951), p. 104.

29. *Virginia v. Tennessee*, 148 U.S. 503 at 520, 13 S.Ct. 728 at 735 (1893).

30. *Safe and Timely Interstate Placement of Foster Children Act of 2006*, 120 Stat. 508, 42 U.S.C. §1305.

31. *United States Steel Corporation v. Multistate Tax Commission*, 434 U.S. 452 at 473, 98 S.Ct. 789 at 813 (1978).

32. *Tobin v. United States*, 306 F.2d 270 at 272–74 (D.C. Cir 1962).

33. *Hinderlider v. La Plata River and Cherry Creek Ditch Company*, 304 U.S. 92, 58 S.Ct. 803 (1938), and *Cuyler v. Adams*, 449 U.S. 433, 101 S.Ct. 703 (1981).
34. *Murdock v. City of Memphis*, 7 U.S. 590, 20 Wallace 590 (1874).
35. *Congressional Record*, April 2, 1941, pp. 3285–286. President Roosevelt signed a resolution granting consent to a modified Republican River Compact, 57 Stat. 86 (1943).
36. 1 Stat. 122 (1790), 28 U.S.C. §1738; 12 Stat. 298 (1804), 28 U.S.C §1738; and *Full Faith and Credit for Child Support Orders Act of 1994*, 108 Stat. 4063, 28 U.S.C. §1738B.
37. *Sosna v. Iowa*, 419 U.S. 393, 95 S.Ct. 553 (1975).
38. *Williams v. North Carolina*, 325 U.S. 226, 65 S.Ct. 1092 (1945).
39. *Defense of Marriage Act of 1996*, 110 Stat. 2419, 1 U.S.C. §1.
40. *Goodridge v. Department of Health*, 440 Mass. 309, 798 N.E.2d 941 (2003). See also Daniel Smith, Matthew DeSantis, and Jason Kassel, "Same-Sex Marriage Ballot Measures and the 2004 Presidential Election," *State and Local Government Review* 38, no. 2, 2006, pp. 78–91.
41. *Massachusetts Laws of 1913*, chap. 360, §2, *Massachusetts General Laws*, chap. 207, §11.
42. *Advisory Opinion of the Justices*, 440 Mass. 1201, 802 N.E.2d 565 (2004).
43. "Vt. Court Asserts Jurisdiction in Dispute," *Washington Post*, August 5, 2006, p. A3.
44. *Paul v. Virginia*, 75 U.S. 168, 8 Wallace 168 (1868).
45. *Ward v. Maryland*, 79 U.S. 418, 12 Wallace 418 (1870).
46. *Toomer v. Witsell*, 334 U.S. 385, 68 S.Ct. 1156 (1948).
47. *Austin v. New Hampshire*, 420 U.S. 656, 95 S.Ct. 1191 (1975).
48. *Sturgis v. Washington*, 414 U.S. 1057, 94 S.Ct. 563 (1973).
49. *Baldwin v. Montana Fish & Game Commission*, 436 U.S. 371 at 388, 98 S.Ct. 1852 at 1861(1978).
50. *Supreme Court of New Hampshire v. Piper*, 470 U.S. 274, 105 S.Ct. 1272 (1985).
51. *Bank of Augusta v. Earle*, 38 U.S. 519, 13 Peters 519 (1839).
52. *McCarran-Ferguson Act of 1945*, 59 Stat. 33, 15 U.S.C. §1011.
53. *Rendition Act of 1793*, 1 Stat. 302, 18 U.S.C. §3182
54. *Pacileo v. Walker*, 449 U.S. 86,101 S.Ct. 308 (1980).
55. *Hall v. State*, 114 N.C. 909, 19 S.E. 602 (1894).
56. *Kentucky v. Dennison*, 65 U.S. 66, 24 Howard 66 (1861).
57. *Puerto Rico v. Branstad*, 483 U.S. 219, 107 S.Ct. 2802 (1987).
58. "Act Aiding Sale of State Wines Is Struck Down," *New York Times*, January 31, 1985, p. B3.
59. *Reeves Incorporated v. Stake*, 447 U.S. 429, 100 S.Ct. 2271 (1980).
60. *Department of Revenue v. Kuhnlein*, 646 So.2d 717, 63 USWL 2271 (Fla. 1994).
61. *City of Virginia Beach v. International Family Entertainment, Incorporated*, 263 Va. 501, 561 S.E.2d 696 (Va. 2002).
62. *Gibbons v. Ogden*, 22 U.S. 1, 9 Wheaton 189 (1824).
63. *Surface Transportation Assistance Act of 1982*, 96 Stat. 2097, 23 U.S.C. §101.
64. *Bacchus Imports, Limited v. Dias*, 468 U.S. 263, 104 S.Ct. 3049 (1984).
65. *Farmland Dairies v. Commissioner of New York State Department of Agriculture*, 650 F. Supp. 939 (E.D. NY 1987).
66. *West Lynn Creamery Incorporated v. Healy*, 512 U.S. 1986, 114 S.Ct. 2205 (1994).

67. *Private Truck Council v. Secretary of State*, 503 A2d 214, 54 USLW 2327 (Me. 1986).
68. *Jenkins Act of 1940*, 63 Stat. 884, 69 Stat. 627, 15 U.S.C. §375.
69. *Contraband Cigarette Act of 1978*, 92 Stat. 2463, 18 U.S.C. §2341.
70. *USA Patriot and Improvement and Reauthorization Act of 2005*, 120 Stat. 221, 18 U.S.C. §§2341(2), 2341(b).
71. *Restatement in the Courts* (St. Paul, MN: American Law Institute Publishers, 2007).
72. Jack L. Walker, "The Diffusion of Innovations Among the American States," *The American Political Science* Review 63, September 1969, pp. 880–99.

CHAPTER 8

1. Joseph F. Zimmerman, *Measuring Local Discretionary Authority* (Washington, DC: U.S. Advisory Commission on Intergovernmental Relations, 1981).
2. John F. Dillon, *Commentaries on the Law of Municipal Corporations* (Boston: Little, Brown and Company, 1911).
3. *City of Clinton v. Cedar Rapids and Missouri Railroad Company*, 24 Iowa 455 at 461 (1868).
4. *Merriam v. Moody's Executors*, 25 Iowa 163 at 170 (1868).
5. *Atkins v. Kansas*, 191 U.S. 107 at 220–21, 24 S.Ct. 124 at 126 (1903).
6. *Trenton v. New Jersey*, 262 U.S. 182, 43 S.Ct. 534 (1923).
7. *Constitution of the State of Michigan*, Art. IV, §30 (1850).
8. *Constitution of the Commonwealth of Massachusetts*, Art. LXXXIX of the articles of amendment, §8.
9. *Farrington v. Pinckney*, 1 N.Y. 2d 74, 133 N.E.2d 817 (1956).
10. *Adler v. Deegan*, 251 N.Y. 467, 167 N.E. 705 (1929).
11. Terrence P. Haas, "Constitutional Home Rule in Rhode Island," *Roger Williams University Law Review* 11, Spring 2006, p. 719.
12. Jefferson B. Fordham, *Model Constitutional Provisions for Municipal Home Rule* (Chicago: American Municipal Association, 1953).
13. *Constitution of Illinois*, Art. VII, §6.
14. *Missouri Constitution of 1875*, Art. IX, §16.
15. Zimmerman, *Measuring Local Discretionary Authority*.
16. *Constitution of West Virginia*, Art. 9, §12.
17. *In re 1975 Tax Assessment Against Oneida Coal Company*, 138 W.Va. 485, 360 S.E.2d 560 (1987).
18. *Allegheny Pittsburgh Coal Company v. County Commission*, 488 U.S. 336, 109 S.Ct. 633 (1989).
19. *Albany Area Builders Association v. Guilderland*, 141 A.D.2d 293, 534 N.Y.S.2d 791 (N.Y. A.D. 1988).
20. *Albany Area Builders Association v. Guilderland*, 74 N.Y.2d 372, 546 N.E.2d 920 (1989).
21. *Communities in Fiscal Distress: State Grant Targeting Provides Limited Help* (Washington, DC: U.S. General Accounting Office, 1985), p. 23.
22. *Size Can Make a Difference—A Closer Look* (Washington, DC: U.S. Advisory Commission on Intergovernmental Relations, 1970).

23. Sam Roberts, "When a Student Is Counted as 94% of One," *New York Times*, February 11, 1988, p. B1.
24. *Serrano v. Priest*, 5 Cal.3d 584, 5 Cal.Rptr. 601 (1971).
25. *Horton v. Meskill*, 32 Conn.Supp. 377, 332 A2d 113 (1974).
26. *Sam Antonio Independent School District v. Rodriguez*, 411 U.S. 1, 93 S.Ct. 1278 (1973); Edgewood *Independent School District v. Kirby*, 777 S.W.2d 391, 56 ED. Law Rep. 663 (Tex., 1989).
27. *Minnesota Statutes*, chap. 473F.
28. Bob DeBoer, "Minnesota's Fiscal Disparities Program Continues to Strength Regional Economies," *Minnesota Journal* 23, August/September 2006, pp. 7 and 11.
29. *New York Laws of 1975*, chap. 168–69, 868–70, and *New York Public Authorities Law*, §3033.
30. *New York Laws of 1975*, chap. 871.
31. *New York Laws of 1995*, chap. 187; *New York Laws of 2000*, chap. 84; and *New York Laws of 2005*, chap. 182.
32. *Florida Laws of 1970*, chap. 243, and *New York Laws of 1972*, chap. 28. See also Joseph F. Zimmerman, *Pragmatic Federalism: The Reassignment of Functional Responsibility* (Washington, DC: U.S. Advisory Commission on Intergovernmental Relations, 1976).
33. *Minnesota Statutes*, §14.091.
34. *New Hampshire Laws of 2003*, chap. 108.
35. *Massachusetts Acts of 1889*, chap. 479; *Massachusetts Acts of 1893*, chap. 407; and *Massachusetts Acts of 1895*, chap. 488.
36. *Massachusetts Acts of 1901*, chap. 168, and *Massachusetts Act of 1919*, chap. 350.
37. *Massachusetts Act of 2003*, chap. 41.
38. *New York Laws of 1960*, chap. 671, *New York Private Housing Finance Law*, §§40–61.
39. *New York Laws of 1967*, chap. 717.
40. *Minnesota Statutes*, chap. 473.121 *et seq.*
41. *Minnesota Laws of 1974*, chap. 422, *Minnesota Statutes*, §§473.121 *et seq.*

CHAPTER 9

1. *Americans with Disabilities Act of 1990*, 104 Stat. 327, 42 U.S.C. §12101.
2. Harold J. Laski, "The Obsolescence of Federalism," *New Republic* 98, May 3, 1939, pp. 363–39, and Harold J. Laski, *The American Democracy: A Commentary and an Interpretation* (New York: Viking Press, 1948), p. 139.
3. Joseph F. Zimmerman, "Congressional Devolution of Powers," a paper presented at a conference on The Federal Nations of North America sponsored by the Eccles Centre for American Studies at the British Library and the Institute for American Studies, London University, London, England, March 19, 2007.
4. Herbert Wechsler, "The Political Safeguards of Federalism: The Role of the States in the Composition and Selection of the National Government," *Columbia Law Review* 54, 1953, pp. 544–45.
5. Richard H. Leach, *American Federalism* (New York: W.W. Norton and Company, Incorporated, 1970), p. 221.

6. Ibid., p. 228.

7. *Marine Sanctuaries Act Amendments of 1984*, 98 Stat. 2296, 16 U.S.C. §1431; *Coast Guard Authorization Act of 1984*, 98 Stat. 2861, 46 U.S.C. §2302; *Abandoned Shipwreck Act of 1987*, 102 Stat. 432, 43 U.S.C. §2101; and *Riegle-Neal Interstate Banking and Branching Efficiency Act of 1994*, 108 Stat. 2343, 2352; 12 U.S.C. §§215, 1831u.

8. 1 Stat. 54 (1789) and *Shipping Statute of 1983*, 97 Stat. 553, 46 U.S.C. §8501.

9. *McCarran-Ferguson Act of 1945*, 59 Stat. 33, 15 U.S.C. §1011.

10. *Submerged Lands Act of 1953*, 67 Stat. 29, 43 U.S.C §1301.

11. *Interstate Horseracing Act of 1978*, 92 Stat. 1813, 15 U.S.C. §3004.

12. *Low-Level Radioactive Waste Policy Act of 1980*, 94 Stat. 3347, 42 U.S.C. §2021d.

13. *Vessel Safety Standards Act of 1983*, 97 Stat. 553, 46 U.S.C. §4305.

14. *Liability Risk Retention Act of 1986*, 100 Stat. 3170, 15 U.S.C. §3901.

15. *Financial Institutions, Reform, Recovery, and Enforcement Act of 1989*, 103 Stat. 183, 12 U.S.C. §1811.

16. *Hotel and Motel Fire Safety Act of 1990*, 104 Stat. 747, 5 U.S.C. §5701.

17. *Federal Fire Prevention and Control Act of 1974*, 88 Stat. 1535, 15 U.S.C. §2224.

18. *Bacchus Imports, Limited v. Dias*, 468 U.S. 263, 104 S.Ct. 3049 (1984).

19. *Unfunded Mandates Act of 1995*, 109 Stat. 48, 2 U.S.C. §1501.

Bibliography

BOOKS AND REPORTS

Anderson, William. *Intergovernmental Relations in Review*. Minneapolis: University of Minnesota Press, 1960.

Barnes, Jeb. *Overruled? Legislative Overrides, Pluralism, and Contemporary Court-Congress Relations*. Stanford: Stanford University Press, 2004.

Barton, Weldon V. *Interstate Compacts in the Political Process*. Chapel Hill: University of North Carolina Press, 1967.

Beard, Charles A. *An Economic Interpretation of the Constitution of the United States*. New York: The Macmillan Company, 1913.

Beyond Preemption: Intergovernmental Partnerships to Enhance the New Economy. Washington, DC: National Academy of Public Administration, 2006.

Bingham, David A. *Constitutional Municipal Home Rule in Arizona*. Tucson: Bureau of Business and Public Research, University of Arizona, 1960.

Bogen, David S. *Privileges and Immunities: A Reference Guide to the United States Constitution*. Westport, CT: Praeger Publishers, 2003.

Brown, Robert E. *Charles Beard and the Constitution*. Princeton: Princeton University Press, 1956.

Bryce, James. *The American Commonwealth*, 3rd ed. 2 vols. New York: The Macmillan Company, 1900.

Cahill, Sean. *Same-Sex Marriage in the United States: Focus on the Facts*. Lanham, MD: Lexington Books, 2004.

Calhoun, John C. *Disquisition on Government*. New York: Political Science Classics, 1948.

Carson, Hampton L. *The History of the Supreme Court of the United States with Biographies of All the Chief and Associate Justices*, vol. I. Philadelphia: A. R. Keller Company, 1892.

City-State Relations. Philadelphia: Institute of Local and State Relations, 1937.

Clark, Gordon L. *Judges and Cities: Interpreting Local Autonomy*. Chicago: University of Chicago Press, 1985.

Clark, Jane P. *The Rise of a New Federalism: Federal-State Cooperation in the United States.* New York: Columbia University Press, 1938.

Cleary, Edward J. *The Oranco Story: Water Quality Management in the Ohio Valley Under an Interstate Compact.* Baltimore: Johns Hopkins University Press, 1967.

Commager, Henry S., ed. *Documents of American History to 1898,* 8th ed. New York: Appleton-Century-Crofts, 1968.

Conlan, Timothy. *From New Federalism to Devolution: Twenty-Five Years of Intergovernmental Reform.* Washington, DC: Brookings Institution Press, 1998.

Corwin, Edward S. *The Commerce Power Versus States' Rights.* Princeton: Princeton University Press, 1936.

———. *National Supremacy: Treaty Power vs. State Power.* New York: Henry Holt, 1913.

Dillon, John F. *Commentaries on the Law of Municipal Corporations.* Boston: Little Brown and Company, 1911.

Doig, Jameson W. *Empire on the Hudson: Entrepreneurial Vision and Political Power at the Port of New York Authority.* New York: Columbia University Press, 2001.

Drury, James W. *Home Rule in Kansas.* Lawrence: Governmental Research Center, University of Kansas, 1965.

Elazar, Daniel J. *American Federalism: A View from the States,* 3rd ed. New York: Harper and Row Publishers, 1984.

———. *The American Partnership: Intergovernmental Cooperation in Nineteenth Century United States.* Chicago: University of Chicago Press, 1962.

———. *Exploring Federalism.* Tuscaloosa: University of Alabama Press, 1987.

Elliot, Jonathan, ed. *The Debates in the Several State Conventions on the Adoption of the Federal Constitution,* 2nd ed., 5 vols. Philadelphia: J. P. Lippincott & Company, 1876.

Ensuring the Future Prosperity of America: Addressing the Fiscal Future. Washington, DC: National Academy of Public Administration, 2005.

Epstein, David F. *The Political Theory of the Federalist.* Chicago: University of Chicago Press, 1984.

Farrand, Max. *The Fathers of the Constitution.* New Haven: Yale University Press, 1921.

———. ed. *The Records of the Federal Convention of 1787.* New Haven: Yale University Press, 1966.

The Federalist Papers. New York: New American Library, 1961.

Fleenor, Patrick. *How Excise Tax Differentials Affect Cross-Border Sale of Beer in the United States.* Washington, DC: Tax Foundation, 1999.

———. *How Excise Tax Differentials Affect Interstate Smuggling and Cross-Border Sales of Cigarettes in the United States.* Washington, DC: Tax Foundation, 1998.

Ford, Paul L., ed. *The Writings of Thomas Jefferson,* vol. 9. New York: G. P. Putnam, 1898.

Fordham, Jefferson B. *Local Government Law: Legal and Related Materials.* Rev. ed. Mineola, NY: Foundation Press, 1975.

———. *Model Constitutional Provisions for Municipal Home Rule.* Chicago: American Municipal Association, 1953.

Frankfurter, Felix. *The Commerce Clause Under Marshall, Taney, and Waite.* Chapel Hill: University of North Carolina Press, 1937.

Friedrich, Carl J. *Trends of Federalism in Theory and Practice.* New York: Frederick A. Praeger, 1968.

Goldwin, Robert A., ed. *A Nation of States: Essays on the American Federal System*, 2nd ed. Chicago: Rand McNally College Publishing Company, 1974.

Goodnow, Frank J. *Municipal Home Rule: A Study in Administration*. New York: Columbia University Press, 1895.

Graves, W. Brooke. *American Intergovernmental Relations: Their Origins, Historical Development, and Current Status*. New York: Charles Scribner's Sons, 1964.

———, ed. "Intergovernmental Relations in the United States." *Annals of the American Academy of Political and Social Science* 207, January 1940, pp. 1–218.

———. *Uniform State Action: A Possible Substitute for Centralization*. Chapel Hill: University of North Carolina Press, 1934.

Grodzins, Morton. *The American System: A New View of Government in the United States*. Chicago: Rand McNally & Company, 1966.

Haider, Donald. *When Governments Come to Washington: Governors, Mayors, and Intergovernmental Lobbying*. Riverside, NJ: Free Press, 1974.

Hardy, Paul T. *Interstate Compacts: The Ties That Bind*. Athens: Institute of Government, University of Georgia, 1982.

Hill, Melvin B. *State Laws Governing Local Government Structure and Administration*. Athens: Institute of Government, University of Georgia, 1978.

Hunt, Gaillard, ed. *The Writings of James Madison*. New York: G. P. Putnam's Sons, 1901.

Interstate Compacts and Agencies. Lexington, KY: Council of State Governments, 2003.

Jacobs, Clyde E. *The Eleventh Amendment and Sovereign Immunity*. Westport, CT: Greenwood Press, 1972.

Jackson, Robert H. *Full Faith and Credit: The Lawyer's Clause of the Constitution*. New York: Columbia University Press, 1945.

Jensen, Merrill. *The Articles of Confederation*. Madison: The University of Wisconsin Press, 1940.

Kaminski, John P. and Gaspare J. Saladino. *The Documentary History of the Ratification of the Constitution*. Madison: State Historical Society of Wisconsin, 1981.

Keith, John P. *City and County Home Rule in Texas*. Austin: Institute of Public Affairs, University of Texas, 1951.

Ketchum, Ralph. *The Anti-Federalist Papers and the Constitutional Convention Debates*. New York: New American Library, 1986.

Kettle, Donald F. *The Regulation of American Federalism*. Baton Rouge: Louisiana State University Press, 1983.

Key, V. O., Jr. *The Administration of Federal Grants to States*. Chicago: Public Administration Service, 1937.

Kincaid, John, ed. "American Federalism: The Third Century." *Annals of the American Academy of Political and Social Science* 509, May 1990, pp. 11–152.

Kolin, Stanley. *Interstate Sanitation Commission: A Discussion of the Development and Administration of an Interstate Compact*. Syracuse, NY: Syracuse University Press, 1954.

Koza, John F., Barry Fadem, Mark Grueskin, Michael S. Mandell, Robert Richie, and Joseph F. Zimmerman. *Every One Equal: A State-Based Plan for Electing the President by National Popular Vote*. Los Altos, California: National Popular Vote Press, 2006.

Krane, Dale, Platon N. Rigos, and Melvin B. Hill, Jr. *Home Rule in America: A Fifty-State Handbook*. Washington, DC: CQ Press, 2001.

Laski, Harold J. *The American Democracy: A Commentary and an Interpretation*. New York: The Viking Press, 1948.

Leach, Richard H. *American Federalism*. New York: W. W. Norton Company, Incorporated, 1970.

———, ed. "Intergovernmental Relations in America Today." *Annals of the American Academy of Political and Social Science* 416, November 1974, pp. 1–169.

———. and Redding S. Sugg, Jr. *The Administration of Interstate Compacts*. Baton Rouge: Louisiana State University Pres, 1959.

Lepawsky, Albert. *Home Rule for Metropolitan Chicago*. Chicago: University of Chicago Press, 1935.

Liner, E. Blaine, ed. *A Decade of Devolution: Perspectives on State-Local Relations*. Washington, DC: Urban Institute Press, 1989.

MacMahon, Arthur W., ed. *Federalism: Mature and Emergent*. Garden City, NY: Doubleday and Company, 1955.

Madison, James. *Journal of the Federal Convention*. Chicago: Albert, Scott & Company, 1893.

Main, Jackson T. *The Antifederalists: Critics of the Constitution 1781–1788*. Chapel Hill: University of North Carolina Press, 1961.

Martin, Roscoe C. et al. *River Basin Administration and the Delaware*. Syracuse, NY: Syracuse University Press, 1960.

Maxwell, James A. *Tax Credits and Intergovernmental Relations*. Washington, DC: Brookings Institution, 1962.

Melnick, R. Shep. *Regulation and the Courts: The Case of the Clean Air Act*. Washington, DC: Brookings Institution, 1983.

Mitchell, Jerry, ed. *Public Authorities and Public Policy: The Business of Government*. New York: Greenwood Press, 1992.

Morley, Felix. *Federalism and Freedom*. Chicago: Henry Regnery Company, 1959.

Mott, Rodney L. *Home Rule for America's Cities*. Chicago: American Municipal Association, 1949.

Munro, William B. *The Government of the United States*. New York: The Macmillan Company, 1937.

Nagle, Robert F. *The Implosion of American Federalism*. New York: Oxford University Press, 2002.

New Hampshire Municipal Bond Bank: 1980s Series A Bonds. New York: Goldman Sachs, 1980.

Noonan, John T. *Narrowing the Nation's Power: The Supreme Court Sides with the States*. Berkeley: University of California Press, 2002.

Petersen, John E. et al. *Credit Pooling to Finance Infrastructure: An Examination of State Revolving Funds and Substate Credit Pools*. Washington, DC: Government Finance Officers Association, 1988.

Policy Positions: 1980–81. Washington, DC: National Governors Association, 1980.

Reagan, Michael D. and John G. Sanzone. *The New Federalism*, 2nd ed. New York: Oxford University Press, 1981.

Report of the Committee on State-Urban Relations. Chicago: Council of State Governments, 1968.

Restatement in the Courts. St. Paul, MN: American Law Institute Publishers, 2007.

Ridgeway, Marian E. *Interstate Compacts: A Question of Federalism*. Carbondale: Southern Illinois University Press, 1971.

Riker, William H. *Federalism: Origin, Operation, Significance*. Boston: Little Brown and Company, 1964.

Sandler, Ross and David Scoenbrod. *Democracy by Decree: What Happens When Courts Run Government*. New Haven: Yale University Press, 2003.

Sato, Sho and Arvo Van Alstyne. *State and Local Government Law*. Boston: Little Brown and Company, 1970.

Saxon, John L. *Enforcement and Modification of Out-of-State Child Support Orders*. Chapel Hill: Institute of Government, University of North Carolina, 1994.

Scott, James A. *The Law of Interstate Rendition Erroneously Referred to as Interstate Extradition: A Treatise*. Chicago: Sherman Hight, Publisher, 1917.

Shalala, Donna E. *The City and the Constitution: The 1967 New York Convention's Response to the Urban Crisis*. New York: National Municipal League, 1972.

Sherk, George W. *Dividing the Waters: The Resolution of Interstate Water Conflicts in the United States*. Boston: Kluwer Law International, 2000.

State-Local Relations. Chicago: Council of State Governments, 1946.

Stewart, William H. *Concepts of Federalism*. Lanham, MD: University Press of America, 1984.

Story, Joseph. *Commentaries on the Constitution of the United States*. Boston: Hilliard, Gray, and Company, 1833.

Sugg, Redding S., Jr. and George H. Jones. *The Southern Regional Education Board: Ten Years of Regional Cooperation in Higher Education*. Baton Rouge: Louisiana State University Press, 1960.

Thursby, Vincent V. *Interstate Cooperation: A Study of the Interstate Compact*. Washington, DC: Public Affairs Press, 1953.

Tocqueville, Alexis de. *Democracy in America*. New York: Vintage Books, 1954.

Voit, William, Jr. *The Susquehanna Compact*. New Brunswick, NJ: Rutgers University Press, 1972.

Walker, David B. *The Rebirth of Federalism*. New York: Chatham House Publishers, 2000.

———. *Toward a Functioning Federalism*. Cambridge, MA: Winthrop Publishers, 1981.

Walker, Robert H., ed. *The Reform Spirit in America: A Documentation*. New York: G. P. Putnam's Sons, 1979.

Warren, Charles. *Congress, the Constitution, and the Supreme Court*. Boston: Little, Brown, and Company, 1925.

Wasby, Stephen L. *The Supreme Court in the Federal Judicial System*, 3rd ed. Chicago: Nelson-Hall, 1988.

Water Wars. Lexington, KY: The Council of State Governments, 2003.

Wheare, Kenneth C. *Federal Government*, 4th ed. New York: Oxford University Press, 1964.

Wood, Robert C. *1400 Governments*. Cambridge: Harvard University Press, 1961.

Wright, Deil S. *Understanding Intergovernmental Relations*, 3rd ed. Pacific Grove, CA: Brooks/Cole Publishing, 1988.

Young, James T. *The New American Government and Its Work*, 3rd ed. New York: The Macmillan Company, 1936.

Zimmerman, Joseph F. *Congressional Preemption: Regulatory Federalism.* Albany: State
    University of New York Press, 2005.
———. *Federal Preemption: The Silent Revolution.* Ames: Iowa State University Press,
    1991.
———. *The Government and Politics of New York State,* 2nd ed. Albany: State Univer-
    sity of New York Press, 2008.
———. *Home Rule in Massachusetts: Some Historical Perspectives.* Albany: Graduate
    School of Public Affairs, State University of New York at Albany, 1970.
———. *The Initiative: Citizen Law-Making.* Westport, CT: Praeger Publishers, 1999.
———. *Interstate Cooperation: Compacts and Administrative Agreements.* Westport, CT:
    Praeger Publishers, 2002.
———. *Interstate Disputes: The Supreme Court's Original Jurisdiction.* Albany: State Uni-
    versity of New York Press, 2006.
———. *Interstate Economic Relations.* Albany: State University of New York Press, 2004.
———. *Interstate Relations: The Neglected Dimension of Federalism.* Westport, CT: Praeger
    Publishers, 1996.
———. *The Initiative: Citizen Law-Making.* Westport, CT: Praeger Publishers, 1999.
———. *The Recall: Tribunal of the People.* Westport, CT: Praeger Publishers, 1997.
———. *The Referendum: The People Decide Public Policy.* Westport, CT: Praeger Pub-
    lishers, 2001.
———. *The Silence of Congress: State Taxation of Interstate Commerce.* Albany: State
    University of New York Press, 2007.
———. *State-Local Relations: A Partnership Approach,* 2nd ed. Westport, CT: Praeger
    Publishers, 1995.
Zimmerman, Joseph F. and Wilma Rule, eds. *The U.S. House of Representatives: Reform
    or Rebuild?* Westport, CT: Praeger Publishers, 2000.
Zimmermann, Frederick L. and Mitchell Wendell. *The Interstate Compact Since 1925.*
    Chicago: The Council of State Governments, 1951.
———. *The Law and Use of Interstate Compacts.* Lexington, KY: The Council of State
    Governments, 1976.

PUBLIC DOCUMENTS

*An Advisory Committee Report on Local Government Submitted to the Commission on Inter-
    governmental Relations.* Washington, DC: U.S. Government Printing Office, 1955.
American Federalism: Toward a More Effective Partnership. Washington, DC: U.S. Advi-
    sory Commission on Intergovernmental Relations, 1975.
Boyd, Eugene. *American Federalism, 1776 to 1995.* Washington, DC: Congressional
    Research Service, 1995.
*Categorical Grants: Their Role and Design. The Intergovernmental Grant System: An Assess-
    ment and Proposed Policies.* Washington, DC: U.S. Advisory Commission on Inter-
    governmental Relations, 1978.
*Community Development Block Grants: Program Offers Recipients Flexibility but Oversight
    Can Be Improved.* Washington, DC: U.S. Government Accountability Office, 2006.
Community Development: Oversight of Block Grant Monitoring Needs Improvement. Wash-
    ington, DC: U.S. General Accounting Office, 1991.

Commission on Intergovernmental Relations: A Report to the President for Transmittal to the Congress. Washington, DC: U.S. Government Printing Office, 1955.

Communities in Fiscal Distress: State Grant Targeting Provides Limited Help. Washington, DC: U.S. General Accounting office, 1985.

Cuciti, Peggy L. Federal Constraints on State and Local Governments. Washington, DC: Congressional Budget Office, 1979

Dairy Industry: Estimated Impacts of Dairy Compacts. Washington, DC: U.S. General Accounting Office, 2001.

Devolving Federal Program Responsibilities and Revenue Sources to State and Local Governments. Washington, DC: U.S. Advisory Commission on Intergovernmental Relations, 1986.

Education Block Grant Alters State Role and Provides Greater Local Discretion. Washington, DC: U.S. General Accounting Office, 1984.

Environmental Protection: Overcoming Obstacles to Innovate State Regulatory Programs. Washington, DC: U.S. General Accounting Office, 1978.

The Federal Influence on State and Local Roles in the Federal System. Washington, DC: U.S. Advisory Commission on Intergovernmental Relations, 1981.

Federal-Interstate Compact Commissions: Useful Mechanisms for Planning and Managing River Basin Operations. Washington, DC: U.S. General Accounting Office, 1981.

Federal Mandate Relief for State, Local, and Tribal Governments. Washington, DC: U.S. Advisory Commission on Intergovernmental Relations, 1996.

Fiscal Balance in the American Federal System. Washington, DC: U.S. Advisory Commission on Intergovernmental Relations, 1967.

Formula Grants: 2000 Census Redistributes Federal Funding Among States. Washington, DC: U.S. General Accounting Office, 2003.

General Revenue Sharing: An ACIR Re-evaluation. Washington, DC: U.S. Advisory Commission on Intergovernmental Relations, 1974.

Hearings Before the Subcommittee on Air and Water Pollution of the Committee on Public Works, United States Senate on "Problems and Progress Associated with Control of Automobile Exhaust Emissions." Washington, DC: U.S. Government Printing Office, 1967.

House Committee on Education and Labor, Report to Accompany H.R. 3530, 99th Congress, 1st Session. Washington, DC: U.S. Government Printing Office, 1985.

How Revenue Sharing Formulas Distribute Aid: Urban-Rural Implications. Washington, DC: U.S. General Accounting Office, 1980.

Intellectual Property: State Immunity in Infringement Actions. Washington, DC: U.S. General Accounting Office, 2001.

Interstate Tax Competition. Washington, DC: U.S. Advisory Commission on Intergovernmental Relations, 1981.

Libonati, Michael E. Local Government Autonomy: Needs for State Constitutional, Statutory, and Judicial Clarification. Washington, DC: U.S. Advisory Commission on Intergovernmental Relations, 1993.

Mandates: Cases in State-Local Relation. Washington, DC: U.S. Advisory Commission on Intergovernmental Relations, 1990.

Memorandum Regarding Final Orders: Civil Action No. 72–911–G. Boston: U.S. District Court, 1985.

North American Free Trade Agreement Coordinated Operational Plan Needed to Ensure Mexican Truck's Compliance with U.S. Standards. Washington, DC: U.S. General Accounting Office, 2002.

O'Hare, Robert J. M. Local Structure: Home Rule. Boston, MA: Department of Community Affairs, 1969.

Posner, Paul L. Federal Assistance: Grant System Continues to Be Highly Fragmented. Washington, DC: U.S. General Accounting Office, 2003.

———. Regulatory Programs: Balancing Federal and State Responsibilities for Standard Setting and Implementation. Washington, DC: U.S. General Accounting Office, 2002.

Revising the Municipal Home Rule Amendment. Washington, DC: U.S. Advisory Commission on Intergovernmental Relations, 1981.

Sector Study Steering Committee. Municipalities, Small Business, and Agriculture: The Challenge of Meeting Environmental Responsibilities. Washington, DC: U.S. Environmental Protection Agency, 1988.

Size Can Make a Difference—A Closer Look. Washington, DC: U.S. Advisory Commission on Intergovernmental Relations, 1970.

State-Local Relations Bodies: State ACIRs and Other Approaches. Washington, DC: U.S. Advisory Commission on Intergovernmental Relations, 1981.

State and Local Government Finances by Level of Government and By State: 2003–04. Washington, DC: U.S. Bureau of the Census, 2004.

State Taxation of Interstate Mail Order Sales. Washington, DC: U.S. Advisory Commission on Intergovernmental Relations, 1992.

Stenberg, Carl W. State Involvement in Federal-Local Grant Programs: A Case Study of the "Buying In" Approach. Washington, DC: U.S. Advisory Commission on Intergovernmental Relations, 1970.

Stephenson, John B. Great Lakes: A Coordinated Strategic Plan and Monitoring System Are Needed to Achieve Restoration Goals. Washington, DC: U.S. General Accounting Office, 2003.

U.S. Bureau of the Census. Expenditure of General Revenue Sharing and Antirecession Fiscal Assistance Funds 1977–78. Washington, DC: U.S. Government Printing Office, 1980.

Water Infrastructure: Information on Federal and State Financial Assistance. Washington, DC: U.S. General Accounting Office, 2002.

Welfare Reform: With TANF Flexibility, States Vary in How They Implement Work Requirements and Times Limits. Washington, DC: U.S. General Accounting Office, 2002.

Zimmerman, Joseph F. Federal Preemption of State and Local Authority. Washington, DC: U.S. Advisory Commission on Intergovernmental Relations, 1990.

———. Federally Induced Costs Affecting State and Local Governments. Washington, DC: U.S. Advisory Commission on Intergovernmental Relations, 1994.

———. Measuring Local Discretionary Authority. Washington, DC: U.S. Advisory Commission on Intergovernmental Relations, 1981.

———. Pragmatic Federalism: The Reassignment of Functional Responsibility. Washington, DC: U.S. Advisory Commission on Intergovernmental Relations, 1976.

———. State Mandating of Local Expenditures. Washington, DC: U.S. Advisory Commission on Intergovernmental Relations, 1978.

Zimmerman, Joseph F. and Sharon Lawrence. *Federal Statutory Preemption of State and Local Authority: History, Inventory, and Issues.* Washington, DC: U.S. Advisory Commission on Intergovernmental Relations, 1992.

ARTICLES

"Act Aiding Sale of State Wines Is Struck Down." *New York Times,* January 31, 1985, p. B3.

Adams, Kristen D. "Interstate Gambling: Can States Stop the Run for the Border." *Emory Law Review* 44, Summer 1995, pp. 1025–067.

Adler, Matthew D. "State Sovereignty and the Anti-Commandeering Cases." *Annals of the American Academy of Political and Social Science* 574, March 2001, pp. 158–72.

Agranoff, Robert. "Managing Within the Matrix: Do Collaborative Intergovernmental Relations Exists?" *Publius: The Journal of Federalism* 31, September 2001, pp. 31–56.

Alexander, James R. "State Sovereignty in the Federal System: Constitutional Protections Under the Tenth and Eleventh Amendments?" *Publius: The Journal of Federalism* 16, Spring 1986, pp. 1–15.

Althoff, Megan M. "The National Bank Act's Federal Preemption of State Electronic Funds Transfer Acts." *Corporation Law* 25, Summer 2000, pp. 843–65.

Althouse, Ann. "How to Build a Separate Sphere: Federal Courts and State Power." *Harvard Law Review* 100, May 1987, pp. 1485–1538.

Arneson, Ben A. "Federal Aid to the States." *American Political Science Review* 16, August 1922, pp. 443–54.

Baer, Jon A. "Municipal Debt and Tax Limits: Constraints on Home Rule." *National Civic Review* 70, April 1981, pp. 204–10.

Baker, Al. "Telecommuter Loses Case for Benefits." *New York Times,* July 3, 2003, pp. B1, B6.

Baker, Thomas E. "A Catalogue of Judicial Federalism in the United States." *South Carolina Law Review* 46, Summer 1995, pp. 835–75.

Baker, William C. "30 Years After the Clean Water Act: Chesapeake's Still Waiting." *Bay Journal* 13, September 2003, pp. 20–21.

Baranski, Jason. "Is Local Government the Equivalent of State Government for Purposes of the Market Participant Exception to the Dormant Commerce Clause." *Dickinson Law Review* 104, Summer 2000, pp. 687–705.

Barnett, James D. "Cooperation Between the Federal and State Governments." *National Municipal Review* 17, May 1928, pp. 283–91.

———. "The Delegation of Legislative Power by Congress to the States." *American Political Science Review* 2, 1908, pp. 347–77.

Baybeck, Brady and William Lowry. "Federalism Outcomes and Ideological Preferences: The U.S. Supreme Court and Preemption Cases." *Publius: The Journal of Federalism* 30, Summer 2000, pp. 73–97.

Beaverstock, Jeffrey U. "Learning to Get Along: Alabama, Georgia, Florida, and the Chattahoochee River Compact." *Alabama Law Review* 49, Spring 1998, pp. 993–1007.

Benjamin, Elizabeth. "State Do-Not-Call List Goes Federal." *Times Union* (Albany, NY), July 8, 2003, p. B2.

Bingham, David A. "No Home Rule in West Virginia." *National Civic Review* 60, April 1980, pp. 213–14.

Bork, Robert H. and Daniel E. Troy. "Locating the Boundaries: The Scope of Congress's Power to Regulate Commerce." *Harvard Journal of Law and Public Policy* 25, Summer 2002, pp. 849–93.

Braden, George B. "Umpire to the Federal System." *University of Chicago Law Review* 10, October 1942, pp. 27–48.

Brilmayer, Lea. "Federalism, State Authority, and the Preemptive Power of International Law." *The Supreme Court Review* 1994, pp. 295–343.

Brown, George D. "Binding Advisory Opinions: A Federal Court's Perspective on the State School Finance Decisions." *Boston College Law Review* 35, May 1994, pp. 543–68.

———. "The Ideologies of Forum Shopping: Why Doesn't A Conservative Court Protect Defendants?" *North Carolina Law Review* 71, March 1993, pp. 659–720.

Buckley, James L. "The Trouble with Federalism: It Isn't Being Tried." *Commonsense* 1, Summer 1978, pp. 1–17.

Byeznski, Lynn. "Judge Raises Taxes to Pay for School Bias Remedy." *National Law Journal* 10, October 5, 1987, p. 25.

Cabraser, Elizabeth J. "The Class Action Counterreformation." *Stanford Law Review* 57, April 2005, pp. 1475–1520.

Calande, Pauline E. "State Incorporation of Federal Law: A Response to the Demise of Implied Federal Rights of Action." *Yale Law Journal* 94, April 1985, pp. 1144–163.

Cao, Lan. "Illegal Traffic in Women: A Civil RICO Proposal." *Yale Law Journal* 96, May 1987, pp. 1297–1322.

Carstens, Anne-Marie. "Lurking in the Shadows of Judicial Process: Special Masters in the Supreme Court's Original Jurisdiction Cases." *Minnesota Law Review* 86, February 2002, pp. 625–704.

Carvajal, Alejandr. "State and Local 'Free Burma' Laws: The Case for Sub-National Trade Barriers." *Law and Policy in International Business* 19, Winter 1998, pp. 257–74.

"Charting No Man's Land: Applying Jurisdictional and Choice of Law Doctrines to Interstate Compacts." *Harvard Law Review* 111, May 1998, pp. 1991–2008.

Cho, Chung-Lae and Deil S. Wright. "Managing Carrots and Sticks: Changes in State Administrators' Perceptions of Cooperative and Coercive Federalism During the 1990s." *Publius: The Journal of Federalism* 31, Spring 2001, pp. 57–80.

Clermont, Kevin M. and Theodore Eisenberg. "Exorcising the Evil of Forum-Shopping." *Cornell Law Review* 80, September 1995, pp. 1507–530.

Cohen, William. "Congressional Power to Validate Unconstitutional State Laws: A Forgotten Solution to an Old Engine." *Stanford Law Review* 35, February 1983, pp. 387–422.

Collins, Michael G. "Article III Cases, State Court Duties, and the Madisonian Compromise." *Wisconsin Law Review* 1995, pp. 39–97.

Conlin, Timothy J. and Francois Vergniolle de Chantel. "The Rehnquist Court and Contemporary American Federalism." *Political Science Quarterly* 116, 2001, pp. 753–75.

"The Coming of Copyright Perpetuity." *New York Times*, January 16, 2003, p. A28.

Conlan, Timothy J. and Francois Vergniolle de Chantel. "The Rehnquist Court and Contemporary American Federalism." *Political Science Quarterly* 116, 2001, pp. 253–75.

"Conn. to Send 500 Inmates to Va. to Ease Overcrowding." *Union Leader* (Manchester, NH), October 26, 1999, p. A3.

Corwin, Edward S. "National-State Cooperation—Its Present Possibilities." *Yale Law Journal* 46, February 1937, pp. 599–623.

———. "The Passing of Dual Federalism." *Virginia Law Review* 36, February 1950, pp. 1–24

Coyle, Marcia. "States' Immunity Redux." *National Law Journal* 21, March 29, 1999, pp. 1, A9.

Crihfield, Brevard and H. Clyde Reeves. "Intergovernmental Relations: A View from the States." *Annals of the American Academy of Political and Social Science* 416, November 1974, pp. 99–107.

Davis, Mary J. "Unmasking the Presumption in Favor of Preemption." *South Carolina Law Review* 53, Summer 2002, pp. 967–1030.

DeBoer, Bob. "Minnesota's Fiscal Disparities Program Continues to Strengthen Regional Economies." *Minnesota Journal* 23, August/September 2006, pp. 7, 11.

Dees, Morris. "Finding the Forum for Victory." *National Law Review* 13, February 11, 1991, pp. S3–4.

Diamond, Martin. "What the Framers Meant by Federalism." In Goldman, Robert A., ed., *A Nation of States: Essays on American Federalism*, 2nd ed. Chicago: Rand McNally College Publishing Company, 1974, pp. 25–42.

Dinan, John. "Congressional Responses to the Rehnquist Court's Federalism Decisions." *Publius: The Journal of Federalism* 32, Summer 2002, pp. 1–24.

Dodge, William S. "Congressional Control of Supreme Court Appellate Jurisdiction: Why the Original Jurisdiction Clause Suggests and 'Essential Role.'" *Yale Law Journal* 100, January 1991, pp. 1013–031.

Donohue, Laura K. and Juliette N. Kayyem. "Federalism and the Battle Over Counterterroist Law: State Sovereignty, Criminal Law Enforcement, and National Security." *Studies in Conflict and Terrorism* 25, January–February 2002, pp. 1–18.

Douglas, Paul H. "The Development of a System of Federal Grants-in-Aid I." *Political Science Quarterly* 35, June 1920, pp. 255–71.

———. "The Development of a System of Federal Grants-in-Aid II." *Political Science Quarterly* 35, December 1920, pp. 522–44.

Dunham, Allison. "A History of the National Conference of Commissioners on Uniform State Laws." *Law and Contemporary Problems* 30, Spring 1965, pp. 233–49.

Durham, G. Homer. "Politics and Administration in Intergovernmental Relations." *Annals of the American Academy of Political and Social Science* 207, January 1940, pp. 1–6.

Eastman, John C. "Re-entering the Arena: Restoring a Judicial Role for Enforcing Limits on Federal Mandates." *Harvard Journal of Law and Public Policy* 25, Summer 2002, pp. 931–52.

Eichorn, L. Mark. "*Cuyler v. Adams* and the Characterization of Compact Law." *Virginia Law Review* 77, October 1991, pp. 1387–410.

"Employees of Professional Sports Franchises Paying Income Taxes in Up to 20 States as State Governments Compete for Funds." *Tax Features* 46, September 2002, pp. 4–5.

Fallon, Richard H., Jr. "Reflections on the Hart and Wechsler Paradigm." *Vanderbilt Law Review* 47, May 1994, pp. 953–87.

"Federal Judge Orders a Panel to Monitor State Schools for Retarded." *Boston Globe*, March 16, 1986, p. 16.

Feron, James. "Yonkers Council, in a 4 to 3 Vote, Defies Judge on Integration Plan." *New York Times*, August 2, 1988, p. 1.

Ferris, Charles D. and Terrence J. Leahy. "Red Lions, Tigers, and Bears: Broadcast Content Regulation and the First Amendment." *Catholic University Law Review* 38, Winter 1989, pp. 299–327.

"Fighting Federal Mandates." *New York Times*, August 16, 1980, p. 20.

Finnegan, Michael C. "New York City's Watershed Agreement: A Lesson in Sharing Responsibility." *Pace Environmental Law Review* 14, Summer 1997, pp. 577–644.

Fisk, Catherine L. "The Last Article About the Language of ERIS Preemption? A Case Study of the Failure of Textualism." *Harvard Journal of Legislation* 33, Winter 1996, pp. 35–103.

Flango, Victor E. "Litigant Choice Between State and Federal Courts." *South Carolina Law Review* 46, Summer 1995, pp. 961–77.

Florestano, Patricia S. "Past and Present Utilization of Interstate Compacts in the United States." *Publius: The Journal of Federalism* 24, Fall 1994, pp. 13–25.

Fordham, Jefferson B. "Home Rule—AMA Model." *National Municipal Review* 44, March 1955, pp. 137–42.

"Forum Shopping Reconsidered." *Harvard Law Review* 103, May 1990, pp. 1677–696.

Frankfurter, Felix and James M. Landis. "The Compact Clause of the Constitution—A Study in Interstate Adjustments." *Yale Law Journal* 34, May 1925, pp. 685–758.

Friedman, Barry. "The Law and Economics of Federalism: Valuing Federalism." *Minnesota Law Review* 82, December 1997, pp. 317–412.

Frost, Amanda. "Judicial Review of FDA Preemption Determinations." *Food and Drug Law Journal* 54, 1999, pp. 367–88.

Garrett, Elizabeth. "States in a Federal System: Enhancing the Political Safeguards of Federalism? The Unfunded Mandates Reform Act of 1995." *Kansas Law Review* 45, July 1997, pp. 113–83.

Gausman, Carlton J. "The Interstate Compact as a Solution to Regional Problems: The Kansas City Metropolitan Culture District." *Kansas Law Review* 45, May 1997, pp. 897–920.

Gold, H. David. "Analyzing the Law, Regulation, and Policy Affecting FDA-Regulated Product." *Food and Drug Law Review* 59, 1004, pp. 93–132.

Goodman, Frank, ed. "The Supreme Court's Federalism: Real or Imagined?" *The Annals of the American Academy of Political and Social Science* 574, March 2001, pp. 9–194.

Grad, Frank P. "Home Rule and the New York Constitution." *Columbia Law Review* 66, June 1966, pp. 1145–163.

Graves, W. Brooke. "The Future of the American States." *American Political Science Review* 30, February 1936, pp. 24–50.

———. "State Constitutional Provisions for Federal-State Cooperation." *Annals of the American Academy of Political and Social Science* 18, September 1935, pp. 142–48.

Green, Tristin K. "Complete Preemption: Removing the Mystery from Removal." *California Law Review* 86, March 1998, pp. 363–95.

Greenhouse, Linda. "Justices Reject Campaign Limits in Vermont Case." *New York Times*, June 27, 2006, pp. 1, A14.

———. "Justices Uphold Most Remapping in Texas by G.O.P." *New York Times*, June 29, 2006, pp. 1, A22.

Grey, Betsy J. "Make Congress Speak Clearly: Federal Preemption of State Tort Remedies." *Boston University Law Review* 77, pp. 559–627.

Grogan, Colleen M. "The Influence of Federal Mandates on State Medicaid and AFDC Decision-Making." *Publius: The Journal of Federalism* 29, Summer 1999, pp. 1–30.

Gulick, Luther. "Reorganization of the State." *Civil Engineering* 3, August 1933, pp. 419–26.

Harris, Joseph P. "The Future of Federal Grants-in-Aid." *The Annals of the American Academy of Political and Social Science* 207, January 1940, pp. 14–26.

Hass, Terrence P. "Constitutional Home Rule in Rhode Island." *Roger Williams University Law Review* 11, Spring 2006, pp. 677–718.

Heim, Michael R. "Home Rule: A Primer." *Journal of the Kansas Bar Association* 74, January 2005, pp. 26–38.

Heron, Kevin J. "The Interstate Compact in Transition: From Cooperative State Action to Congressionally Coerced Agreements." *St. John's Law Review* 60, Fall 1985, pp. 1–25.

Hill, Rebecca L. "California v. F.E.R.C.: Federal Preemption of State Water Laws." *Journal of Energy, Natural Resources, and Environmental Laws* 12, No. 1, 1992, pp. 261–83.

Hill, Kim Q. and Patricia A. Hurley. "Uniform State Law Adoptions in the American States: An Exploratory Analysis." *Publius* 18, Winter 1988, pp. 117–26.

Hoffman, David K. "State Income Taxation of Nonresident Professionals." *Tax Foundation Special Report*, July 2002, pp. 1–6.

Holcombe, Arthur N. "The Coercion of States in a Federal System." In MacMahon, Arthur ed. *Federalism: Mature and Emergent*. Garden City, NY: Doubleday and Company, 1955, 137–56.

Hu, Winnie. "Judge Approves Settlement in Yonkers Desegregation Suit." *New York Times*, March 27, 2002, p. B6.

Hughes, David W. "When NIMBYs Attack: The Heights to Which Communities will Climb to Prevent the Siting of Wireless Towers." *Journal of Corporation Law* 23, Spring 1998, pp. 469–500.

Jackson, Robert H. "The Supreme Court and Interstate Barriers." *Annals of the American Academy of Political and Social Science* 207, January 1940, pp. 70–78.

Jackson, Vicki C. "Federalism and the Court: Congress as the Audience." *Annals of the American Academy of Political and Social Science* 574, March 2001, pp. 145–57.

Janson, Donald. "Iowa Is Called Aggressor State: Nebraska Fears Shooting War." *New York Times*, July 26, 2964, pp. 1, 24.

Kearney, Richard C. and John J. Stucker. "Interstate Compacts and the Management of Low Level Radioactive Wastes." *Public Administration Review* 45, January/February 1985, pp. 210–20.

Kelly, Janet M. "The States on Unfunded Mandates: Where There's a Will, There's a Way." *South Carolina Policy Forum* 8, Winter 1997, pp. 29–34.

Kelly, Matthew J. "Federal Preemption by the Airline Deregulation Act of 1978: How Do State Tort Claims Fare?" *Catholic University Law Review* 49, Spring 2000, pp. 873–902.

Kerr, Timothy. "Cleaning Up One Mess to Create Another: Duplicative Class Actions, Federal Courts' Injunctive Power, and the Class Action Fairness Act of 2005." *Hamline Law Review* 29, Spring 2006, pp. 218–58.

Key, V. O., Jr. "State Legislation Facilitative of Federal Action." *Annals of the American Academy of Political and Social Science* 509, January 1940, pp. 7–13.

Kincaid, John, ed. "American Federalism: The Third Century." *Annals of the American Academy of Political and Social Science* 509, pp. 1–152.

———. "From Cooperative to Coercive Federalism." In John Kincaid, ed., "American Federalism: The Third Century." *Annals of the American Academy of Political and Social Science* 509, May 1990, pp. 139–52.

Koch, Edward I. "The Mandate Millstone." *The Public Interest* 61, Fall 1980, pp. 42–57.

Koenig, Louis W. "Federal and State Cooperation Under the Constitution." *Michigan Law Review* 36, March 1938, pp. 752–85.

Kravitz, Mark R. "Removal Remands." *National Law Journal* 23, June 25, 2001, p. A10.

Laski, Harold J. "The Obsolescence of Federalism." *The New Republic* 98, May 1939, pp. 362–69.

Lawson, Gary and Patricia B. Granger. "The 'Proper' Scope of Federal Power: A Jurisdictional Interpretation of the Sweeping Clause." *Duke Law Journal* 43, November 1993, pp. 267–336.

Leach, Richard H., ed., "Intergovernmental Relations in the United States." *Annals of the American Academy of Political and Social Science* 416, November 1974, pp. 1–193.

Ledewitz, Bruce. "The Role of Lower State Courts in Adapting State Law to Changed Federal Interpretations." *Temple Law Review* 67, Fall 1994, pp. 1003–015.

Lee, Carol F. "The Political Safeguards of Federalism? Congressional Responses to Supreme Court Decisions on State and Local Liability." *Urban Lawyer* 20, Spring 1988, pp. 301–40.

Luken, Susan M. "Irreconcilable Differences: The Spending Clause and the Eleventh Amendment: Limiting Congress's Use of Conditional Spending to Circumvent Eleventh Amendment Immunity." *University of Cincinnati Law Review* 70, Winter 2002, pp. 693–714.

Macey, Jonathan R. "Federal Deference to Local Regulators and the Economic Theory of Regulation: Toward a Public-choice Explanation of Federalism." *Virginia Law Review* 76, March 1990, pp. 165–91.

———. "Origin of the Blue Sky Laws." *Texas Law Review* 70, December 1991, pp. 347–96.

MacManus, Susan A. "Mad About Mandates; The Issue of Who Should Pay for What Resurfaces." *Publius: The Journal of Federalism* 21, Summer, 1991, pp. 59–75.

McCoy, Charles S. "Federalism: The Lost Tradition?" *Publius: The Journal of Federalism* 31, Spring 2001, pp. 1–14.

Meese, Edwin, III. "The Attorney General's View of the Supreme Court: Toward a Jurisprudence of Original Intention." *Public Administration Review* 45, November 1985, pp. 701–04.

Nathan, Richard P. "The New Federalism Versus the Emerging New Structuralism." *Publius: The Journal of Federalism* 5, Summer 1975, pp. 111–29.

Nathan, Richard P., and Paul R. Dommel. "Federal-Local Relations Under Block Grants." *Political Science Quarterly* 93, Fall 1978, pp. 421–42.

———— and John R. Lago. "Intergovernmental Fiscal Roles and Relations." *Annals of the American Academy of Political and Social Science* 509, May 1990, pp. 36–47.

Nelson, Caleb. "Preemption." *Virginia Law Review* 86, March 2000, pp. 225–305.

Nichol, Gene R., Jr. "Federalism, State Courts, and Section 1983." *Virginia Law Review* 73, September 1987, pp. 959–1010.

Northrop, Patricia T. "The Constitutional Insignificance of Funding for Federal Mandates." *Duke Law Journal* 46, February 1997, pp. 903–30.

O'Brien, David M. "The Rehnquist Court and Federal Preemption: In Search of a Theory." *Publius: The Journal of Federalism* 23, Fall 1993, pp. 25–31.

————. "The Supreme Court and Intergovernmental Relations: What Happened to 'Our New Federalism'?" *Journal of Law and Politics* 9, Summer 1993, pp. 609–37.

Patchel, Kathleen. "Interest Group Politics, Federalism, and the Uniform Laws Process: Some Lessons from the Uniform Commercial Code." *Minnesota Law Review* 78, November 1993, pp. 83–164.

Pemberton, Jackson. "A New Message: On Amendment XVII." *The Freeman* 26, November 1976, pp. 654–60.

Penny, Michael. "Application of the Primary Jurisdiction Doctrine to Clean Air Act Citizen Suits." *Boston College Environmental Affairs Law Review* 29, 2002, pp. 399–426.

Percy, Stephen L. "ADA, Disability Rights, and Evolving Regulatory Federalism." *Publius: The Journal of Federalism* 23, Fall 1993, pp. 87–105.

Petragnani, Amy M. "The Dormant Commerce Clause: On Its Last Leg." *Albany Law Review* 57, Fall 1994, pp. 1215–253.

Powell, H. Jefferson. "The Original Understanding of Original Intent." *Harvard Law Review* 98, March 1985, pp. 885–948.

"The Power of Congress to Subject Interstate Commerce to State Regulation." *University of Chicago Law Review* 3, 1935, pp. 636–40.

Radish, Martin H. and Steven G. Sklaver. "Federal Power to Commandeer State Courts; Implications for the Theory of Judicial Federalism." *Indiana Law Review*, 1998, pp. 71–110.

Rehnquist, William H. "The Changing Role of the Supreme Court." *Florida State University Law Review* 14, Spring 1986, pp. 1–13.

Revesz, Richard L. "Rehabilitating Interstate Competition: Rethinking the 'Race-to-the-Bottom' Rationale for Federal Environmental Regulation." *New York University Law Review* 67, December 1992, pp. 1210–254.

Ribstein, Larry E. and Bruce H. Kobayashi. "An Economic Analysis of Uniform State Laws." *Journal of Legal Studies* 25, January 1996, pp. 131–87.

Rich, Michael J. "Targeting Federal Grants: The Community Development Experience, 1950–86." *Publius: The Journal of Federalism* 21, Winter 1991, pp. 29–49.

Roberts, Sam. "When a Student Is Counted as 94% of One." *New York Times*, February 11, 1988, p. B1.

Robinson, Richard S. "Preemption, the Right of Publicity, and a New Federal Statute." *Cardozo Arts and Entertainment Journal* 16, 1998, pp. 183–206.

Santora, Marc. "Rowland Vows to Shut Down Cross-Sound Cable That Helps Power Long Island." *New York Times*, September 6, 2003, p. B6.

Schneeweiss, Jonathan. "Watershed Protection Strategies: A Case Study of the New York City Watershed in Light of the 1996 Amendments to the Safe Drinking Water Act." *Villanova Environmental Law Journal* 8, 1997, pp. 77–119.

Scicchitano, Michael J. and David M. Hedge. "From Coercion to Partnership in Federal Partial Preemption: SMCRA, RCRA, and OSHA Act." *Publius: The Journal of Federalism* 23, Fall 1993, pp. 107–21.

Sentell, R. Perry, Jr. "Local Government Litigation: Some Pivotal Principles." *Mercer Law Review* 55, Fall 2003, pp. 1–34.

Sherk, George W. "Resolving Interstate Water Conflicts in the Eastern United States: The Re-Emergence of the Federal-Interstate Compact." *Water Resource Bulleting* 30, June 1994, pp. 397–408.

Siegel, Norman E. "FIFRA and Preemption: Can State Common Law and Federal Regulations Coexist? *Papas v. Upjohn Co.*, 925 F.2d 1019." *Washington University Journal of Urban and Contemporary Law* 41, Spring 1992, pp. 257–70.

Simmons, Peter. "Home Rule and Exclusionary Zoning: An Impediment to Low and Moderate Income Housing." *Ohio State Law Journal* 33, 1972, pp. 621–38.

Sinozich, Paula A., ed. "The Role of Preemption in Administrative Law." *Administrative Law Review* 45, Spring 1993, pp. 107–224.

Smith, Daniel A. "Same-Sex Marriage Ballot Measures and the 2004 Presidential Election." *State and Local Government Review* 38, no. 2, 2006, pp. 78–91.

Smith, Stephen F. "Proportionality and Federalization." *Virginia Law Review* 91, June 2005, pp. 879–951.

Spence, David B. "The Law, Economics, and Politics of Federal Preemption Jurisprudence: A Quantitative Analysis." *California Law Review* 87, October 1999, pp. 1125–1206.

Squire, Ryan C. "Effectuating Principles of Federalism; Reevaluating the Federal Spending Power as the Great Tenth Amendment Loophole." *Pepperdine Law Review* 25, 1998, pp. 869–937.

Stenberg, Carl W. "Running Clean in the American States: Experience with Public Funding of Elections." In Philip J. Davies and Bruce I. Newman, eds., *Winning Elections with Political Marketing*. Binghamton, NY: The Haworth Press, Incorporated, 2006, pp. 211–26.

Stephens, G. Ross. "State Centralization and the Erosion of Local Autonomy." *Journal of Politics* 36, February 1974, pp. 44–76.

Stevens, Ted. "The Internet and the Telecommunications Act of 1996." *Harvard Journal on Legislation* 35, Winter 1998, pp. 5–31.

Strahan, Philip E. "The Real Effects of U.S. Banking Deregulation." *Federal Reserve Bank of St. Louis Review* 85, July/August 2003, pp. 111–28.

Swindler, William F. "Our First Constitution: The Articles of Confederation." *American Bar Association Journal* 69, February 1981, pp. 166–69.

Syles, Richard T. "Nuclear Power Plants and Emergency Planning: An Intergovernmental Nightmare." *Public Administration Review* 44, September-October 1984, pp. 393–401.

Teske, Paul and Andrey Kuljiev. "Federalism, Preemption, and Implementation of the Telecommunications Act." *Publius: The Journal of Federalism* 30, Winter/Spring 2000, pp. 53–67.

————, Michael Mintrom and Samuel Best. "Federal Preemption and State Regulation of Transportation and Telecommunications." *Publius: The Journal of Federalism* 23, Fall 1993, pp. 71–85.

Thompson, Walter. "The Trend Toward Federal Centralization." *The Annals of the American Academy of Political and Social Science* 113, May 1924, pp. 172–82.

Thrash, Thomas W. "Federal Automotive Safety Standards and Georgia Products Liability Law: Conflict or Coexistence?" *Georgia State Bar Journal* 26, February 1990, pp. 107–12.

Trinchero, Mark P. and Holly R. Smith. "Federal Preemption of State Universal Service Regulations Under the Telecommunications Act of 1996." *Federal Communications Law Journal* 51 March 1999, pp. 303–47.

Tubbesing, Carl. "The Dual Personality of Federalism." *State Legislatures* 24, April 1998, pp. 14–18.

Vairo, Georgene M. "Forum Selection: Judge Shopping." *National Law Journal* 23, November 27, 2000, p. A16.

————. "Forum Selection: Removal Traps." *National Law Journal* 23, July 9, 2001, p. A14.

————. "An Update on Removal." *National Law* Journal 26, October 14, 2002, p. B8.

Vaishnav, Anand. "City Defends Assignment Plan: US Court Hears School Lawsuit." *Boston Globe*, February 11, 2003, p. B2.

Van Hernel, Peter J. "A Way Out of the Maze: Federal Agency Preemption of State Licensing and Regulation of Complementary and Alternative Medicine Practitioners." *American Journal of Law & Medicine* 27, No. 2–3, 2001, pp. 329–44.

Vazqiez, Carlos M. "Treaties and the Eleventh Amendment." *Virginia Journal of International Law* 42, Winter 2002, pp. 713–42.

"Vt. Court Assets Jurisdiction in Dispute." *Washington Post*, August 5, 2006, p. A3.

Wald, Matthew L. "Indian Point Report Contradicts Experts on Effect of Attack." *The New York Times*, January 21, 2003, p. B5.

————. "Indian Point Security Test Is Called Too Easy." *The New York Times*, September 16, 2003, p. B5.

Walker, Jack L. "The Diffusion of Innovations Among the American States." *The American Political Science Review* 63, September 1969, pp. 880–99.

Wallick, Ruth. "GATT and Preemption of State and Local Laws." *Government Finance Review* 10, October 1994, pp. 46–47.

Warren, Charles. "New Light on the Federal Judiciary Act of 1789." *Harvard Law Review* 37, 1923–24, pp. 93–132.

Warren, Manning G., III. "Reflections on Dual Regulation of Securities: A Case Against Preemption. *Boston College Law Review* 25, 1984, pp. 495–538.

————. "Reflections on Dual Regulation of Securities: A Case for Reallocation of Regulatory Responsibilities." *Washington University Law Quarterly* 78, Summer 2000, pp. 497–512.

Warren, William T. "Free Trade and Federalism." *State Legislatures* 22, May 1996, pp. 12–16.

Wechsler, Herbert. "The Political Safeguards of Federalism: The Role of the States in the Composition and Selection of the National Government." *Columbia Law Review* 54, 1953, pp. 543–60.

Williamson, Richard S. "Block Grants—A Federalist Tool." State Government 54, No. 4, 1981, pp. 114–17.
———. "The Self-Government Balancing Act: A View from the White House." National Civic Review 71, January 1982, pp. 19–22.
Willing, Richard. "Attitudes Ease Toward Medical Marijuana." USA Today, May 29, 2003, p. A4.
Wilson, James G. "The Eleventh Amendment Cases: Going 'Too Far' with Judicial Neo-federalism." Loyola of Los Angeles Law Review 33, June 2000, pp. 1687–717.
Winkler, John W., III. "Dimensions of Judicial Federalism." Annals of the American Academic of Political and Social Science 416, November 1974, pp. 67–76.
Winter, Greg. "Schools Resegregate, Study Finds." New York Times, January 21, 2003, pp. A14.
Yoo, John C. "The Judicial Safeguards of Federalism." Southern California Law Review 70, July 1997, pp. 1311–1405.
Young, Ernest A. "Dual Federalism, Concurrent Jurisdiction, and the Foreign Affairs Exception." George Washington Law Review 69, February 2001, pp. 139–88.
Zeigler, Donald H. "Gazing into the Crystal Ball: Reflections on the Standards State Judges Should Use to Ascertain Federal Law." William and Mary Law Review 40, April 1999, pp. 1143–221.
Zimmerman, James. "Restrictions on Forum-Selection Clauses in Franchise Agreements and the Federal Arbitration Act: Is State Law Preempted?" Vanderbilt Law Review 51, April 1998, pp. 759–86.
Zimmerman, Joseph F. "A Beginner's Guide to Interstate Compacts." Journal of Insurance Regulation 22, Spring 2004, pp. 66–75.
———. "Child Support: Interstate Dimensions." Publius: The Journal of Federalism 24, Fall 1994, pp. 45–60.
———. "Congressional Preemption During the George W. Bush Administration." Publius: The Journal of Federalism 37, Summer 2007, pp. 432–52.
———. "Congressional Preemption: Removal of State Regulatory Powers." PS: Political Science and Politics, 38, July 2005, pp. 375–78.
———. "Congressional Preemption and the States. The Book of the States 2006. Lexington, KY: The Council of State Governments, 2006, pp. 26–29.
———. "Congressional Regulation of Subnational Governments." PS: Political Science & Politics 26 (June 1993): 177–81.
———."The Development of Local Discretionary Authority in New York." Publius: The Journal of Federalism 13, Winter 1983, pp. 89–103.
———. "The Discretionary Authority of Local Governments." Urban Data Service Report 13, November 1981, pp. 1–13.
———. "Election Systems and Representative Democracy: Reflections on the Voting Rights Act of 1965." National Civic Review 83, Fall 1995, pp. 287–309.
———. "Eliminating Disproportionate Representation in the House." In Zimmerman, Joseph F. and Wilma Rule, eds. The U.S. House of Representatives: Reform or Rebuild? Westport, CT: Praeger Publishers, 2000, pp. 163–86.
———. "Evolving State-Local Relations." The Book of the States 2002 Edition. Lexington, KY: The Council of State Governments, 2002, pp. 33–39.
———. "Federal Judicial Remedial Power: The Yonkers Case." Publius: The Journal of Federalism 20, Summer 1990, pp. 45–61.

————, ed. "Federal Preemption." *Publius: The Journal of Federalism* 23, Fall 1993, pp. 1–121.

————. "Federal Preemption Under Reagan's New Federalism." *Publius: The Journal of Federalism* 21, Winter 1991, pp. 7–28.

————. "The Federal Voting Rights Act and Alternative Election Systems." *William & Mary Law Review* 19, Summer 1978, pp. 621–60.

————. "Financing National Policy Through Mandates." *National Civic Review* 81, Summer-Fall 1992, pp. 367–73.

————. "Interstate Compacts: School Districts." *Current Municipal Problems* 29, No. 3, 2003, pp. 314–21.

————. "Interstate Cooperation: The Roles of the State Attorneys General." *Publius: The Journal of Federalism* 24, Winter 1998, pp. 71–89.

————, ed. "Interstate Relations." *Publius: The Journal of Federalism*, Fall 1994, pp. 1–114.

————. "Interstate Relations Trends." *The Book of the States 2005*. Lexington, KY: The Council of State Governments, 2005, pp. 36–41.

————. "Mandating in New York State." In *State Mandating of Local Expenditures*. Washington, DC: U.S. Advisory Commission on Intergovernmental Relations, 1978, pp. 69–85.

————. "Maximization of Local Autonomy and Citizen Control: A Model." *Home Rule and Civil Society*, 1989, pp. 175–88.

————. "The Metropolitan Area Problem." *Annals of the American Academy of Political and Social Science* 416, November 1974, pp. 133–47.

————. "National-State Relations: Cooperative Federalism in the Twentieth Century." *Publius: The Journal of Federalism* 31, Spring 2001, pp. 15–30.

————. "The Nature and Political Significance of Preemption." *PS: Political Science and Politics* 38, July 2005, pp. 359–62.

————. "The 104th Congress and Federalism." *Current Municipal Problems* 23, No. 4, 1997, pp. 494–514.

————. "Overview of Voting Rights Laws." In *Communities & The Voting Rights Act.* Denver: National Civic League, 1996, pp. 8–16.

————. "Preemption in the U.S. Federal System." *Publius: The Journal of Federalism* 23, Fall 1993, pp. 1–13.

————. "Regulating Intergovernmental Relations in the 1990s." *The Annals of the American Academy of Political and Social Science* 509, May 1990, pp. 48–72.

————. "Regulation of Professions by Interstate Compact." *The CPA Journal* 74, May 2004, pp. 23–28.

————. "Relieving the Fiscal Burdens of State and Federal Mandates and Restraints." *Current Municipal Problems* 19, No. 2, 1992, pp. 216–24.

————. "The Role of the State Legislature in Air Pollution Abatement." *Suffolk University Law Review* 5, Spring 1971, pp. 850–77.

————. "The State Mandate Problem." *State and Local Government Review* 19, Spring 1987, pp. 78–84.

————. "Trends in Congressional Preemption." *The Book of the States 2003*. Lexington, KY: The Council of State Governments, 2003, pp. 32–37.

————. "Trends in Interstate Relations: Political and Administrative Cooperation." *The Book of the States*. Lexington, KY: The Council of State Governments, 2002, pp. 40–47.

———. "Trends in State-Local Relations." *The Book of the States 2004*. Lexington, KY: The Council of State Governments, 2004, pp. 28–33.

Zimmermann, Frederick L. "Intergovernmental Commissions: The Interstate-Federal Approach." *State Government* 42, Spring 1969, pp. 129–30.

———. "The Commission on Interstate Cooperation." *State Government* 33, Autumn 1960, pp. 233–42.

UNPUBLISHED MATERIALS

"Address of William Bradford Reynolds, Assistant Attorney General, Civil Rights Division, Counselor to the Attorney General, United States Department of Justice before the Conservative Law Students—A Federalist Society Chapter, Washington University, St. Louis, Missouri, October 28, 1987."

Baer, Jon A. "Municipal Debt and Tax Limitations in New York State: A Constraint on Home Rule." Albany: Graduate School of Public Affairs, State University of New York at Albany, 1980.

Bork, Robert H. "The Constitution, Original Intent, and Economic Rights." Presented at the University of San Diego Law School, November 18, 1985.

Bowman, Ann O'M. "Interstate Equilibrium: Competition and Cooperation in the U.S. Federal System." Presented at the annual meeting of The American Political Science Association, Philadelphia, Pennsylvania, August 28, 2003.

Brennan, William, Jr. "The Constitution of the United States: Contemporary Ratification." Presented at a text and teaching symposium, Georgetown University, Washington, DC, October 12, 1985.

Crotty, Patricia M. "The New Federalism Game: Options for the States." Presented at the annual meeting of the Northeastern Political Science Association, Philadelphia, November 14–16, 1985.

Hyde, Albert C. "The Politics of Environmental Decision Making: The Non-Decision Issue." Albany: Unpublished PhD Diss., State University of New York at Albany, 1980.

"Members Certify GLBA Reciprocity Requirement Met." News release issued by the National Association of Insurance Commissioners, Kansas City, MO, September 10, 2002.

Nickerson, Brian J. "Interest Group Involvement in New York State Public School Aid: Litigation and Lobbying." Albany: Unpublished PhD Diss., State University of New York at Albany, 2002.

Reynolds, William Bradford. "The Bicentennial: A Constitutional Restoration." Presented at the University of Texas, Austin, Texas, February 19, 1987.

"Statement of William Bradford Reynolds, Assistant Attorney General, Civil Rights Division Before the Committee on Labor and Human Resources, Subcommittee on Labor, U.S. Senate Concerning Impact of *Garcia v. San Antonio Metropolitan Transit Authority* on September 10, 1985."

Stenberg, Carl W. "Federal-Local Relations in a Cutback Environment: Issues and Future Directions." Presented at the Annual Conference of the American Politics Group of the United Kingdom Political Studies Association, Manchester, England, January 4, 1980.

Zimmerman, Joseph F. "Achieving State Insurance Regulatory Uniformity: The Interstate Compact." Presented at an Interstate Compact Symposium: Strengthening State Regulation of Insurance, San Diego, CA, December 7, 2002.

———. "Congressional Devolution of Powers to the States." Presented at a conference on The Federal Nations of North American sponsored by the Eccles Center for American Studies at the British Library and Institute for American Studies, London University, London, England, March 19, 2007.

———. "Congressional Preemption: Regulatory Federalism." Presented at the annual meeting of the American Political Science Association, Chicago, Illinois, September 4, 2004.

———. "Federalism in the United States of America." Presented at Moscow State University, Moscow, U.S.S.R., June 4, 1990.

———. "Formal and Informal Interstate Cooperation." Presented at the annual meeting of the American Political Science Association, San Francisco, September 1, 2001.

———. "How Perfect Is the Economic Union? Interstate Trade Barriers." Presented at the annual meeting of the American Political Science Association, Philadelphia, Pennsylvania, August 28, 2003.

———. "The Interstate Agreement for the Popular Election of the President of the United States." Presented at the annual conference of the American Politics Group, University of Leicester, Leicester, England, January 5, 2007.

———. "The Interstate Compact." Presented at the annual meeting of the American Political Science Association, Philadelphia, Pennsylvania, August 30, 2006.

———. "Interstate Cooperation: The Roles of the State Attorneys General." Presented at the annual meeting of The American Political Science Association, Washington, DC, August 28, 1997.

———. "Interstate Disputes: The Supreme Court's Original Jurisdiction." Presented at the annual meeting of the American Political Science Association, Washington, DC: September 2, 2005.

———. "The Interstate Insurance Product Regulation Compact." Presented at a meeting of the National Conference of State Legislatures Executive Committee's Task Force to Streamline and Simplify Insurance Regulation, New York, New York, March 22, 2003.

———. "Interstate Trade Barriers: Their Erection and Removal." Presented at the annual conference of the American Politics Group of the United Kingdom Political Studies Association, University of Reading, Reading, England, January 4, 2003.

———. "Powers of Municipal Governments in the United States of America." Presented at the Kyungham Local Community Research Center, Chinju, Republic of Korea, May 27, 1996.

———. "Regulatory Federalism: Congressional Preemption." Presented at the annual conference of the American Politics Group of the United Kingdom Political Studies Association, Oxford University, Oxford, England, January 3, 2004.

———. "State Taxation of Interstate Commerce: The Silence of Congress." Presented at the annual conference of the American Politics Group of the United Kingdom

Political Studies Association, Manchester Metropolitan University, January 6, 2006.

———. "The Supreme Court's Original Jurisdiction: Interstate Disputes." Presented at the annual meeting of the American Political Science Association, Washington, DC, September 2, 2005.

———. "The United States Federal System: A Kaleidoscopic View." Presented at the Rothermere American Institute, Oxford University, Oxford, England, November 23, 2004.

Index

247

Made in the USA
Lexington, KY
13 October 2010